T0369930

Advance Praise for *My Family and I*

"*My Family and I* is a remarkable and thought-provoking book that offers an intimate exploration of race, identity, and the pursuit of beloved community in contemporary America. Gussow eloquently argues that the reification of so-called racial identities reflects long-standing divisions that we must acknowledge, do not need to maintain, and should arguably destroy."

–Dr. Sheena Michele Mason, author of *The Raceless Antiracist: Why Ending Race Is the Future of Antiracism*

"In an America increasingly divided by the clash between those who seek power in the reductive, skin-deep world of identity politics and those who wish to remain within our greater humanity, Adam Gussow's *My Family and I* offers a powerful argument for the latter. Gussow's refusal to betray his humanity for this nefarious ideology is what gives this book of his its enduring and enlightening power. Most of all, it gives us hope."

–Eli Steele, filmmaker and director of *Resegregating America* (2021), *What Killed Michael Brown?* (2020), and *How Jack Became Black* (2018)

"Gussow's harrowing account of attending an anti-racist workshop is an edgy parable on the dangers of thinking in racial categories. He is a first-rate scholar whose earlier work probed racial wounds in the American past, but his stimulating new study lets us see that racial healing can be on the horizon in our society."

–Charles Reagan Wilson, editor-in-chief, *The New Encyclopedia of Southern Culture*

"*My Family and I* is an unflinchingly challenging, provocative book that demands nuanced, careful thought. As an Ashkenazi Jewish and Black woman, I am grateful for the challenge that Adam Gussow's book provides, and for the ways in which I was forced to consider my own belief systems as I read. What a gift."

–Marra B. Gad, author of *The Color of Love: A Story of a Mixed-Race Jewish Girl*

"Adam Gussow's quest to prove the possibility of a transracial beloved community takes him on a transformative odyssey from the streets and clubs of Harlem to Princeton to a revelatory life in contemporary Mississippi, playing and teaching the blues. More than a memoir, the lived experience of *My Family and I* boldly challenges racial orthodoxy at a critical moment in American history."

–Jerry Wasserman, author of *Life Could Be a Dream: African American Blues, R&B, Gospel & Doo Wop, 1946-56*

My
Family & I
A Mississippi Memoir

My Family & I

A Mississippi Memoir

ADAM GUSSOW

EMANCIPATION
BOOKS

EMPANCIPATION BOOKS
An Imprint of Post Hill Press
ISBN: 979-8-88845-765-8
ISBN (eBook): 979-8-88845-766-5

My Family and I:
A Mississippi Memoir
© 2025 by Adam Gussow
All Rights Reserved

Cover Design by Conroy Accord

Leaving Here Walking
Words and Music by James Olin Burns
Reprinted by Permission of James Olin Burns / Velrone Music and Delmark Records LLC
All Rights Reserved

Don't Know Why
Words and Music by Jesse Harris
Copyright © 2002 Sony Music Publishing (US) LLC and Beanly Songs
All Rights Administered by Sony Music Publishing (US) LLC, 424 Church Street, Suite 1200,
Nashville, TN 37219
International Copyright Secured All Rights Reserved
Reprinted by Permission of Hal Leonard LLC

This book, as well as any other Emancipation Books publications, may be purchased in bulk quantities at a special discounted rate. Contact orders@posthillpress.com for more information.

All people, locations, events, and situations are portrayed to the best of the author's memory. While all of the events described are true, many names and identifying details have been changed to protect the privacy of the people involved.

No part of this book may be reproduced, stored in a retrieval system, or transmitted by any means without the written permission of the author and publisher.

Post Hill Press
New York • Nashville
posthillpress.com

Published in the United States of America
1 2 3 4 5 6 7 8 9 10

For Sherrie

Something must have gone wrong
It's taking way too long
—Sterling Magee, "Freedom For My People"

Table of Contents

WOKENESS, HETERODOXY, AND DREAMS DEFERRED

RECLAMATION

Author's Note

When used as racial and/or ethnic identifiers, the words *black* and *white* are rendered here in lowercase rather than uppercase. This is a deliberate decision by the author, made with full recognition of the cultural and political ramifications of such a lexical choice and with sincere respect for those who have made other choices.

In the aftermath of George Floyd's death in May 2020 and the nationwide protests that followed, the *New York Times*, the *Associated Press*, the *Chicago Manual of Style*, and many other organizations announced that they would henceforth be capitalizing *Black* in all contexts where it served as a racial and ethnic identifier. Many academics in the social sciences had already been capitalizing the word for years; many in the academic humanities who had not necessarily been doing so now embraced the rapidly consolidating new consensus.

Contrarian voices within the black intelligentsia, including Glenn Loury ("Why I Don't Capitalize Black"), John McWhorter ("Why I'm Not Writing 'Black'"), Chloé Valdary ("Black People are Far More Powerful than Critical Race Theory Preaches"), Thomas Chatterton Williams, and Kmele Foster, remained unpersuaded.

Although I briefly went along with the new consensus, I ultimately reverted to familiar practice, except in certain specific academic contexts where I've decided to make nice. "Familiar practice," I should note, was an uncontroversial norm for many decades. Black journalist Isabel Wilkerson's *Caste: The Origins of Our Discontents*, for example, published in August 2020 but written in the run-up to that epochal summer, used the lower-case *black*, as did her Pulitzer Prize–winning *The Warmth of Other Suns*, published a decade earlier. My rejection of *Black* and *White*, at bottom, traces to my growing embrace of a race-abolitionist perspective and my continuing faith in the beloved community ideal.

I view race, which is to say the reification of racial difference and embrace of racial identifiers, as the foundation of American racism—a perspective I learned from Williams's *Self-Portrait in Black and White: Unlearning Race* and, behind that, Karen and Barbara Fields's *Racecraft: The Soul of Inequality in American Life*. My wife and son have blessed me with a household in which black and white, as terms of racial art, have faded badly, losing their existential weight in the face of the merely human—whatever about us is most loveable, maddening, sustaining, productive of zany joy. Capitalizing *Black* and *White* adds nothing to the collective life we have created and, in my view, takes us as a country in precisely the wrong direction, as though the No Man's Land separating two exhausted armies on the verge of declaring a truce were suddenly to sprout a tall and slippery border wall, rendering a truce that much more unlikely.

Still, I respect your choices about such things, if they're different from mine. I hope you'll extend me, and this book, the same consideration.

Prologue:
White Antiracist Allies
in Training

If we—and now I mean the relatively conscious
whites and the relatively conscious blacks,
who must, like lovers, insist on, or create, the
consciousness of the others—do not falter in
our duty now, we may be able, handful that we
are, to end the racial nightmare, and achieve our
country, and change the history of the world.

—James Baldwin, *The Fire Next Time*

I've waited more than two decades to tell this story. I'm not particularly eager to tell it—Sherrie and I have been happily married for many years; Shaun is tall, strong, and thriving—and several good friends have counseled me not to. But this isn't about me. It's about the country we want our children to inherit. That America—the prophetic America envisioned by Martin Luther King, Jr., and kept alive by John Lewis—needs more of us to step forward and say, "We *can* create the beloved community. But the path you have chosen is the wrong one, doomed to divide and dishearten. And silence is no longer an option."

Some people, when they're cornered, fight or flee. I did both. After getting home from Seattle, I dumped my research materials in a drawer and tried to move on. I did a good job of erasing the names and faces of my antagonists. But I can't forget the primal scene: how it felt to be silenced and abused by a circle of my fellow citizens. That memory has gained power through the years, haunting me like an omen, slowly coming into alignment with the present moment. The virus I confronted back then, not the virus of racism but the virus of a certain kind of blunt-force antiracist work engaged in by those convinced of their own righteousness, has spread so rapidly across our country over the past few years that it is threatening to drown us all—although there have been recent signs, thankfully, of a broad-based resistance. So I'm going to share my story, reconstructing it as best I can from the materials I've got on hand. (I have changed the names of the principal actors and altered several relevant details, including the location of the workshop, to preserve anonymity.)

When people survive trauma, their memories are often fragmented, discontinuous, incomplete. What happened to me out in Seattle hardly merits the term *traumatic*. Nobody laid a hand on me. It was just angry talk. I don't have nightmares, although I get skittish when I hear people proclaiming the importance of being "a good white ally." Considering the long tenure of my interracial marriage and the loving and supportive household Sherrie and I have established, that's a curious response. But what happened was disturbing enough at the time that the two white women who ran the workshop yanked things to a stop. Holding up their hands to silence us, insisting on a time-out, they seemed puzzled, disconcerted. This wasn't how things were supposed to go. The "safe, non-judgmental space" they'd described in their advertising had dissolved into *Lord of the Flies*. They apologized privately to me later, after apologizing to the group.

I heard the term *struggle session*—the humiliations vented upon hapless citizens of Communist China during the Cultural Revolution—for the first time in the fall of 2020, not long after George Floyd died with a knee on his neck out in Minneapolis and Ibram X. Kendi's *How To Be an Antiracist* was trading places with Robin DiAngelo's *White Fragility* at the top of the bestseller lists. When I saw the photo of a cringing Chinese man surrounded by his sneering fellow citizens, a light went on.

"Jesus," I thought. "That's what it was." I'd never had a word for what happened to me back then. It felt marginally better to have a word for it. But I still felt sick. And I feel a duty to warn. Because where I found myself, more than twenty years ago, is where we are all headed. If they could do to me what they did in that workshop classroom, given the life I'd lived to that point, they're going to knock you flat. But I did resist, and it made a difference.

The events I'm about to relate took place in the fall of 2003, when I'd had my tenure-track job at the University of Mississippi for about a year. I'd moved down to Oxford from New York City—a former touring blues musician turned scholar of African American literature; author of a book on southern violence and the blues; a single man in his mid-forties looking to get married and settle down.

Although compelled by the subject of racial violence, I'd also reached a breaking point. I'd learned far more during my dissertation research about spectacle lynching than I'd ever wanted to. Luther Holbert in Doddsville, Mississippi; Jesse Washington in Waco, Texas; Claude Neal in Marianna, Florida. Extended ritual torture at the hands of white mobs in the service of a hardened racial order that inflicted terror to maintain black subservience. Charred black bodies strung up in town squares, tossed off the backs of trucks on the black side of town. Body parts—fingers, ears, penis—snipped or hacked off living people and burnt corpses alike; pickled in jars; traded like sacred relics. Nothing in my prior educational history, nothing in my small-town, downstate New York upbringing, had prepared me to encounter this sordid, horrific chapter of American history. I'd waded into deep waters, determined to wring meaning from white racist practices that sought the spiritual annihilation of black blues subjects. I'd cooled myself out by chain-smoking cigarettes during the weekly commute from my uptown Manhattan apartment down to Princeton, fleeing as I did so from the live-in relationship I'd established several years earlier with a younger woman, an unemployed Jewish sketch comedian whom I no longer loved and whose disdain for me finally matched my own for her.

If I'd been honest with myself, I would have acknowledged that my weathervaning erotic imagination, always askew from the blonde-babe American ideal, had slowly pivoted during those years towards a dark goddess whose embrace, I imagined, would heal all that needed healing, in the world and in me. I was a mess, frankly. But I was lucid and productive, and I soldiered on. The girlfriend moved out, the dissertation got written, the new millennium arrived.

The beating heart I'd always been able to count on, the receptacle into which I'd dumped the slow-motion catastrophe that was my spiritual life, finally rebelled one night in Florida in the spring of 2000. I was visiting with a friend at his weekly gig, a gifted young blues harmonica player named Jason Ricci, chain-smoking Dunhills as I watched him throw down with his band. When he brought me onstage at the end, we battled furiously on an up-tempo groove, the protégé doing his best to upstage his mentor. It was only later, as I slumped in his van, that I felt the dark splotch slowly spreading across my chest, tightening and deepening—a coronary spasm, it turned out, that put me in intensive care at Delray Beach Medical Center for the next four days. I'd had a minor heart attack.

The day Jason walked me out of the hospital back into the Florida sunlight was also the day he put his mother's heavily underlined copy of Pema Chödrön's *When Things Fall Apart: Heart Advice for Difficult Times* into my hands. I'd recently started attending worship services at a New Age church, Interfaith Fellowship in New York, so I had no trouble integrating Chödrön's blunt, sensible Tibetan Buddhism, her emphasis on clarity and self-acceptance, with *A Course in Miracles* and the other non-judgmental, sometimes loopy, unabashedly utopian ideas that circulated within our congregation. After I returned the following Sunday morning and testified during Sharing Time to my shattering and rebirth, one of my fellow pilgrims, a woman in flowing silks with long wispy hair, drifted towards me and took my hand.

"The opening of the heart chakra," she assured me, "is a very powerful thing."

That was the beginning of a critical turn in my thinking—about race, America, and the work I was supposed to be doing. A decision to reorient my research in the direction of healing, rather than probing, racial wounds. My heart led the way and I followed it. I quit smoking; I started running again—miles and miles into the Mississippi countryside, after I moved down here. Fifteen miles every Sunday morning. Thankful for the new life, the fresh start I'd been blessed with.

It was during this period that I began to outline a book on the many ways in which Americans, black and white, were engaging the project of racial reconciliation in turn-of-the-millennium America: the post–Rodney King, post-OJ era in which President Clinton had staged his "Initiative on Race" and jazz musician James McBride had published his bestselling memoir, *The Color of Water: A Black Man's Tribute to His White Mother*.

Many Americans at the time were pursuing this sort of transracial fellowship work, a surprisingly broad range of approaches that led my literary agent to ask for a book proposal. I called my new project *Dreams of Beloved Community: Racial Healing in Contemporary America*. "King's dream is not dead," I insisted, "but it has been splintered into a thousand different dreams, like the oddly-angled facets of a large rough diamond that hasn't quite caught the eye of the American public":

> Some modes of racial healing and racial reconciliation
> are faith-based, drawing on Christian theology, Quaker
> and Unitarian-Universalist promptings of conscience,
> New Age spirituality, and Baha'i belief in the so-called
> "family of man." Some are decidedly secular, drawing
> on the languages of law, peace studies, social psychol-
> ogy, psychotherapy, and leftist politics. Some see racism
> as America's primal sin, in profound need of collective
> white atonement; others, such as Kokomon and Aeeshia

Clottey's "attitudinal healing," are premised on a radical forgiveness that relinquishes all such racial accountings for the sake of a release from the wounds engendered by American history. Some varieties of racial reconciliation, particularly those propagated by evangelical Christian groups such as Promise Keepers and Mission Mississippi, are premised on a reification of race—as in the statement, "The races must learn to get along." Others are premised on the spiritual non-validity of racial distinctions, as in the statement, "Spirit has no color."

Some efforts at reconciliation, which I term "site-specific commemorations," are distinctly local: they assemble interracial coalitions in a particular town for the purpose of commemorating and reframing grievous acts of racial violence, such as the quadruple lynching at Moore's Ford Bridge in Monroe, Georgia in 1946. Others, modeling themselves on ad campaigns of the "Colors of Benneton" variety, are capital-driven, with regional and national ambitions: the "NuSouth" line of clothing, for example, in which two young entrepreneurs from Charleston, South Carolina—one white, one black— came up with a logo that crosses the Confederate flag with the black, red, and green of the African liberation movement to create a "new unifying symbol" for the fractious US South.

Some who write about racial healing, such as Nathan Rutstein, founder of the Institutes for the Healing of Racism, invoke the language of epidemiology as they prescribe ways of confronting and curing the so-called "disease" of racism among whites. Others, such as the Rev. Clarence Williams, founder of the Institute for Recovery from Racisms and author of *Racial Sobriety: A Journey from Hurts to Healing*, use rhetoric drawn from the 12-step recovery movement to help alleviate the suffering and diminished sense of self-worth that white racism has produced in black people. Finally, I've been surprised at how frequently interracial families and the biracial/multiracial children they produce turn out to be agents for racial healing. The struggle for beloved community within the sacred bond of such marriages and the life narratives they produce (Elizabeth Alexander, Shirlee Taylor Haizlipp, Barbara and David Douglass, Rebecca Walker) turns out to be a crucial thematic on the post-Civil Rights movement, post-OJ landscape.

Racial healing? Beloved community? It all seems so quaint now, so early-2000s. (Google Ngram has 2002 and 2007 as the peak years for "racial healing" and 2004 as the peak year for "beloved community.") My agent never did place the project. But I was nothing if not sincere. I fervently believed in King's dream of an America where racial brotherhood was a reality, and integration, "genuine intergroup and interpersonal living," was made flesh. I knew we could solve America's problems if we could establish that sort of common ground: rout the lingering shadows of the color line and spiritually commit to each other's well-being. If we did that, there was nothing we couldn't achieve.

Sherrie and I were engaged by that point. Forget about furtive yearnings for the dark goddess: this was *life*, bold, beautiful, and impossibly sweet! This was love in action, thoroughgoing integration in all dimensions. I'd bought her the diamond ring; we were planning our wedding for the following summer. A Match.com success story, we were one more "swirl" couple in an America where, as of the year 2000 census, one could self-identify, if one wanted, as black *and* white. Which was great. After so much bitterness, violence, and division, race—racial polarity, racial division—was finally beginning to loosen its hold. We felt blessed to be living at this moment. Our child, the son or daughter we planned to have, would have choices.

ADAM GUSSOW

I had lived a version of that integrated, reconciled life during my decade as a street musician and touring blues performer, working side by side with Mississippi-born Harlem bluesman Sterling Magee, a.k.a. "Mr. Satan." The creative partnership we sustained over the years, an unlikely father-and-son act animated by a power-sharing arrangement based in mutual respect, taught me something about the dimensions of the possible within America's tortured racial purview. I planned to carry forward what I'd learned there into the sweeter, gentler project of making my new marriage work.

Of all the modalities of racial healing I was researching back in 2003, the one that left me most skeptical was the one grounded in a desire to reify racial difference, to make it a "thing," rather than ameliorating and dissolving it in a way that facilitated brotherhood. By that point I had read Elisabeth Lasch-Quinn's scathing neoconservative critique, *Race Experts: How Racial Etiquette, Sensitivity Training, and New Age Therapy Hijacked the Civil Rights Revolution* (2001) and, at the other extreme, Derald Wing Sue's *Overcoming Our Racism: The Journey to Liberation* (2003), with its hectoring evocation of microaggressions and white privilege. Sue, anticipating Kendi two decades later, anchors his diagnosis not just in a reification of white racial identity—whiteness is static, self-evident, "pure"—but in a totalizing conception of whiteness-as-racism that is essentially theological: a spiritual stain, a contemporary reimagining of original sin. "Although it is an unpleasant conclusion for you," he lectures his hapless white reader, "it is inescapable that you are racist, whether knowingly or unknowingly, intentionally or unintentionally."

No fan of Sue, I was also familiar with, and generally approved of, the insurgent academic discipline of whiteness studies, precisely because its grittiest work—Matt Wray's and Annalee Newitz's *White Trash: Race and Class in America*, for example—undercut facile generalizations about "white privilege" by taking class and region into account. Hillbillies are stigmatized comic underdogs, not blithe beneficiaries of white privilege. But I remained leery of the weird congruence between the legions of diversity trainers inventoried by Lasch-Quinn, who reified whiteness and its hardwired sinfulness as a way of somehow—eventually, mysteriously, far down the line—getting *beyond* whiteness, and on the other hand, Nazis and other white identitarians who proudly proclaimed their whiteness while rejecting the stigma attached to it. Diametrically opposed in every other respect, on this point they made common cause: they were determined to keep "whiteness" alive.

Skeptical or not, I thought it was my duty to investigate this quadrant of the contemporary race-healing beat. So I settled on a workshop called "White Antiracist Allies in Training," to be held in Seattle at Education For Progress, an organization founded by John Mott, a legendary Quaker activist. The workshop was being run by a pair of white female facilitators, Jane Holloway and Leah Benowitz, who had come to "the work," as they called it, from somewhat different points on the social justice spectrum. Holloway, a native of England, had been involved with community organizing and direct action, including a stint with the Women's Peace Camp at Greenham Common, a group of radical feminists who had chained themselves to the fence of a British military base in 1982 to protest the Reagan-era deployment of nuclear-tipped cruise missiles. Benowitz came from the world of nonprofit and corporate diversity training and was a certified Reiki practitioner. I'd attended a handful of workshops over the preceding decade, all of them at the Omega Institute in Rhinebeck, NY—the Opening the Heart workshop, Marianne Williamson on *A Course in Miracles*, David Deida on sacred sexuality—although none of them had focused on race. But I was familiar with, and comfortable with, the encounter-group model, the idea that "doing the work" required a willingness to take risks, go deep, expose wounds, sit with discomfort, shed tears.

Holloway and Benowitz were warmly receptive when I emailed them, told them about my project, and asked if I might join their October workshop as a participant/observer for the purpose of research. It was important to all three of us that I show up wholeheartedly, an equal among peers, not simply sit on the margins and take notes—something that would increase participant self-consciousness and interfere with the work. With a few basic ground rules in place, we were ready to go. I paid my registration and bought a round-trip ticket to Seattle.

Before proceeding, I need to make clear that I bear these facilitators no ill will. Quite the opposite: although I disagree with their methods, I respect them highly. They aren't just competent professionals but exquisitely attentive to the complexities of the antiracist work they have trained themselves and many others to do. In our recorded telephone postmortem, conducted two days after I arrived home, they spoke with me for almost two hours, thoughtfully and in good faith. It's impossible not to admire them.

But I'm also struck by a paradox and the questions it raises. How could two such skilled antiracist facilitators nevertheless have precipitated such a trainwreck—short-lived, to be sure, but with effects that have lingered through the decades? And if this could happen under their supervision, what sort of havoc is being wrought across contemporary America when less skilled, less thoughtful and resilient facilitators engage in the same sort of work? Or is the work itself the problem? What if "white antiracist training," as they conceived of it, is critically flawed in some way, so that what might at first glance appear to be a bug is in fact a feature, a fatal error in the program?

By the time we'd all filtered into the conference room for our Friday evening start, there were twenty of us sitting in a large horseshoe-shaped circle.

"Welcome, white people!" Jane and Leah said cheerfully, standing at the blackboard.

Jane had an English accent and a gentle, soothing voice with some residual tensile strength. Leah, dark haired, had a hint of urban tough girl, South Philly or Brooklyn, but with edges carefully smoothed. We were four men and sixteen women, most of us in our late teens or early twenties, except that three or four I'd initially taken to be young women were considerably more gender-indeterminate: skinny, boyish, wearing baseball caps turned backward. Nowadays I would recognize them as members of the trans/non-binary/genderqueer spectrum and would be unsurprised if they said their pronouns were *they* and *their*. Back in 2003 I had no such words. I simply took note of their presence, part of the varied cohort that had shown up for the workshop, some of them featuring aggressively razored haircuts and tattoos. I was, at forty-five, one of the oldest people in the room.

Our text for the weekend was a hundred-page spiral bound notebook authored by our facilitators, "White Antiracist Allies in Training: A Workshop Manual." Paging through it now, I'm simultaneously impressed by the way it anticipates our current moment and depressed at the socio-therapeutic blitzkrieg it represents: micro-subdividing and problematizing every conceivable way in which somebody labeled "white" might relate to abstract conceptions of racial difference (meaning stereotypes) and actual people of color. The highly compressed ten-part summary of US history subtitled "Histories and Practices that Formed the U.S. Concept of Race and Racism," which begins with "Colonization" and "African Enslavement" and ends with "The Civil Rights Movement" and "The Struggle Continues," contains some notable inaccuracies. "By 1800," the authors write, "10–15 million African slaves are in North America" (the US Census of 1800 lists 893,605 enslaved black people, most of whom were born in America, not Africa; only 388,000 African slaves were shipped directly to North America during the slave trade, with another 60–70,000 imported from the Caribbean). "Africa," they claim, "lost up to 50 million people to slavery" (the actual figure is roughly half this many, and only if one supplements the twelve million enslaved people shipped from sub-Saharan Africa to the New World with the six million sent across the Indian Ocean to points East and the eight million "lost" to slavery within the African continent, including Muslim North Africa).

At the time I didn't notice these inaccuracies. What I did notice were the misspelled names of two African American notables: Carter G. Woodson, the originator of Negro History Week (later Black History Month)—called "Washington" in the manual—and the singer Pearl Bailey, whose last name was misspelled "Baily."

What quickly became evident, both in the casual chit-chat among participants and in the responses we made as Jane and Leah worked their way into the manual's densely packed material, is that few of my fellow workshoppers had much lived experience with actual black people. Nor were they conversant with African American history and culture in the way that I'd managed to accrue by dint of my academic training—including two years at Vassar in a visiting Africana Studies position—and my career as a blues performer. This didn't surprise me. Wasn't the whole point of the workshop to help inexperienced white people push beyond stereotypes, fears, and fantasies in a way that prepared them to deal constructively, rather than incompetently, with their black fellow citizens? Maybe I could be of service here, even as I conducted my participant/observer research.

What did surprise me, as self-disclosures slowly painted our collective portrait, is that a number of participants—young, female, more LGBTQ than not, highly politicized, brittle rather than resilient—seemed to view this workshop as a way of exploring grievances, especially revolving around gender and sexuality, that had nothing to do with the lives of black people.

Just as curious was the way in which my own conversational style, which had been shaped by the call-and-response aesthetics and ritual affirmations of fellowship that lay at the core of my blues musician's life, seemed to grate against their sensibilities, especially those who saw themselves as most distinct from me on the intersectional grid in which we'd been schooled early on. One of the worst things I could do as a white ally in training, I discovered, was to say "I hear you" or "I can imagine how that must feel" when somebody confessed to a wound or shared any sort of negative experience. This was considered presumptuous. Even worse was commiserating—responding to such a share not just by verbally validating it, but by confiding a wound or negative experience of my own, one white person to another. To do this was actually to *invalidate* the other person, rather than affirming them, by daring to suggest that my straight white male pain was in any way equivalent to their gay white female pain.

Although most people are familiar at this point with the basic outlines of intersectionality, a theory of social power and subjectivity propounded by critical legal theorist Kimberlé Crenshaw in 1989, in 2003 I wasn't yet familiar with the term, and neither Crenshaw nor the word *intersectionality* were mentioned in our training manual. But one of our first lessons put forward what I can now plainly see was a simplified version of intersectional theory.

Jane and Leah had framed our weekend's work through the lens of a single page headlined "Power Grid & Social Rank." "Each of us," it began, "has many group identities in society. These group identities determine our social rank in U.S. culture. Following are some examples of group identities and the relative power those identities are given."

Across the top were the categories "Race," "Class," "Gender," and "Sexual Orientation," plus "Etc." Running down the left side of the page were two categories: "More Power" and "Less Power." The quadrant bracketed by "Race" and "More Power" contained a short stack of words: "European," "American," "(white)." "Upper," "Middle," "Male," and "Heterosexual" fill out the "More Power" line. "African American," "Latino/a," "Asian," "Native American," "Working," "Poor," "Female," and "Homosexual" fill out the "Less Power" line.

I knew where we were headed the moment I saw the chart. It was a primitive, brutalist reduction of intersectional theory; it doesn't capture Crenshaw's foundational point, which has to do with the way in which a black female legal complainant's intersecting blackness and femaleness may effectively place her beyond the legal protections conferred separately on blacks and women. Nor does it make a space for trans and genderqueer identities. But it did what it was designed to do. It took a room full of self-identified white people and, rather than joining them in community, taught them to slice and dice themselves and each other into component parts. As Jane and Leah worked the chalkboard, I could feel everyone making macro- and micro-assessments about where each participant should be placed in our new hierarchy of virtue. Since we were all white people—surprise!—race couldn't be a part of that process. We were guilty as charged there: cast helplessly into the "More

Power" quadrant. This clarified the activist-in-training pecking order. (Presumed) class, gender, and sexual orientation suddenly took on preternatural importance.

If I'd brought with me any residual notion that a workshop called "White Antiracist Allies in Training" would anchor itself in a shared desire to find common ground with one's racial peers as a way of raising our collective game and being a credit to our race, that quickly evaporated. We'd been thrown into a state of nature, a Hunger Games for edgy activists. Dr. Gussow—white, male, Princeton educated (therefore presumptively Upper or Middle), presumably heterosexual, twice as old as the median workshopper—had drawn the short straw. There was a weird kind of frost in the room, a shiver of stigma that the researcher in me noted silently.

It wasn't yet clear how all this was going to play out. I did, however, find myself protesting silently—not the first straight white guy in my position, I suspect—about the degree to which the harsh contours of the Power Grid (and the subsequent lessons on "Rank Awareness" and "White Privilege") couldn't begin to map the way in which race, power, privilege, and rank actually functioned in the spaces that had formed me.

As a half-Jewish Princeton freshman with no trust fund or prep school connections, vividly sensing my exclusion from the socially rarefied world of the Prospect Street eating clubs, I'd peddled hoagies door to door at night—"Hoagie Man!"—and cleaned filthy dorm bathrooms as part of the custodial crew to pay my bills while working my way out of a remedial writing class to become an English major. One of my junior-year roommates, installed after the two lacrosse-playing sophomores I'd signed on with were booted for physically threatening me, was a pedigreed gay black man from Atlanta with two middle initials and a hyphenated last name. Charming but aloof, he clearly viewed me as the most hilarious sort of white suburban primitive. My harmonica teacher during the mid-1980s, Nat Riddles, was a black New Yorker, six years older than me and far more accomplished, who saw something worth nourishing and took me under his wing like a kid brother.

During the decade I spent as a working blues musician in Harlem and on tour—the first four years in an all-black space, the last seven in predominantly white spaces—I was the junior partner to a voluble, indomitable black man who called most of the shots. Both my dissertation director, Arnold Rampersad, and Erroll McDonald, the editor of my 1998 memoir of life as a blues musician, *Mister Satan's Apprentice*, were intimidatingly urbane and erudite black men who had far more class and access to power than I ever would. My entire adult life had been shaped by accomplished older black men: men who effortlessly outranked me, held the keys to new worlds, modeled dynamism and finesse, inspired me to excel and persist, taught me some of what they knew, and let me figure out the rest.

I didn't need training on how to live and work with black people. White people, on the other hand, could be a challenge.

The trainwreck, as I've called it, occurred mid-morning on Saturday, the second day of the workshop. Three months later, I wrote my literary agent a succinct description:

> I am, by most reckonings, straight, white, and male. When I described during a "circle share" the way in which I had willingly surrendered power to several black students during an African American literature class I was currently teaching and the exhilarating outcome for both the students and myself, my remarks ended up precipitating not merely anger among white female workshop participants but an improvised show-trial in which Holloway and Benowitz allowed me to select one ally (gay and female and a genuinely supportive advocate) and then deliberately arrayed the entire circle against me so that each member could express and "process" their anger. The outcome of this exercise surprised and dismayed everybody in the room; Holloway ultimately apologized to the group, and to me, for her

miscalculation, one that did at least as much to exacerbate as to heal whatever wounds, racial and otherwise, we had brought with us to the workshop.

This compressed narrative raises as many questions as it answers. What sorts of thoughts, experiences, fears, wounds, were my fellow workshoppers sharing before I shared my own story? Why did *that* story, of all stories, an account of fruitful interracial collaboration intended to inspire and instruct, piss everybody off? By what rationale did Holloway and Benowitz think it was advisable to silence me, forcing me to sit quietly in my chair, defended only by my hastily appointed ally, while each member of the group was invited to have at me, at whatever length and in whatever fashion they felt moved to do so? And, crucially, just how bad did things have to get, and in what way, to convince Holloway not just to stop the proceedings, but to apologize to all of us for what suddenly felt to her like a mistake, a significant professional misjudgment?

Many details remain hazy. This is what happens when people go numb and shut down. But I remember a few things. I remember more now than I did twenty years ago, because I recently discovered a worksheet in the notes I shoved into that desk drawer long ago. So this is the moment to come clean and tell the truth.

The truth is, I lied to my agent. More precisely, I didn't tell her the whole truth. Or maybe I'd already repressed that part of what happened and simply didn't remember.

The truth is that the "circle share" story wasn't what set people in an uproar. It just got the ball rolling. Placing the whole burden of what happened next on that one story was a convenient fiction—a screen memory that, by skating me away from the shoals of moral complexity, exempted me for two decades from the need to confront what I said during the next round of circle-sharing and the cascading outrage it provoked.

When things fall apart, they fall apart quickly. When the mob comes for you—you!—it can take your breath away.

But that was then. This is now. And the people in that room no longer have the power to scare me, silence me, or shame me.

The circle-share story I initially offered up was about a classroom experience at the University of Mississippi, something that had taken place literally the day before I flew out to Seattle. My English Department colleague, Ethel Young-Minor, was on maternity leave that fall; she and my chair had asked me to step in and cover the African American lit survey. I was honored to be subbing for my black colleague, understandably concerned that the predominantly black class might not accept me in that role, yet eager to share my perspective on a range of classic texts—*Their Eyes Were Watching God, A Raisin in the Sun, Dutchman, Beloved*—and just as eager to hear what my students had to say about them. One young woman, a spirited, bluntly outspoken black Mississippian named Joshlyn, was so inspired by Hansberry's play that she told us a story about a café in Winona, on the edge of the Delta, that was still segregated.

"Still white-folks-only in the year 2003," she said. "Do you *believe* that shit? We ought to take a bus down there, all of us, and integrate it. I'm serious."

I knew she was. "Come up with a plan," I told her after class. "Find out a little more about what's going on down there. I'll give you the floor at the beginning of the next class."

When the class reconvened, I slid to the side of the room and she jumped up from her desk, skipped down the steps, and took the stage along with a male friend. She had a big gleeful smile.

"Brothers and sisters," she announced, "we have a *plan*."

She roused the class like a preacher, call and response style. People were hooting and giving Black Power salutes. It was a revolutionary moment; it energized us for the Black Arts Movement writers we were about to discuss. We never did go to Winona. But the fact that we *thought* about going down there like freedom riders—whites as well as blacks—and that I'd given Joshlyn space to share her dream, loosened everybody up and made us feel like a team.

It quickly became clear that I had managed to mightily offend several of the gender-fluid young workshoppers with backwards baseball caps.

"That's *so* white savior," said one of them. "You realize that, right?"

"White what?" It took me a moment to understand. "White *savior*? Heck no. I was trying to empower my black students, not save them."

"The inspirational teacher," snorted another, glancing at Holloway for confirmation that she'd pegged me correctly. "Your students must love you."

Things simmered along uneasily for the next ten or fifteen minutes. Then Jane and Leah asked us to pause, as they'd done more than once between their mini-lectures, and engage in a reflective exercise. Take out a sheet of blank paper, they said, and sketch a capsule history of your racial education—the messages you took in, both early and in later years, that led to your understandings about race, especially black people and white people. This racial programming can come from parents and other family, from friends and acquaintances, from religious traditions, educational institutions, public interactions, the mass media. Be honest. Go deep. Touch your own discomfort—that's how you'll know you're doing the work.

So I went to work. I wrote about my longstanding sense of being mixed, a tough Russian-Lithuanian Jewish/Scotch-Irish-Dutch mutt, and proud of that: son of a Jewish father and Protestant mother who'd married at a time when such interfaith marriages were unusual. Wincing a little, I wrote about the two black women, Marie and Hazel, who had worked in sequence for my Jewish grandparents as cooks and housekeepers down in the city. Marie, dark and quiet, I hardly remembered, but Hazel—boisterous, assertive, a Barbadian immigrant almost as light as my grandmother—had been there from the time I was ten. She'd stayed on through the decades, stayed on after my grandmother and then my grandfather got Alzheimer's—took control of the household with my father's blessings, hired additional caregivers, and nursed them both to dignified deaths.

Summoned to the city on the day my grandmother died, my father and I had walked into my grandparents' bedroom. My grandmother was lying on the bed, eyes closed, her face smoother than I'd ever seen it. Hazel came in behind us. "I was holding her hand when she died. She was breathing a little rough. I told her, 'Betty, you can let go now. It's okay. You gonna be okay.' That's when things smoothed out. I thought she'd passed, but I wasn't sure. So I took a little mirror from beside the bed—a little cosmetic mirror, like you'd have in a purse—and put it under her nose. To see if it fogged. When it didn't fog up, I knew."

"Thank you, Hazel," my father said.

"Then I shed a tear myself, and I pushed her eyelids and mouth closed. I smoothed out her face and wrapped it in a sheet so it could set."

She took a deep breath. "She died at *home*. I made sure a that. It wasn't gonna be some dirty, stinky old nursing home for this one. 'Hazel,' she used to tell me, before the Alzheimer's got real bad, 'Don't let them take me to some old nursing home fit for a dog, like Geraldo is always busting on TV.'" She laughed loudly and her voice caught, like she was crying. "Not this one. I loved her like my own mother. That's the truth."

I sketched several other stages in my racial education—Martin Luther King, Jr.'s assassination and the shadow his loss had thrown across our household; my musical mentors Nat and Mr. Satan, the richness of their teaching and the chance they'd given me to grow; the lessons in intellectual fearlessness I'd absorbed from Rampersad and historian Nell Painter at Princeton, along with the deep heartache engendered by racial division after the Rodney King beating and trial, the LA riots, the OJ Simpson trial and verdict. But my mind kept drifting back to one foundational memory: the sound of raucous laughter, my grandmother's and Hazel's, emanating from the warm, fragrant kitchen on Sutton Place. Two women joying in each other's company.

Although my kid brother and I had grown up poor out in the boonies, my grandmother was rich, the epitome of "privileged," thanks to my grandfather's successful career as a publisher of business magazines. She wore mink stoles; she knew salesmen by name at Saks Fifth Avenue and had season tickets to the Met. But she was a peasant woman in every other respect—a shopkeeper's daughter who'd sold apples out of a storefront shop in Harlem, back when Harlem was still Jewish. When she and my grandfather flew first class on Pan Am, she stole the little salt and pepper shakers they gave you with dinner. She had a whole drawer full of them back at Sutton Place. Loot! She was loud, uncouth, uncultured, direct. She'd slap her hands together, call you a stinker, toss off some Yiddish: putz, schlemiel.

"Your grandmother would talk to anybody," Hazel used to chuckle. "Right on the street. Didn't make no difference who you were."

When it came time to share, I could have picked anything on my list. Others ahead of me spoke of growing up in all-white towns in Oregon and Massachusetts; watching *Sanford and Son*, *The Jeffersons*, and *Good Times* on TV; listening to Michael Jackson and Whitney Houston; wishing they could be friends with Oprah. I could have spoken about King's death—or recapitulated some of the material I'd worked through in *Mister Satan's Apprentice*. But I thought a little bravery was called for.

I was also—if I'm being honest—fed up by this point with the premise of the workshop, which viewed American race relations as a boobytrapped No Man's Land populated by clueless whites and wounded blacks facing each other across an unbridgeable divide. The life I'd lived, not to mention my ongoing romance with Sherrie, undercut this harsh, reductionist vision at every turn. I had no intention of bringing Sherrie into the conversation, but Hazel and my grandmother were on my mind. So I spoke briefly about their relationship—the private black-Jewish alliance they'd forged in that kitchen, the sounds of nurturance I'd absorbed as a young man when I'd visited the Sutton Place apartment with my parents. This was one early chapter of my racial education, I said, and it had given me hope.

To judge from the frost that audibly ricocheted around the circle, you'd have thought I was James Earl Ray himself, lowering my Remington Gamemaster after blowing a hole through Martin Luther King's jaw. I had unconsciously intended to provoke—I realize that now—and I succeeded. Whispers, then angry murmurs, began to fill the space. Colonialist. Patriarchal. False consciousness. Rich kid. Mammy!

"Hazel wasn't my *mammy*," I heard myself saying. "She was my grandparents' housekeeper. But she was much more than that, and you can't—"

The room began to throb.

"—patterns of behavior reported by people of color around white privilege behavior," Benowitz was saying. "Sometimes that bothers—"

"Unbelievable," hissed one of my gender-fluid antagonists. "Fucking unbelievable."

"It's not as simple as you think," I protested, half-smiling. "You hear 'Barbados' and you think 'black,' but Hazel was mixed, and proud of it. She was part-Jewish! She used to talk about how she was light, like her mother, because her *mother's* mother had married the Jewish man who owned the plantation in her town, after he left his wife for her. She could cook better gefilte fish than my grandmother."

As anger and offense rippled around the circle, I shivered awake, aware for the first time of the gaping hole that had opened before me. No longer the researcher as fly-on-the-wall, no longer a minor irritant, I had suddenly become the main event. Jane and Leah were conferring, then holding up their hands. The suddenness of my silencing was shocking, as was the quiet earnestness, the conviction of rightness, that animated both of them. For the next twenty minutes, they explained, after selecting one person as my advocate, I would sit mute in my chair. Each of my fellow workshoppers would be given the floor, in whatever order they felt like speaking, and would be allowed to unburden themselves of the bad feelings my share had produced at whatever length they desired. No reply or cross-talk was permitted. When the group process was complete, we would adjourn for lunch and engage in silent reflection.

Here I began to shut down. The gay white female ally I chose seemed genuinely concerned on my behalf, although I can't remember what she said in my defense. Nor do I remember how, or even whether, we were allowed to confer. Only recently have I come to understand that the deep structure of this harangue-and-submit ritual derives not from Esalen and other forms of encounter-group work, but from Maoist struggle sessions during the Chinese Cultural Revolution. I have no reason to believe that Holloway and Benowitz were conscious of this parallel, much less adapting it to their needs. What I do know is that at some point they grew alarmed by what they had unleashed.

What does evil sound like, feel like, once set into motion? I knew even as it happened that the scapegoating I was being subjected to was wrong in a way that couldn't possibly contribute to the creation of a better America.

I certainly didn't use the word *evil* during our follow-up phone call two days later. We were all making nice at that point. Our voices were mellow and well-modulated. A mistake had been made, an apology publicly tendered. The ship had been righted, the workshop rescued from disaster. By the time we left Education for Progress at 5:00 PM on Saturday, the dust had settled. Everybody was more or less okay. I'd managed to find a little time outside the back door with Chris, one of my gender-fluid antagonists, and we'd made peace—even shared a brief hug. I'd probably talked a little more than I should have, we agreed. Holloway, Benowitz, and I chuckled about this on the phone: the professor's eternal sin. No hard feelings.

But in the end it was hard feelings—my hard feelings—that had turned the tide. This I remember well. I broke the spell of the struggle session in the simplest possible way: by getting angry.

Because as I sat there in the circle, silenced, *allowing* myself to be silenced, slowly chilling with fear, playing along with the ritual, trying to be a good boy as the solicited bitterness of my fellow workshoppers poured down on me from all sides, there came a moment when something inside me suddenly sparked and I thought, "Wait a minute." In that split second, the slippage between the actual scale of my offense, whatever it was, and the anger being funneled in my direction became impossible to ignore. I was being crucified for the sins of American history, transformed into a convenient dumping ground for every disappointment my fellow citizens had brought through the door. I was Thomas Jefferson raping Sally Hemings, Simon Legree flogging Uncle Tom, Shylock demanding his pound of flesh. *This* was the work?

My heart flamed. I'm not a rageful man, but I've got a fuse, and it occasionally melts. I may have risen to my feet; I may have leaned forward in my chair. I can't remember. But I remember what I said. It was a strange thing for a white guy to say. But it was true to the life I had lived, including four years as a street musician on 125th Street, one block down from the Apollo Theater.

"You couldn't do this in Harlem," I said loudly, suddenly furious, waving my hand at the circle, shocking them into silence. "That's not how things work down there. Everybody gets a chance to say their piece. You want me to be *silent* while you dump on my ass? That's the *whitest* goddamn thing I've ever heard of!"

I said more, but that was enough.

Antiracist Struggle Session 1.0: that's what I was introduced to one October morning in 2003. I was an unwitting pioneer; a test-pilot for the United States of Wokeness that many in my left-of-center cohort would have our nation become. What I was briefly subjected to in that anti-whiteness workshop represents a beta version of the humiliations, reductionist schematics, and compelled "trainings" to which diversity consultants have been subjecting whiteness-carriers ever since George Floyd's death in the summer of 2020. Say what you want about the stories I shared—about the students I sought to serve in an African American literature class, about the intricacies of my black-Jewish family circle. There was room there for a deeper conversation; for exploration and thoughtful critique. But that is not how our workshop organizers set us up. The whole thrust of their work, with its emphasis on iden-tity-based hierarchies of virtue, discernment of microaggressions, and attribution of racial bad faith, was designed to do exactly what it did: spring-load us in the direction of scapegoating, rather than knitting us into a trust-based community.

Reflecting on this experience two decades later, I have no trouble discerning its prophetic shadow in the skewed racial dynamics that unfolded in the summer of 2020 and beyond. Muckraking journal-ist Chris Rufo's July 2020 dispatch, "Cult Programming in Seattle," for example, describes a training session on "Interrupting Internalized Racial Superiority and Whiteness": "The trainers explain that white peo-ple have internalized a sense of racial superiority, which has made them unable to access their 'humanity' and caused 'harm and violence' to people of color. The trainers claim that 'individualism,' 'perfectionism,' 'intellectualization,' and 'objectivity' are all vestiges of this internalized racial oppression and must be abandoned in favor of social-justice principles.... As part of this process, white employees must abandon their 'white normative behavior' and learn to let go of their 'comfort,' 'physical safety,' 'social status,' and 'relationships with some other white people.'"

At Cherokee Middle School in Springfield, Missouri, according to Rufo, trainers took a slightly different approach, forcing teachers to watch a silent nine-minute video of Floyd being choked to death under officer Derek Chauvin's knee, his final cries for his mother highlighted on the screen, before announcing the day's agenda: oppression, white supremacy, and systemic racism. Then they provided the teachers with an eerily familiar "oppression matrix" that defined "White People," "Male assigned at birth," "Heterosexuals," and "Adults," among other categories, as "Privileged Social Groups" and "Asian, Black, Latina/o, Native People," "Female assigned at birth," "Lesbians, Gay Men," and "Elders, Young People" as "Oppressed Social Groups."

Elders *and* young people are oppressed? *Adults* are the problem?

Such essentialist reductions—hammered into rigid templates that blind us to our common humanity, transforming Floyd into a sacrificial victim and leveraging his death like an activist battering ram—are deployed in a way that snares their intended targets in a double bind: damned if you remain silent ("White silence is violence!"), damned if you object ("White fragility!").

Then there are Regina Jackson and Saira Rao, the African American and Indian American co-founders of Race2Dinner, who have profitably reengineered the struggle session so that it nestles within the confines of a dinner party. Profiled in a *Guardian* story titled "Why liberal white women pay a lot of money to learn over dinner how they're racist," Jackson and Rao used to charge liberal white women $2,500 for the privilege of hosting seven other white women at a dinner in their home, but the price has doubled since George Floyd's death. All eight participants must read Robin DiAngelo's *White Fragility* before assembling on game day. Then Jackson and Rao show up, dinner and wine are served, and the difficult conversation—the ritual shaming—begins. "White women are trained to be nice," Jackson tells a reporter. "And part of that niceness means you don't come to a beautifully prepared dinner table and then leave because something upsets you. So we know they'll stay, so that's why we use the dinner."

Rao doesn't coddle her clients. "All white women are Karens," she says, using the hip term for clueless entitled white women. "White liberal women are some of the most dangerous people out there. Because they are the ones changing their Instagram profile to the black box and posting pictures of their kids with lemonade stands for Black Lives Matter and End Asian Hate. But when it comes time to speak up for Black women at work or Asian women at work or Latina women at work: Silent. Silent. Silent."

Rao uses the high-priced Race2Dinner table as her pulpit, a staging area for humiliations that may, if the white women are willing to be re-educated, literally save them from themselves. "The way you just spoke to me was straight-up white supremacy," she lectures one faltering middle-aged matron. "You actually just answered with racism."

After I flew home from Seattle, after the agreed-upon phoner with Jane and Leah had been taped, I kept puttering away on research for my book about racial healing. Something had shifted, though. After Sherrie and I got married the following June and began to live a life outside the Power Grid—a joyful, playful life of shared purpose—the book project came to seem secondary, even unneeded. I wrote one long article, a study of New Age visions of racial healing; the peer reviewer for *American Literary History* mocked it viciously, claiming I was trying to hoax the publication, as physicist Alan Sokal had notoriously hoaxed a leftist cultural studies journal five years earlier. "I could give you lots of 'evidence' to suggest that this is a send up," s/he wrote, "but let this suffice to say NO—unless you want to go the *Social Text* scandal route." I finally got the point: what I had written was literally unthinkable. Racial *healing*? Come on, dude. You can't be serious.

So I gave up on the book and fled from what had happened in Seattle. I'd always considered myself politically progressive—not a marcher or joiner, but somebody committed to the African American freedom struggle and determined to make the world a better place. Yet I knew that what I'd encountered in that activist community wasn't something I wanted any part of. So I pivoted once again, around the time our son was born, and spent the next seven years writing a book about the devil and the blues: not just a subject whose legitimacy no scholar could question, but a broad-ranging field of research into which I could retreat from the culture wars and cultivate more music-focused concerns.

When Shaun turned out to be musically gifted I bought him a trumpet, then an electric bass, then a trombone, a sax, a high-tension marching snare drum—any instrument he wanted—and watched him blossom. I taught him the blues scale. He taught me how to hear the marches of John Phillip Sousa in a new way. I pulled out my parents' old Herb Alpert records; he sputtered through "Tijuana Taxi" and "Spanish Flea" while Sherrie and I drank margaritas on our shady back porch, looking out at the creek and reminiscing about "The Dating Game."

Even as we lived out our own little Mississippi-style experiment in beloved community, I watched our country slowly come undone. I watched the promised racial harmony of the Obama years dissolve in violence and rancor, beginning with the shootings of Gabby Giffords and Trayvon Martin. Sandy Hook Elementary School was next, then Michael Brown and the others. Obama was followed by Trump. We know how that worked out. I outraged and lost Facebook friends on both left and right when I dared to suggest that Trump himself wasn't racist, just happy for the support of racists who said nice things about him. Then came the "Unite the Right" rally in Charlottesville in the summer of 2017, in which a who's who of white identitarian groups—the alt-right, neo-Confederates, neo-fascists, white nationalists, neo-Nazis, Klansmen, and various right-wing militias—joined forces to chant "Jews will not replace us" and a white nationalist rammed a car into a crowd of counter-protestors, killing one woman and injuring many others. It became harder to reason with my friends on the left, not just because overt racism *had* been unleashed, but because Trump's election had driven progressives off the deep end, leading them to form mobs, topple statues, cancel perceived heretics at the slightest whiff of wrongthink, and jettison the author of "The Emancipation Proclamation" as an evil man. "In some circles," reported CNN, "'Honest Abe' is increasingly becoming Racist Abe."

I sympathize with young people, including my son, who must wrangle the world we've bequeathed to them. I applaud the work of those determined to give a fuller and more accurate accounting of our history, one that acknowledges failures and avoids triumphalist cliches. We're living through a time of mourning, engaged in a national reckoning about race. People are waking up to the inequities that have warped our justice system, the lack of police accountability that haunts many communities. These are good and needed developments. But the question of how to create the humane multiracial America that most of us want to live in remains far more vexed than the legions of diversity trainers, equity assessors, and critical race theorists would have us believe.

Where will they place Shaun in their Power Grid? Will the National Museum of African American History & Culture decide that he shows incriminating "signs of whiteness" such as "individualism," "hard work," and "delayed gratification"? My beloved wife exemplifies all those qualities: she's a hard-working individual, decidedly her own person, who knows how to take care of business. Will they banish her too, or summon her to a state-sponsored struggle session? Will they send someone to knock on our front door and teach us, calmly and self-assuredly, that we are not, in fact, members of the same human family, bound in holy matrimony and committed to mutual care, but representatives of distinct races, each with its own historical inheritance and appropriate cultural manifestations, carefully slotted into pre-approved levels within the prevailing hierarchy of virtue? White replacement theorists on the far right are already hard at work on this project. Now we're supposed to submit to attacks from the left?

I've read and taught Toni Morrison's *Beloved*. So I'm familiar with the figure of Schoolteacher, the well-educated white man who arrives at the Sweet Home plantation in Kentucky in the 1850s to take charge after the master dies. Cold, sadistic, utterly convinced of his superiority, he studies the slaves, assaying their "qualities" with a pseudo-scientific precision that Morrison means us to see, through the eyes of an enslaved woman named Sethe, as sickeningly inhumane. "No, no," Sethe overhears Schoolteacher tell his two nephews, "That's not right. I told you to put her human characteristics on the left; her animal ones on the right. And don't forget to line them up."

Sethe, pregnant with her fourth child and beaten mercilessly for helping her two sons and daughter escape Sweet Home, flees the plantation not long after this. She's haunted by Schoolteacher's chart. The columns that divide, with considered precision. When Schoolteacher later tracks her down in Ohio, she slits her daughter's throat rather than allowing her to be taken back to a place where she will be subjected to that Grid. She knows it is evil. I share her revulsion. When something like that has you and your family in its sights, your flesh and blood, the people you would kill for, you do what you need to do.

Those who have brought intersectional theory into the public square after developing it in academic and activist circles over the past thirty years would have us reconstruct the totality of our social relations in line with its dictates: in K-12 schools and universities, in the corporate and nonprofit worlds, at all levels of government, in every conceivable quadrant of organized social life. I think that's a recipe for disaster. I'm convinced we can do better. But of course, I'm just a straight white cisgendered male, and an aging one at that. *And* I live in Mississippi. So nothing I say should be taken seriously.

What do you think? What will you do when you find yourself sitting inside the charmed circle? Will you be fragile or fierce? Will you speak up or remain silent?

My family and I are right here, waiting for you.

Introduction

> You live as if you're already there, that you're already in
> that community, part of that sense of one family, one
> house. If you visualize it, if you can even have faith that
> it's there, for you it is already there. And during the
> early days of the movement, I believed that the only
> true and real integration for that sense of the beloved
> community existed within the movement itself. Because
> in the final analysis, we did become a circle of trust, a
> band of brothers and sisters. So it didn't matter whether
> you were black or white. It didn't matter whether
> you came from the North to the South, or whether
> you're a Northerner or Southerner. We were one.
>
> —John Lewis (2016)

I n the spring of 2014, on the fiftieth anniversary of Mississippi's
Freedom Summer, I taught a course in the University of Mississippi
Honors College about the events of that turbulent time. Although
I am a blues scholar and, more broadly, a scholar of African American
literature and culture, I have long been fascinated by the early years
of the civil rights movement, especially Mississippi between 1961 and
1964, a dark period indeed when white supremacist reaction was murderous and anyone seeking to improve the lives of Mississippi's black

folk would have been forgiven for losing hope. What I found impossible to understand was the way Dave Dennis, John Lewis, Chuck McDew, Anne Moody, Bob Zellner, and those other early SNCC activists, led by Fannie Lou Hamer and Bob Moses but with the guidance and assistance of Ella Baker, Amzie Moore, and countless others, managed to conquer the fear that the entire system of racialized disciplinary violence, head-lined by the Klan and underwritten by the White Citizens' Council, was trying to inflict on them. Somehow they managed to walk forward into the teeth of that violence, and they remained nonviolent while doing so.

It became clear to me that the concept of beloved community, a brotherhood and sisterhood grounded in love, was a key to the spiritual and, ultimately, political power they wielded, however compromised the latter may have seemed at the time. They had changed my adopted state for the better. They had broken open the closed society. They had made my marriage, my wife's and son's flourishing, our familial flourishing, possible. We owed them a debt that could never fully be repaid. But we could, if we were willing, try to understand and honor the ideals that guided them.

This book's yearning toward beloved community speaks not just to our own troubled and perilous American moment but to the world into which I was born, more than six decades ago. The dream of beloved com-munity always takes shape in the face of what would oppose it: violent words, threats, and actions; the reification of racial difference and the creation of racial hierarchies; closed-hearted subjugation; the calculated infliction of fear; the narrowing of acceptable speech until politically efficacious silencing has been achieved. Light shines most powerfully in the presence of darkness. And the recurrent, chronic, dispiriting pres-ence of darkness is no reason to discount, much less ignore, the power of the dream to light the way.

I grew up in an unabashedly progressive family. My late father, Alan Gussow, worked for Robert Kennedy's 1968 presidential campaign out in Oregon and was a delegate for George McGovern at the Democratic National Convention in 1972. My mother, Joan Dye Gussow, nutri-tion educator and agribusiness gadfly, friend of Michael Pollan and Bill

McKibben, has been called the godmother of the locavore movement. "The movement," meaning the Civil Rights movement and its evolution into protest against the war in Vietnam, was a frequent subject of conversation in our household during the late '60s and early '70s, although I was far more invested at the time in boyhood pursuits: butterfly and snake collecting, go-karts, pulling wheelies on my bicycle with the purple banana seat and hi-rise handlebars. But I shared the desolation that haunted our household in the spring of 1968 when Martin Luther King, Jr., and then Bobby Kennedy were assassinated within the space of two months. America had done this: killed our brightest stars, our best hopes. I was ten years old and felt this.

1968 was also my introduction to the cyclical nature of American progress, the boomerang of history, as Ralph Ellison might have called it. Because things *had* improved thanks to the struggle for civil rights— although of course more improvement, more forward motion, were required, and reversals were always possible. In 1958, the year I was born, a Gallup poll showed that only 4 percent of Americans approved of marriage between blacks and whites. Yet 1958 was also the year that Mildred and Richard Loving, an interracial couple from rural Virginia, chose love and marriage across the color line, forming a beloved community of two that expanded into a family of five. Yes, they were persecuted by a Virginia court: forced to live out of state, prevented from cohabiting as husband and wife in their own hometown. But they ultimately triumphed with the help of the US Supreme Court in *Loving v. Virginia* (1967), a landmark decision that repealed anti-miscegenation statutes nationwide and paved the way for marriages like my own. By 2021, the same Gallup poll found that 94 percent of Americans approved of black-white intermarriage: an astonishing inversion of the earlier attitudinal snapshot.

The Afropessimist perspective articulated by Frank Wilderson, Saidiya Hartman, Christina Sharpe, and Isabel Wilkerson, among others, which views American history as a domain shaped by an intractable anti-blackness that forecloses all talk of temporal progress in racial matters, refuses to applaud that sort of good news. In *Caste: The Origins of*

Our Discontents (2020), for example, Wilkerson invokes the 4 percent approval figure from Gallup's 1958 poll by way of arguing that African Americans form a sort of untouchable caste, permanently beneath and exiled from the perquisites of the white American caste, but she fails to cite subsequent Gallup polls tracking the wholesale reversal of this don't-mix-the-races attitude among whites over the following decades. (Blacks had always viewed interracial marriage more favorably, but they, too, had come around.) To allow such an incontestably positive development into her analysis would have forced her to consider the possibility that neither race nor caste is as wholly intractable or determinative as she believes, and that racial pessimism is not the only valid orientation towards American experience.

My family and I know this. I have written this memoir to bear witness to what we know. But I am also a realist, and I recognize that the beloved community my family and I have created is imperiled by a range of recent developments. I have written *My Family and I* not just to share the good news of what is possible in contemporary America, but to engage deeply with what shadows, troubles, and impinges upon our national life and one family's pursuit of happiness down in Oxford, Mississippi.

In 1957, the year before Mildred and Richard Loving married and shortly after the founding of the Southern Christian Leadership Conference, Martin Luther King, Jr., spelled out his dream for the first time. "The ultimate aim of SCLC," he wrote, "is to foster and create the 'beloved community' in America where brotherhood is a reality... SCLC works for integration. Our ultimate goal is genuine intergroup and interpersonal living—*integration*." King took pains to distinguish between desegregation and integration. Desegregation, King explained, "will only create a society where men are physically desegregated and spiritually segregated, where elbows are together and hearts apart. It gives us social togetherness and spiritual apartness." Integration, in his view, was much more than that.

My Family and I makes no pretense at offering an in-depth study of King's thoughts on the subject, much less an historical or theological survey of the beloved community ideal. Others, especially Charles Marsh with *The Beloved Community: How Faith Shapes Social Justice, From the Civil Rights Movement to Today* (2005), have done a much better job of that. My own understanding is primitive, eclectic, but workable. It views beloved community as grounded in love—not just the selfless *agape* that King and Lewis spoke of, but the somewhat less exalted but passion-driven *philia*, the joy in shared endeavor that breaks down social distinctions and transforms fellow citizens into thriving communities. Grooving to music, as musician and audience, can do that; so can the collective practice of taekwondo; so can full-throated participation in a graduate seminar, if conditions are right. All three activities are imaged in the pages that follow. Since slavery and segregation were grounded in violence, a violence used to maintain racial separation and subordination, and since beloved community represents the aspirational endpoint of a process dedicated to healing the long traumatic tail of those two things, an embrace of nonviolence is a critically important constituent of beloved community, as is an egalitarian outlook dedicated to diminishing the practical importance of racial difference.

Food—breaking bread with friends and family—is, or can be, another important touchstone of beloved community, as King famously suggested in his 1963 "I Have a Dream" speech. "I have a dream," he declaimed, "that one day on the red hills of Georgia sons of former slaves and the sons of former slave-owners will be able to sit down together at the table of brotherhood." An attentive reader of *My Family and I* will pick up on moments that example this bountiful-table idea. The presence of peace, more broadly, is a sign of beloved community, testifying to the presence of mutual care and acceptance of our flawed but shared humanity. The opposite of peace—tension, uncertainty, anxiety; a compulsion to racialize, judge, rage, wreak violence—can help us see not just the absence of beloved community in specific social contexts, but the presence of what is inimical to beloved community in the world at large.

If SCLC's ultimate goal in the late 1950s, as King noted, was "genuine intergroup and interpersonal living—*integration*," then integration, as a social ideology with political force, has an almost laughably outdated sound in our own time. This is largely because it was stigmatized, dislodged, and run out of town in the mid-1960s by the Black Power movement and its anti-colonialist analysis. SNCC's retreat from a transracialist ethos, visible by the fall of 1964, came to a head with a 1967 vote to exclude whites from the organization—a development, we should not forget, that Fannie Lou Hamer, John Lewis, and Bob Moses all objected to.

The separatist thrust of Black Power has recently reemerged in attenuated form in the curious social formation known as "racial affinity groups," a form of antiracist behavioral modification that temporarily segregates, by race, the employees of a given organization, the better to facilitate—or so it is argued—the "difficult conversations" and urgently needed consciousness-raising required of blacks without the potentially toxic and disabling presence of whites. Not only does this practice stand at the farthest possible remove from King's dream of beloved community, but it fails to make a space for the glorious and expanding tribe of "black" and mixed-race Americans, including Thomas Chatterton Williams, Kmele Foster, Starlette Thomas, Eli Steele, and my son, who, happy to check two boxes or no boxes, have little patience with what feels to them like a creaky old paradigm, "race," that has outlived its usefulness. Some refer to this development as race abolitionism. Inaya Folarin Iman and Sheena Mason, with her "theory of racelessness," are eloquent spokeswomen for this loosely organized movement. *My Family and I* contributes to the race abolitionist project by offering autobiographical testimony that living one's life in accord with the movement's insights is a realizable ambition, not a utopian fantasy.

While this book has irritable things to say about contemporary elite circles dominated by a particular kind of progressive illiberalism, it doesn't spend much time discussing, or worrying about, the broad spectrum of white identitarians and white supremacists hovering on the right: the Richard Spencers, Stephen Millers, Jared Taylors, and Dylann

Roofs of the world. I know they're out there; I see them for who they are. Spencer and Miller were a grad student and undergrad at Duke, respectively, when the Duke lacrosse "rape" case roiled our mass media environment for months before imploding, making clear to many—and to me for the first time—that some elements of our academic left are profoundly troubled. But I share nothing else with Spencer or Miller, or with Taylor or Roof or any other white man who reifies and embraces his "own" race to prattle of "race-realism" and the "Great Replacement," or who simply hates black people and wants to abuse them or see them dead. The latter sort of old-school white racists do show up when I write in "Harlem Awakening" of New York City's tortured racial atmosphere in the late 1980s and early 1990s; Howard Beach, Bensonhurst, and Crown Heights each saw racial murders during this era—Italian on black in the first two cases, black on Jewish in the third. Some may presume that an interracial family living in contemporary Mississippi and traveling throughout the Deep South would feel imperiled by an ongoing threat of racist disrespect and intimidation. We don't feel that way, because our long experience has taught us, after some initial uncertainty and with a couple of minor exceptions, that we don't need to. That's a pleasant surprise.

The memoir you are holding in your hands is an offering: my attempt, as a citizen of the imperfect country we both love, to help you see our America in a new way. "Double-consciousness" is the phrase W. E. B. DuBois used; this is sort of like that. We are an unfinished people. A passion project filled with loose ends. *At* loose ends. Our passions are disordered. We could use some guidance. All I've got by way of advice is the life I've lived and a few ideas about what it means. So that's where my offering begins: with a mid-career restart in the summer of 2002 and scenes from the life of my family. Maybe you'll figure something out, whoever you are, when I share what I'm about to share.

I want to tell you about the woman I love and the son we both love. We have a good life. (What I share of my wife here, I should add, is what she wanted shared; I'm truly grateful for her generosity, since she

xlix

values her, and our family's, privacy.) But I also want to help you see why I've spent most of the last decade worried about where we're headed—not my family, but the country. Harlem, back in the day with Sterling Magee, is a part of all this, because that's where I began to figure out who I was and what I wanted. The third section of this book, "Wokeness, Heterodoxy, and Dreams Deferred," offers time-stamped dispatches from the front lines of the culture war: good-faith, sometimes agonized reflections of a skeptical liberal, a scholar of African American literature and culture who was forced with considerable reluctance to take a step toward the center to defend his family against an onslaught of bad ideas and tell complex truths that his progressive peers were unwilling to acknowledge. Although Faulkner has never been a conscious influence on the way I tell stories, it's possible that I've caught a contact high after dwelling for more than two decades in the north Mississippi hill country. Like the blues songs described by Zora Neale Hurston, this book proceeds through incremental repetition: worrying key themes, circling obsessively around the seasons of our discontent, boomeranging back and forth across the decades, struggling for firm grounding in a troubled world.

There is hope in the distance, over the far horizon. But we need to know where we've been before we can fully appreciate where we are.

CHASING THE DREAM

Pea Ridge Road

The bike wreck happened on my fifth day in town, just as I was starting to settle in.

The Allied Van Lines truck hadn't yet shown up with my bed and other worldly possessions, but it was fun sleeping on an air mattress—like camping in the woods, except with air conditioning and no mosquitoes. The katydids of north Mississippi made a huge clattery sound in the trees outside my window, an uncanny echo of hot August nights back in Congers, New York, the tiny downstate hamlet where I'd grown up.

I'd done all the obvious stuff: visited my campus office and checked out the big new iMac; walked over to the Blues Archive, on the second floor of the library, and introduced myself to the blues archivist, Greg Johnson; bought chicken-on-a-stick at Chevron. I'd had drinks at Ajax Diner with Scott Barretta, editor of *Living Blues*, to chat about the "Blues Today" symposium we were organizing for the spring. Clarksdale was sixty-two miles from my front door. The Delta began on the far side of Batesville, twenty-two miles away. Blues country all around me.

What surprised me most was how quickly I'd fallen in love with the landscape. Turning left out of the driveway on my bike, I'd found a hot sunny road that looped past New Hope Missionary Baptist church and the dusty entrance to a construction site, passed through a gauntlet of rangy dogs curled up in front of trailers who leaped up to give chase, then headed up into hills blanketed with dark green kudzu that gave off a sharp tangy scent. A pack of speckled pea hens chased each other through the wooded yard at the crest. It felt good to stand up on the pedals, working the handlebars and sweating in the sun; good to speed downhill, cooling a little as I blew through the woods past old trucks and the occasional pimped-out ride with flashy chrome rims. I'd brought along a local map—I'd already learned to say "La-FAY-ette County," the local pronunciation—and knew that I was on Pea Ridge Road. Tailing down out of the hills after three or four miles, the road T-junctioned into a rural highway; a left turn took you out onto a long flat straight-away past fields thick with dark green cotton plants that hadn't yet burst into fluffy white bolls. Another mile and a half and you hit a bigger two-lane highway, Route 7, and a country store in which older white men sat around a table in back, sipping coffee and chatting like Yoknapatawpha locals while a migrant fresh from New York bought a bottle of cold lemonade up front. I found my way home on back roads, three more miles that ended with a long slow uphill pull past the skate park on South Lamar. Nine miles for the loop.

I can do this, I thought, heart soaring. I can whip myself back into shape. I can live here.

Two days later I biked the Pea Ridge loop for the third day in a row—not in the morning, but later, just before dusk. A light drizzle was starting to fall. Knowing the route now, seeing it in my head, I decided to push harder. I hit it past the dogs—they were a hazard, I'd decided, just waiting to jump me—and hammered the first hill, up over the wooded crest where the speckled pea hens drifted like ghosts through the trees. I wound it out on the first big downhill. The speed was exhilarating. I was starting to get a feel for the bike again.

Ten minutes later, as I came down off the last long hill into the flat stretch before the highway, a glance at my digital speedometer showed twenty-seven miles an hour. I'd just looked back up when I hit a stray bump—a blob of hardened contractor's concrete about the size of a small turtle, I'd discover later—and was thrown into a standing position on the pedals: butt off the seat, hands off the handlebars. The bike and I sailed down the road for one endless second, center bar shuddering between my thighs, before the handlebars spun sideways and I flipped, the pavement coming up and slapping me with a sickening thump. It was as though a giant had grabbed me by the ankles and hammered my head and left shoulder down against the blacktop.

I lay on my back by the side of the road. Dusk was falling. I'd been thrown free of the bike. After discovering that I could still breathe, I slowly sat up and began to assess. The Styrofoam-lined cycling helmet had taken the full brunt of the impact. My zip-up cycling shirt was badly torn; my left shoulder seemed to be broken. I could feel the bone sticking out—my collarbone, I realized—and my hand was bloody when I took it away. I shifted my weight, put my hand on the pavement, and staggered to my feet. My knees were bloody and stinging. My head suddenly felt light. I put my hands on my knees and tried to breathe calmly. Something very bad had happened. But collapsing by the side of a back road in rural Mississippi was not an option.

I stood up and hobbled over to my bike, reached down for the handlebars and raised it to full height. The handlebars were slightly skewed relative to the front fork, but that was all. It could be ridden. I tilted the frame sideways toward the ground, lifted a leg over the lowered seat, then raised the frame back to full height, straddling it, slipping one cycling shoe into a toe clip. Then I was on and moving—pedaling slowly down the road, through the dusk and light mist, toward the highway.

At some point, in the middle of an endless gloomy straightaway, I stopped. I'd ridden as far as I could. Now I would walk. The country store had to be somewhere up ahead.

I limped along the side of the road, wheeling my bike through the darkening drizzle. Then I saw the lights of a car approaching from behind and I turned and put out my thumb. I'd never hitchhiked, but that's what you were supposed to do.

The car slowed, then stopped. The passenger side window rolled down. It was a woman, younger than me. I told her what had happened. I told her where I lived. I would be okay, I said, if I could just get a ride back there. She was staring at me as I spoke.

"I'm sorry for all the blood," I said.

"Just get in," she said, leaning over to yank the door halfway open. "I'll put your bike in the back."

Before moving to Mississippi, I'd made a conscious decision. I had a book coming out that December—my revised dissertation—entitled *Seems Like Murder Here: Southern Violence and the Blues Tradition.* During my last three years in grad school I'd done a deep dive into the history of racial violence in the Deep South. I had a map of Mississippi in my head, one that highlighted the names of towns where lynchings, often gruesome and highly public, had taken place. Duck Hill. Doddsville. Lexington, where B. B. King's spirit had been crushed as a boy. I'd written about Claude Neal in Marianna, Florida; Henry Smith in Paris, Texas. I knew that I was moving to a haunted state with a troubled past—a place that would weigh on me if I allowed it to.

But I'd also become a student of *A Course in Miracles*, with its stress on radical forgiveness, and a fan of Pema Chödrön's teachings on impermanence, nonattachment, and compassion. I wasn't a full-blown New Ager, but I'd been phase-shifted in that direction.

So I'd decided, when I headed south, to start fresh. I knew as much about the bad old days as book learning could teach you. I knew that many people thought of the University of Mississippi as a place scarred by the deadly riot that took place back in 1962 when James Meredith tried to become the first black student to enroll. I knew Faulkner's most famous saying about the state: "The past is never dead. It's not even past." But the *Course* told me that dwelling in the past, using the past to attack the present, would make miracles impossible. It would prevent me from seeing the present, apprehending all of its richness and potential, and dwelling joyfully in it. I was determined to allow miracles to materialize.

And, yes, I knew exactly how loopy that sounded to most people. But I was where I was at that point in my life, and that really was my attitude.

He was the first friend I'd made in Oxford. A small, skinny guy with shaved legs and a big smile, a native of Brandon, down near Jackson, Richard Nye was a competitive biker who lived with his girlfriend in the rental house just down the hill. He'd seen me pumping up my tires on my first morning in town and walked up the driveway to chat. He liked to talk. He had a cocky attitude and a flavorful twang that reminded me of Ross Perot's. He was in his early thirties and had left Ole Miss to train as an elite in-line skater before returning to finish up his degree in accountancy. I showed him my Honda; he showed me his old Toyota. It couldn't hold a candle, he said, to the van he used to drive: the Linear Power Bread Truck.

"Ray Rayfield put a heck of a sound system in that baby. One hundred and fourteen subwoofers. One hundred and fourteen *thousand* watts. The most dangerous thing in the world," he proclaimed, "is a redneck with money."

I didn't know Richard well—I barely knew him at all—but on the night of my wreck, I asked the woman who gave me a lift to drive a hundred feet past my driveway, down to his house. I was alone in town. A competitive cyclist like him would be able to take one look at me and have a pretty good sense of what steps needed to be taken.

Richard and his girlfriend opened their front door.

"Hoo-wee," he said. "What happened to you?"

And just like that, they took me in. "Road rash" was Richard's term for the bloody abrasions on my shoulder, back, knees, and elbows. He made it sound like a rite of passage for any serious rider. When I almost passed out as he began to dab at my wounds, they bundled me into their car and drove me to the emergency room at Baptist Memorial. They waited out front while x-rays were taken and the nurses cleaned me up.

I hadn't broken any bones, but I had a Grade 3 separated shoulder—my shoulder blade had been torn away from the collarbone, permanently lowered one full inch by the impact, leaving the end of the collarbone sticking out: a noticeable bump. I'd be wearing a sling for the next few weeks, but I would probably regain full range of motion, although I'd always have that knob on my shoulder. The flesh wounds would heal if I kept them clean and used ointment. The nurses gave me a couple of Tylenol and a prescription for Vicodin.

That was my welcome to Mississippi. Less than one week in and I was permanently disfigured, incapacitated, and in pain. Broken again. I wouldn't be riding, running, or dating for a while. But I was alive. I did my best to look on the sunny side. Classes didn't start for two weeks.

What happened next was something that might lead people to use the word *angel*, although I was too much of a skeptic even then to imagine that God had sent Richard down for my benefit. But there he was: my nurse. It started with him volunteering that first night to pick up my prescriptions the next morning—the sort of thing a generous neighbor might do. When he stopped by to drop them off, we both realized that there was no way I could twist my arms around to apply ointment to the places where it was needed. So I took off my shirt and he carefully peeled off my bloody dressings, which hurt a lot because the nurse at the hospital who shaved the hair around my wounds hadn't gotten it all.

Richard, it turned out, was familiar with this routine; my yelps just made him laugh.

"Why do you think my legs are shaved?" he said as he worked on my back. "You know you're going down eventually. Road rash is part of the job description. My legs are pre-approved for surgical tape."

I winced and cursed, but I was grateful. "I used to think I had it in me to be a race car driver. I've harbored that dream for years. That fucker is *gone*, baby."

"Nawwwww. Don't give it up."

"No more contact sports for me. You know the worst injury ever suffered by a table tennis player?"

"Gosh dawg, ya got me stumped."

"There were two guys playing in a tournament—I heard this story years ago at a training camp—and one of the guys got so angry at how badly he was playing that he threw his paddle at the net. It bounced up and scored a direct hit on the other guy's crotch."

"Ouch!"

"Took him out."

We told many stories over the next two weeks during his daily morning round. I tried to thank him, but he shrugged it off. Just one man helping another.

In the weeks after my crash, I managed to ease into my new professor's job. I learned how to drive wearing a sling and how to write on the board by slipping it off for thirty seconds at a time. My shoulder ached when I raised my arm, but I could do it.

Thanks to Richard's ministrations, my flesh wounds had begun to heal. But my spirit was troubled. In a moment of carelessness at the bottom of a hill, I'd mutilated myself. I wasn't a vain guy, but still: I'd come south hoping finally to meet the right woman and settle down. Now this. I hadn't quite been transformed into a hunchback, but I had a noticeable bump that showed through my shirts.

My orthopedist in Oxford, Dr. Cooper Terry, advised against surgery. But he sent me to the Campbell Clinic up in Germantown for a second opinion. I'd regained full mobility; I was playing table tennis again. But I still had the bump. It didn't hurt, but I didn't want it. So I drove up.

The consult lasted five minutes. The doctor waved me into his office, asked me to take off my shirt. He looked at my separated shoulder, felt it, asked me if it hurt. It didn't really hurt. I was honest with him about why I was there. I was single and looking. Hoping.

"I wouldn't worry about it," he said. Then he gave me the faintest flicker of a smile. "Some women like bumps."

How I Met My Wife

During several weeks of late-night talks in which I'd rapidly grown infatuated with Vanessa, a Memphis phone-personals hookup I still hadn't met, I'd had one phone conversation with a second potential date. She, too, was a single black female seeking a single white male. She lived in Dallas, worked as an accountant at a major marketing firm, and had an eleven-year-old daughter. We'd only spoken once. I was a newly hired tenure-track assistant professor of English and Southern Studies at the University of Mississippi. I'd just moved down from New York after twenty-two years in Manhattan and, at age forty-four, was determined to find and marry my beloved, whoever she turned out to be.

This goal was accompanied, curiously enough, by a prophecy: one that had presented itself to me quite unexpectedly on the final day of the "Opening the Heart" workshop I'd attended back in July at The Omega Institute, a holistic educational center in upstate New York. I was about to embark on a new phase of my life; I wanted to heal what needed healing and lighten my load. The facilitators had led us through many exercises over the previous two days, most of which involved sitting cross-legged on the floor, gazing into the eyes of our fellow workshoppers—male, female, gay, straight—and letting go. Many tears had been shed. By this point we were blown wide-open and running on fumes. This is when the facilitators gave us pens and paper and asked us to write down our heart's desire, then share it with the person we'd been paired with.

My first thought, jokingly, was, "Heck, man, if I can't get a McLaren F1, I'll take a 'Vette Z06."

Then I felt my heart flower. If I was being honest, I knew exactly what I wanted.

My heart's desire was a life partner: a woman I could love without limits, marry without reservation, and live with in joy, peace, and the fullness of time, until death did us part. I'd had two five-year live-in relationships, and each of them had gone down in flames—although the first, back in my early twenties, had taught me what open-hearted love felt like. My romantic life was the repeated A-line of a blues song. I needed that answering line, and it needed to be a happy blues, not a sad one.

So I wrote down my heart's desire. It came to me with the weird specificity of a fortune teller's vision. "She'll be a Louisiana woman," I wrote. "I don't know if she'll be black or white, but she'll be wearing blue jeans and cowboy boots."

There was more, but that's the part I remember.

Sherrie and I had connected with the help of a new website called Match.com. There were a handful of dating sites like that back in the early aughts. They seemed like a huge improvement over older modes: *Village Voice* personals, bars, friends setting you up. You could select for a wide range of attributes—physical, emotional, economic, political, religious—which made the whole process less of a crapshoot, and you could expand your search as far as you were willing to travel. The profiles had photos and self-descriptions. This was useful because it told you whether the person thought in clichés. I knew I could never marry a woman who said she enjoyed "the finer things in life." I wanted somebody with more imagination than that.

Sherrie's profile was titled "Sassy, Sweet, Sexy & Smart." She had a big, cute smile with white teeth against dark skin, startlingly bright eyes, short dark bobbed hair. She was wearing a lemon yellow singlet and dark shorts and was posed against a white background—hands on hips, arms toned, as though she'd just finished a workout. Dallas was a long way from Oxford: more than 550 miles, according to MapQuest. I'd set that filter pretty high. Everything else looked good. Divorced was no problem; I assumed that somebody in her forties like me might have a divorce and/or a kid. None of us were spring chickens.

In the "About her personality" section, she'd selected "Light-hearted—I like cheerful, gentle fun." "Turn Ons" included "Public Displays of Affection" and "Brainiacs." She'd only checked one item in the "Turn Offs" column: "Sarcasm."

How she describes herself:

Hi there! I'm pleased to give you a glimpse of who I am. I know you've probably read it a million times, but again I'm honest (test me), sincere, attentive and very affectionate. I really like to have fun, laugh uncontrollably, and basically have a good time. Outgoing, confident, intelligent (no brain surgery), I'm a woman who loves life. I'm serious when necessary, but being silly lightens the mood. Since I'm not perfect, I accept constructive criticism and try to improve myself daily. I love sports, especially football. I play a little tennis, rollerblade and run for exercise. If you're the right guy, I just want to be anywhere you are—which means you can take me anywhere and I'd have a good time. But if you want a list, it includes travel, movies, festivals, concerts, anything artsy or cultural, sporting events, church/community activism, whatever. Cuddling, hugging, kissing and handholding are welcomed treasures. I want to share the prime of my life—and beyond!—with the right man.

Evaluating somebody at a distance, how do we know which enumerated qualities, if any, will end up capturing our heart? Compatibility isn't love. Idealized self-portraits aren't love. Truth in advertising makes a difference, though. Sherrie said nothing about her slender wrists and warm hands, or her adorable habit of decorating the interior and exterior of the house to ceremonialize major holidays; I would find all that out later. Kindness, sincerity, self-knowledge, and integrity turn out to have been what I was looking for. But I was also looking for poetry and was struck by that phrase "welcomed treasures."

Match.com allowed you free access, but you had to pay a membership fee to respond. So I'd joined up, paid, and messaged her. We'd exchanged phone numbers, talked once. It wasn't as magical as the talks I'd been having with Vanessa, but it was fun and interesting, and it was clear that this could lead to a date.

I had a gig that Sunday afternoon at Hopson Plantation over in Clarksdale, a pickup gig at an outdoor festival that Scott Barretta had hooked up for me. It was my first blues gig since moving down to Mississippi seven weeks earlier.

We'd had one rehearsal the previous weekend at drummer Sam Carr's house over in Lula, between Clarksdale and Helena, on the edge of a big cotton field. It was a hot day and we sat on the screened-in porch while Sam's wife, a friendly, plain woman named Doris, lounged on the bed just inside, watching TV. I found out later they'd been married for fifty-six years. Sam, a small trim brown man in a sharp-brimmed white hat, was a legend: the best-known Delta blues drummer, son of Robert Nighthawk and a former member of the Jelly Roll Kings with Big Jack Johnson and Frank Frost. The guitarist, who also lived in Lula, was Andrew "Shine" Turner, Ike's second cousin. Roughly my age, he, too, was small, trim, and friendly, with a dark blue trucker's cap and wire-rimmed glasses. The other guitarist—there was no bass—was a white guy named Fred.

It was a low-key rehearsal. We sat around on chairs and an old sofa, swatting away flies, talking and playing through a handful of different shuffles, slow blues, and straight-time grooves. "Blow Wind Blow," "Hoochie Coochie Man," "Got My Mojo Working." Sam was using a very small trap set and the amps were turned down. My New York City groove was a little more forward-leaning than these guys, so I dialed it back and settled in. Sam was blues royalty; his shuffle was the gold standard.

On gig day I drove over to Clarksdale with a sick, hollow feeling in my heart from what had happened, or hadn't happened, with Vanessa the night before. I hadn't been stone-cold blown off like that in a long time. I knew how to do the emotionally bereft thing; I'd done it a dozen times through the years. But this time it really hurt. I didn't want the blues. But there it was. I actually *had* the blues, in a bad way, on the day of my first legit blues gig in Mississippi.

The October afternoon was clear and dry, warm in the sun and cooler in the shade. Shine did most of the singing. He gave me the nod to take solos; otherwise I just settled into the groove, working my harp into the overall texture. I thought about Nat and Sterling and all the other great players whose guidance had brought me to the point where I could walk into a gig like this, on a festival stage in the Mississippi Delta, and handle it. I was one of Sam Carr's Delta Jukes. That fact helped counterbalance the previous night's disaster and the low-level ache in my heart. I was still alone in the world.

After the gig, after I'd packed up, loaded out, and gotten paid, Shine and I were standing by my car as the next band did their thing. He was a likeable guy with an attitude of basic friendliness. I would find out a decade later, when we worked as a duo for a year or two, that he'd been a church musician for a long time, partnered with his wife, a singer. So he was a good man: a man of faith. But he'd also been a blues player for a long time. On this day I took the risk of sharing my pain more openly than I normally would have with somebody I didn't know well.

"Hey, Shine," I said, "something happened yesterday that got me hurting, and I could really use some of your blues wisdom." It was a strange way to put things, but that's what I needed.

He smiled. "Tell me about it."

I told him an abbreviated version of what had happened with Vanessa. He listened patiently. People told longer stories in Mississippi than they did in other places, I'd discovered, and they gave each other the space to do that.

"It hurts, man. I feel like a fool. I went and bought all that stuff—fruit salad, which I made from scratch, and Champagne. I cleaned the house from top to bottom. She was supposed to drive down from Memphis. And then she stood me up. I called her home phone three or four times and left a voicemail. Nothing. She *still* hasn't called back. I feel like a goddamned fool."

"No, I wouldn't do that." He cocked his head, angling the brim of his trucker's cap against the late afternoon sun. "Look at it this way: now you got your place all cleaned up for when the *right* person comes along. Uh huh. So it wasn't wasted work."

I didn't call Sherrie that night, after I got home from the gig, even though I wanted to. I just lazed around the house, thinking about Shine's words and finishing up Arthur Flowers's novel *Another Good Loving Blues*, which I was teaching the next day. Bluesman Luke Bodeen was trying to woo conjure woman Melvira Dupree. They get together in the end, but not before Bodeen tumbles into addiction and despair, gives up on life, then gets disgusted with himself and begins to climb back out. I liked novels that showed somebody persisting in the face of disaster. The blues ethos, I told my students: never give up. When you fall down, don't stay down any longer than you have to. Then pull yourself together and get on with it. That's what I'd done after the bike wreck, with Richard Nye's help. And I was okay. Scarred, with a bump, but everything still worked.

I called Sherrie that evening, after class. We had a great conversation that took us in unexpected directions and convinced us that we should meet. We made a date for Saturday night.

I can't remember which of us came up with the idea of driving in from opposite directions and meeting in Monroe, Louisiana, halfway between Dallas and Oxford. It was 270 miles for me, a little further for her, all on fast highways. It seemed like the sort of crazy romantic thing you could only do in the South. I couldn't imagine somebody back in Manhattan driving that far for a first date. I reserved two rooms at the Days Inn, just east of town on I-20.

"Are we really gonna do this?" I said. "I like your voice, by the way. You have a cute voice."

She laughed. "How can somebody have a cute voice?"

"Damned if I know."

"Awww," she said like Tweety Bird. "Dat's so tweeeeet. Yes, we're gonna do this."

She emailed another photo the next day, a casual group shot from the office. She and her coworkers were gathered in a half circle. She was in the front row, sitting on the floor—legs crossed at the ankles, arms clasped around legs. She was wearing Capri pants and a sweater with the sleeves pushed up. Her horn-rimmed glasses accentuated her jawline. She had full features and a pretty smile. Prettier than I'd realized.

"You wear glasses," I said when we spoke that evening.

"Surprise!" she laughed. "My eyes are terrible, so the prescription is super-strong. I'll be wearing contacts when I see you on Saturday."

When Vanessa finally called on Wednesday evening, the first thing she did was apologize in her husky, sexy voice. I listened to her briefly, letting her talk, breathing calmly. I was surprised by how calm I was.

"Look," I said, "I appreciate your apology. But I'd like you to do me a favor. Please never call me again."

There was a pause.

"I don't…I mean what are you…are you angry at me?"

"No, I'm just not interested in continuing the conversation. Please don't call me again."

I didn't have a cell phone, but Sherrie did, and I stopped once during the drive down from Oxford to call her from a pay phone at a rest area in Vaiden. She was near Longview, she said. On the way!

MY FAMILY & I

I-55 South in Mississippi was fast, uncrowded. The drive gave me a chance to think about who I was at this point in my life—to realize that the sense of strangeness, freedom, and excitement feathering my guts was the same groundlessness I'd felt when leaving New York two months earlier to take the job at Ole Miss. Something genuinely new was about to happen. That was a good thing.

I exited right onto I-220 in Ridgeland and headed west towards Vicksburg, rolling gently downhill past signs for the Lady Luck Casino and the Bottleneck Blues Bar at the Ameristar. I'd been playing one particular CD the whole way down, a two-disc Delmark Forty-Fifth Anniversary blues sampler that Scott had tossed me from the stack in his office at *Living Blues*. I was stuck on Jimmy Burns's "Leaving Here Walking," a shuffle with a repeated minor-key riff that rolled onward, whispering to me:

> I'm gonna leave here walking
> Ain't got time for a bus, train, or plane
> Gonna leave here walking
> Ain't got time for bus, train or plane
> I got a letter, came today
> From my baby, she's so far away
> Said she needs me and I'm still her man
> Said she was sure I would understand
>
> This time tomorrow
> I wanna be way down the road
> This time tomorrow
> I wanna be way down the road
> I wanna be with my baby all alone
> Don't want nobody else hanging around
> She's way down yonder in Dublin, Miss,
> And Lord you know that's way down in Mississippi

The music had a troubled urgency: Burns knew where he was going, needed his woman, needed that fulfillment and completion, but knew things were working against him. I knew that feeling. I'd known it was lurking in the music as long as I'd been playing the music. But something about actually *being* down in Mississippi, pushing down through the state on my way to a big date....

The blues were gut-level dread. For a moment, rolling towards Vicksburg, that's what possessed me. A pair of motel rooms and a woman I'd never met. How could things possibly work out? Only a fool could think that.

I inhaled deeply and surrendered, letting the feeling flow through. I thought about every other lonely guy who'd ever been in my position: all that lost love, all those fuck-ups. But we kept getting up off the floor. Off the pavement. That's what we did.

I turned off the music and wiped my eyes. I was okay. I blew through Vicksburg on I-20 West, the battlefield rippling across the grassy bluff to my right as I crossed the bridge into Louisiana with the oily brown Mississippi swirling down below.

The Days Inn was nondescript. I'd stayed in these places hundreds of times when I was on the road with Sterling and his wife. I'd check in and get the keys, then come back to the car and hand them their set. In this case I told the clerk, a heavyset black man in his thirties, that I had reserved two rooms: one for me and one for a friend. I gave him Sherrie's full name as I handed him my credit card.

"She'll be getting here soon," I explained. "I'd appreciate if you'd let her know what room I'm in."

"You want both sets of keys now?"

I thought for a moment. A single woman would probably prefer the other way. "Can she just pick hers up when she gets here?"

"Sure, no problem."

I'd been sitting in my room for half an hour when there was a knock at the door. I jumped up and opened it. And she was standing there.

"I made it!" she said.

"You made it!"

"Can I come in?"

"Of course, of course," I said, stepping aside, almost tripping as I got out of her way.

I'd heard the cliché "love at first sight" for years. This wasn't exactly that. But it was close. She gave off a power, an aura, standing in the doorway and then moving into the room, that rendered me temporarily speechless. Hollywood tries to represent this phenomenon by backlighting the love object in question and magically slowing down time so that the lovestruck young man momentarily imagines himself frolicking with his beloved in a sun-dappled spring glade before time speeds back up and reality kicks in. There was no spring glade or slow motion here, just a rippingly cute fortysomething black woman with a brown ponytail grinning in a sunlit October doorway, wearing stonewashed blue jeans, cowboy boots, and a top with some sort of relaxed lacing arrangement in the middle. Nothing fancy. Down-home girl.

What had me tongue-tied wasn't just the aura she gave off, but the prophecy that suddenly flashed through my mind—the vision of my heart's desire that I'd shared at the workshop three months earlier. Sherrie was a Texas woman, not the Louisiana woman my prophecy called for: Dallas born and bred. But here she was, wearing blue jeans and cowboy boots, standing in the doorway of a Louisiana motel room. I hadn't told her to dress like that. And it hadn't once occurred to me while planning our date that "Louisiana woman" could mean this.

We made small talk for ten or fifteen minutes.

"You seem a little wired," she said.

"Yeah, that's probably true." We'd barely shaken hands, and I wasn't sure where to sit. I'd shifted places two or three times.

"Let's go get some beer."

"That sounds great," I said, relieved.

It only took a couple of minutes to find an overpass, cross I-20, and pull into a bustling little Chevron. I'd dated interracially before, so I was familiar with the shifting vibes you encountered as you moved through public space together: the looks, the occasional comments, the times when nobody gave a damn. But that was up in New York. I barely had a chance to worry about whether attitudes were different in Louisiana before we were standing in line with a six-pack of Tecate, my blind date and I, and she was asking for "twang."

"What's twang?" I half-whispered in her ear, noticing the shelves of liquor bottles behind the counter. That was something you never got at gas stations up north.

The Arab-looking guy at the register pointed towards a display box filled with green-and-yellow packets: lemon-lime Twang.

"A salty powder," she half-whispered back. "It goes with beer."

It was a curious first date. The beer helped—it was a smart move on her part—but I couldn't tell if we were connecting. You talk at first about the things you both like to do: jogging, rollerblading, tennis. I'd done a lot of the first two back in New York; I'd never been much good at tennis, despite my table tennis skills, but I was game. She wasn't particularly a blues fan, although she wanted to hear me play harmonica, but she loved jazz, especially piano. Smooth jazz, too. Mexican food was a yes! Duncanville, the part of South Dallas where she lived, had some great Tex-Mex restaurants. She mentioned go-karts—she'd seen a track by the side of the highway and thought it looked fun. I'd built a kart when I was a kid, I said. I tried to summarize the story but probably went on too long.

She flashed a smile when I'd finished. "You like to get your hands dirty."

That statement intrigued me, not because she was flirting—she wasn't—but because she'd distilled everything I'd just said, cutting to the chase. She did it again later. She had a gift.

We went out to dinner after a while, ordered mediocre Mexican food at a Chili's, talked about families. Our fathers were both dead—hers when she was young, mine five years earlier. Her mother had raised seven kids on a nurse's salary: two boys and five girls. She had an identical twin sister named Sharon. I told her about my half-Jewish background, the grandparents who were first cousins, my quirky autistic brother, my mother's recent memoir about growing all her own food on the banks of the Hudson River. She seemed interested at first. Then her attention seemed to drift in a way that led me to say, "I think I'm boring you."

"No, I'm fine. I was just thinking about my daughter."

"Did you leave her with a babysitter?"

"She's with my sister Kay." She smiled. "Myla Michelle. That's her name."

"Like *mylar* without the *R*?"

"M-y-l-a. I wanted an original name, but nothing too ghetto fabulous."

Later, back at the room, we were talking about religion. She'd grown up in a heavily religious family, a Pentecostal sect. Very long services every Wednesday and Sunday, an endless list of *don'ts*. Your whole life revolved around church. It was oppressive; she rebelled and went her own way. She still attended a weekly service—Oak Cliff Bible Fellowship, near where she lived—but Pastor Tony Evans's preaching was more laid-back than the stuff she'd grown up on. A thoughtful message, not somebody hollering and whooping. I'd come at religion from the opposite direction: nothing in the way of formal worship service until two years ago, after the heart attack. Now I was a believer—not in specific doctrine, but in the healing power to be found in spirit. Interfaith Fellowship, the worship center I'd joined in New York, had given me a way of translating anybody's religious vocabulary into something I could appreciate. Was God inside us or out there? I didn't know. But I knew *something* was there. Maybe the words "God" and "open heart" were ways of symbolizing the same thing.

It was a heavy topic for a first date—a frank and open exchange, as the diplomats put it, not the sort of playful small talk and seduction rituals that led to a one-night stand. We'd both played it straight. Whatever aura I'd felt when she'd first walked through the door had faded; she was just a cute, funny, thoughtful, lighthearted, and friendly person, and that was enough—or almost enough. Something was missing, though— some sexual spark, some intensity of focus. I couldn't put my finger on it. But I trusted my gut, which was saying, "Just let it be. No big moves."

And so the evening glided along until, around eleven, she suddenly stirred—we'd been relaxing side by side on the bed—and slid onto her feet.

"Time to go," she said, yawning. "Sleepytime for Sherrie." She smiled. "Jog in the morning?"

"Um, sure. Yeah, let's do that."

After a quick round of slightly awkward thank-yous, we hugged: friendly but chaste. And then she left, closing the door softly.

I sat back down on the bed, breathing quietly in the sudden silence. I wasn't sure what had just happened. Had anything happened? We'd spent seven hours together. Now she was gone. It hadn't quite happened. We had a date for tomorrow morning. Maybe things would become clearer then.

There was a knock. I pulled open the door.

"Hey," she said softly.

"Hey."

She took my hand in her warm hand. "Let's try this again."

Then we were kissing. My arms were encircling her waist. Her tongue brushed my mine.

"I like where this is going," I chuckled. "You wanna come back inside and discuss this?"

"Sure."

I gently pulled her across the threshold and shut the door.

"Don't Know Why," the debut single by singer and pianist Norah Jones, was released in July 2002. It entered the Billboard Adult Contemporary chart on August 8 at Number 28. By late October, when I first heard it, it had pushed into the Top 20. Jones, the beautiful, vulnerable, dark-eyed daughter of Indian sitar master Ravi Shankar, ran the table at the Grammy awards in February 2003, winning Record of the Year and Best Female Pop Vocal Performance, along with Album of the Year, Best Pop Vocal Album, and Best New Artist. "Don't Know Why" spent more than a year on the Billboard chart, peaking at Number 4 on April 26, 2003.

Jones was everybody's favorite at that particular moment in American pop musical history. So there's nothing special about the feelings her song stirred in me. Lots of people have precious memories connected with that song.

I remember where I was when I first heard it. I had driven the 270 miles from Monroe back to Oxford in a straight shot—dazed, silent, lost in thought. It was Sunday dusk as I reached town, heading east on Route 6 from Batesville after the long push north on I-55. I was so dazed that I missed my exit on South Lamar. I drove another mile to the next exit, crossed the overpass, and returned to South Lamar. The radio was on by that point, tuned to one of several local stations. Jones's song came on as I hit the off ramp and rose toward the lights of the Chevron that still sits on that corner.

It began with the softest, most diaphanous of guitar cadences, interleaved with tinkly piano—a sound overheard rather than heard, as though spirits were whispering themselves awake in some distant land. Then came that soft silky voice:

> I waited 'til I saw the sun
> I don't know why I didn't come
> I left you by the house of fun
> I don't know why I didn't come
> I don't know why I didn't come
>
> When I saw the break of day
> I wished that I could fly away
> Instead of kneeling in the sand
> Catching teardrops in my hand
>
> My heart is drenched in wine
> But you'll be on my mind
> Forever

Many years later, struggling to understand what had happened that weekend, and on that off-ramp, I found the sheet music on

Musicnotes.com and realized that the opening vocal line, which leaps from the tonic up to the major seventh before worrying the major sixth and fifth, echoes the opening phrase of "Somewhere Over the Rainbow," with its leap from tonic to octave. So perhaps melodic craftsmanship on the part of songwriter Jesse Harris is responsible. Or perhaps it was the gently yearning timbre of Jones's voice, tear-stained with sadness and regret, that reached into my heart and tore it open, so that I paused momentarily at South Lamar, half blind, before veering right into a far corner of the gas station's parking lot, engine idling, to hear the song out.

Maybe my heart was breaking for the guy I'd been all those years, the loser at love whose ship had never quite come in.

Except that this time, impossibly, the ship *had* come in. This time there were no teardrops at the break of day, just two people sharing a room who would end up spending their life together.

Sherrie didn't know that yet. But I knew.

Hollywood loves a good montage sequence. The pages of the calendar flip and blur to denote the passage of time. Hand in hand, the happy couple-in-formation takes a romantic whirl, sometimes involving a carousel. Dialogue is replaced by upbeat music. In *Butch Cassidy and the Sundance Kid*, Paul Newman and Katharine Ross bounce through meadows on a rickety bicycle to the sound of "Raindrops Keep Falling on My Head."

Because Sherrie lived in Texas and I lived in Mississippi, our chief romantic obstacle was distance. Travelocity, we discovered, had a last-minute deal—the Elvis Memphis Getaway Weekend—that would fly her to and from Memphis and throw in a hotel room for two nights at a package price lower than a round-trip ticket alone. We used that a few times. I'd pick her up at Memphis International Airport—long kisses leaning against the car in the underground parking lot—and we'd drive to whatever hotel they'd given us, grinning and chattering as we walked into the front lobby and waited on the check-in line, hand in hand. First time in, we stayed at the hotel Friday night after ribs and blues on Beale

Street, then drove down to Oxford for the Ole Miss vs. Auburn game with a discount CD compilation of seventies funk hits—"Car Wash," "Fire," "Brick House"—bumping through my Honda over the steady low thrum of the Thermal exhaust. The next couple of times we just skipped the hotel and drove the seventy-five miles back to Oxford.

Our second date was the American Studies Association conference in Houston, mid-November. Houston was 225 miles from Dallas. I'd been planning to attend, but this opportunity for a rendezvous was too good to pass up. She said she'd drive down.

She called my hotel room from the road. "I'm about eighty miles out," she said. "I'll be there in an hour."

I thought about her hurtling toward me at eighty miles an hour. My kind of woman.

It took her longer than an hour. But then, once again, came the knock on my door.

"Sorry I'm late," she said, easing toward me for a kiss. "Traffic was bad."

There was a blond streak in her hair. She'd done her hair differently every time I'd seen her. Every version of Sherrie was cute, but it was hard to keep track. She laughed when I said something.

"Change is good," she said, setting down her shoulder bag and hooking a leg around my leg.

"You're messing me up."

"That's the plan."

The Valentine's weekend getaway at Hot Springs, Arkansas, was her idea. She'd been there once before with her niece and nephew, Sasha and Jamarrick. We'd take baths in the old marble bath houses, she promised—they were still single-sex, but fun and relaxing—and stroll the streets. It was 310 miles from Dallas, 270 miles from Oxford: another gasoline-powered tryst.

I was very much in love by this point and wanted to express that with the help of food. At a deli north of the Square I found a pair of box lunches themed for the holiday, complete with Chocolate Volcano desserts that needed to be microwaved to activate their creamy chocolate centers. We would feed each other, I thought, arms interlinked.

"I don't have a microwave oven," I told her on the phone, "so I need you to bring yours. I can't tell you why."

"Whoa-kay."

The weather on day-of was very bad, a rainy slushy wintry mix. I made it to our hotel just before dark, but she'd gotten a late start. She called me from a Love's truck stop in Texarkana—complaining about the roads, apologizing for the delay. "My night vision just isn't very good," she said. "I told you about my eyes."

"Take your time," I soothed, relaxing on the bed. "I'll be here. Just don't have an accident."

Two hours later she called me from downstairs. "I made it."

"Thank god!"

A couple of minutes later she kicked at the door with a muffled thud. "Special delivery!"

I pulled it open. She was holding a large cardboard box in her arms. "Heyyyyy honey—Jesus, I didn't realize it was so big."

"The woman at the front desk looked at me like I was crazy," she chuckled, entering and setting it down with a clanking thump.

The brownies were delicious. But the photos I took the next day sealed the deal. Sherrie sitting across the table at breakfast, crystal goblet of orange juice in her slim-wristed brown hand, eyes slanted out the window, at peace. Sherrie in black windbreaker and charcoal-flecked white slacks, crouching in the clearing of a little forest we'd found in a nearby park, grinning at me. Something about her eyes caught at my heart—not just the warmth, but the slight downward tilt on the outside. Like Ethel Kennedy's eyes, I realized later. The angling didn't bespeak sadness or concern, just anchored her playful spirit in something solid and sustaining, something I could count on.

Although Sherrie had been born and raised in the all-black world of South Dallas, her mainstreamed work life had often put her in situations where she was the only black person in the room. She'd lived in Plano for a while, too, when Myla was a girl, so she had white friends as well as black friends and was comfortable in all-white settings. She was unflappable, in fact. She could walk into any room, anywhere, and be her funny, friendly self. People embraced her for who she was. Appreciating the ease with which she stepped into my world made it easier for me to step into hers.

When Sherrie and I went out to dinner with her family—Myla, Sharon, Sharon's daughters, Pinkie and Sasha, and son, Jamarrick—and we were all sitting around a big table at Los Lupes or Papacito's or Pappadeaux, I was of course *aware* of being the only white person in the group, but that awareness quickly melted under the onslaught of so much familial friendliness extended in my direction and so much playfully ricocheting energy swirling around the circle. Same with dinners at Sherrie's little two-bedroom house in Duncanville when the crew came over. Even Sherrie's code-switching from the way she talked when we were alone into the blacker vernacular she used around kin quickly came to seem natural, like a smooth downshift at the bottom of a hill. On a couple of occasions when I'd been in that environment for a while and was chattering quickly, I accidentally dropped an *s*—saying "he think" instead of "he thinks"—and everybody cracked up. The English professor had been yanked into the black!

The one sticking point in the family was her mother. I'd met Mrs. Gardner once, a brief outdoor greeting after Easter services at her church, but that was the only time. She wasn't interested in having anything to do with me and didn't like the fact that her daughter was dating a white man, much less one from Mississippi. There was one extremely awkward moment where we drove to her house on Easter, I stayed in the car while Sherrie went inside to make sure it was okay for me to come in, and she came back to the car a couple of minutes later, not happy, to say, "We're going back to my house."

Everybody else in the family, including Sherrie's sisters, Kay, Freda, and Bridget, told me not to worry about it. "That's just the way Grandma is," they said. She'd grown up in Waco and picked cotton for white people; maybe that's where it came from. Or maybe she was secretly hurting at the idea that her daughter might end up moving far from home. Sherrie wasn't happy about her mother's attitude, but she refused to give it any power over our relationship. She'd always done her own thing, regardless of what anybody thought.

Doing Dallas with Sherrie always involved lots of driving around town, which meant risking life and limb on an insane set of zig-zagging local highways in close proximity to Dallas drivers, who hammered them all at seventy-five miles an hour. Sherrie had come of age on those roads; she knew when to change lanes, cutting left or right in anticipation of the next merge or exit. Her maroon 1995 Toyota Corolla was nothing special, and it was amazing how much stuff she stored in the trunk, but she drove with a heavy foot and never let anybody push her around—although she never cursed at them, either. I was more of a talker. When we'd take my car, she'd expertly guide me through the maze, giving me the sort of moment-by-moment advisories that we now outsource to our GPS devices. I thought I'd seen every sort of crazy move, living and driving in Manhattan for two decades, but Dallas drivers were a breed apart.

"What the hell was *that*?" I'd say as a white Lexus cut me off, swooping across three lanes on 35 East northbound to exit at Zang Boulevard. "Jesus!"

"You're back in the big city, babe," she'd say, unflappable. "Oxford's a small town."

Our dating life in Dallas took us everywhere, from blues clubs like The Bone in Deep Ellum, where I sat in with the Hash Brown Band, to Sunday morning services at Oak Cliff Bible Fellowship, a black megachurch on the edge of the hood, as Sherrie called it. She was unsentimental about where she'd grown up. She didn't revere it, romanticize it, or deny it. In some ways she felt the same way about it as I felt about Congers, my own tiny hometown in downstate New York. She was *from* there—it had inevitably shaped who she was, it had built in some strengths, including some toughness, she wasn't embarrassed by it—but it didn't define who she had become or where she was headed. It was one more example of the sort of thing that dating websites can't index but that ultimately makes two people compatible.

We went jogging on the winding streets and wide grassy medians of her suburban neighborhood, then sat in her fenced-in back yard sipping iced tea on warm summer evenings while big black grackles made loud ripping sounds in the trees overhead. We loved watching boxing on TV, we discovered, and kibbitzing the whole way through, although neither of us had ever been to the fights. One night we drove thirty miles west to Fort Worth and wandered into the dark cavernous interior of Billy Bob's, "the world's largest honky tonk," a mixed couple braving the cowboy hats, to sip longneck Lonestars and watch a couple of random country acts. It was a world neither of us knew but an adventure worth having, if not repeating.

Much more to our liking was the DFW Auto Show at a convention center downtown. Although the sport-tuning world didn't call to Sherrie, she was a fan of design—she loved to sightsee old Art Deco buildings, for example—and shared my enthusiasm for sexy curves, flashy chrome, candy-apple paint, and the fantasy of streetside dominance. Strolling past the latest low-slung Lamborghini or Corvette Z-1, hands in each other's butt pockets, we'd pause and take photos of each other.

"When are you gonna buy me my 'Vette?" I'd joke.

"Keep hoping."

We chattered, flirted, dreamed.

At some point in the first six months, the word "harmony" drifted into view. That word had never come to mind in connection with any woman I'd dated over the years, including the two I'd lived with. My previous relationships could be characterized by a host of other words, including romance, excitement, passion, drama, insecurity, rage, and disdain. But harmony? That was new. Sherrie and I certainly had romance, excitement, and passion; we also had friendship and a shared sense of humor that kept our hearts light. The harmony I sensed was on a deeper dimension, a kind of unforced spiritual alignment rather than something we had to work for. A lot of it had to do with Sherrie: secure in who she was, devoid of arrogance, cattiness, or cruelty, she gazed on the world—and me—without condemnation or judgment. She had no hunger to refashion the world in accord with her own ideas about how it should be. She just wanted to make it better on a daily basis by bringing her best self to the table. When she fell short of that goal, no worries. She got a good night's sleep and started fresh.

I'd been looking for a woman like that my whole life without realizing it. I thought about Marianne Williamson's warning in *Enchanted Love*: about how tarrying, remaining indecisive while trying to check every box on the marriage bucket list, might give the spaceship a chance to depart with your beloved on board. A leap of faith was required.

My heart had been murmuring all spring, but it spoke more loudly during the week we spent on Monhegan Island, Maine, in late June—fishing, hiking, cooking, sipping wine, cracking steamed lobsters, and necking on the porch as the sun slowly set over Manana Island. As we took the ferry home towards the mainland for the first of what would turn out to be many times, skimming side by side across the salt water, the feeling was so strong and pure that it scared me—until suddenly it didn't.

I'd never asked a woman to marry me; I didn't have a ring or a plan. I didn't even know you were supposed to get down on your knee. I was that kind of overeducated fool. But the next morning, back in the hotel room after breakfast, I couldn't help myself. It took her a moment to realize what was happening.

"Are you asking me to marry you?" she said with a gentle smile.

"Yes!" I said, almost blubbering.

"Sure, honey. Yes. I'd love to do that." Then she chuckled. "I'll drive to Oxford next weekend. But you better have a ring. Girls like diamonds."

"Don't worry," I said. "I'll have a ring."

Race Mixing

Our son, Shaun, the first and only child Sherrie and I would have together, was born late in the afternoon of March 17, 2006, at Baptist Memorial Hospital in Oxford, Mississippi, an emergency C-section that, coming three days earlier than planned, surprised us both. She was forty-five; I was forty-seven. It was a lazy Friday afternoon during Spring Break. I'd been relaxing at a table outside the student union on the University of Mississippi campus, thinking ahead toward Monday, filled with a mixture of apprehension—Was I up to the task? Would bonding happen?—and uncontainable joy, as most first-time fathers are. The pregnancy had been trouble free. All the standard tests suggested a normal child. "Trouble-free" and "normal" were welcome words indeed.

At some point I called home from a pay phone inside the building to check our answering machine. (I had no cell phone and wouldn't acquire my first until the following year, a Walmart burner, not the iPhone that had just debuted.) What greeted me was a series of increasingly panicked messages from Myla, now sixteen, letting me know that her mom's water had broken earlier that afternoon while she was at work on campus and everybody was waiting for me at the hospital, ready to move ahead.

Hazard lights flashing, heart thudding, I raced the two miles that separated me from my family and, after hugging Myla at the Emergency Room entrance and identifying myself as the husband in question, was ushered almost immediately into an operating room and seated in a chair next to the bed that held my wife, who was relieved to see me and whose hand I quickly took. Her body was veiled from the waist down by white tenting that opened out away from me, creating a pop-up operating theater. It was there, after greeting me in his blue scrubs, that the ob-gyn did his work. No fan of natural childbirth, Sherrie had accepted the standard proffer of anesthetics. She was awake and aware, but drowsy. Heart slowly calming after the high-speed drive, I was wide awake as I squeezed her hand, as fully present as a man can be. Wishing I could draw into me some of whatever pain she was sure to incur.

And then, as in the movies, a cry blossomed. Although time blurred, it seemed only a minute or two before a nurse came around the tenting and handed us our son, swaddled in a blanket. White? Blue? Memory fails me. The last thing in the world I was paying attention to was the color of his blanket. *His!* Shaun's! We'd made a kid. His wrinkled, reddened face, viewed in profile, uncannily resembled the ultrasound image we'd been living with for the past few months. He was healthy, the doctor told us with a smile after he'd pulled down his mask. No problems at all.

It was only now, as Sherrie held Shaun in her arms, that I suddenly felt the enormity of what we'd done. The great gift of my rushed entrance into the operating room is that I simply didn't have time to wonder whether the sort of couple we were in Mississippi's eyes—black mother, white father—was of the slightest importance to those who were about to facilitate our son's birth. Now, even as I was swept along in a current of glorious high feeling, I became conscious for the first time that we'd taken a huge, irrevocable step. It was one thing to speak in historical terms about the stigma attached to "race-mixing" in Jim Crow Mississippi, as I did from time to time in the classroom. It was very different to launch a mixed kid into the world of contemporary Mississippi.

Surely things had changed. But Oxford was Faulkner's town, a place where people were fond of quoting his best-known line; "The past is never dead. It isn't even past." At the annual Faulkner & Yoknapatawpha Conference, visiting academics never tired of talking about "blood," meaning race, and "parchmentcolored" Joe Christmas, he of indeterminate racial ancestry who is lynched near the end of *Light in August*. Shortly after I'd moved down from New York to take the job at Ole Miss, I'd been surprised to hear people, from Chancellor Robert Khayat on down, employ the phrase "the races." Meaning white and black. It was a thing, that phrase. Local currency. What passed for common knowledge. Nobody back in New York used that phrase. It would have had no traction for anybody who had ever set foot on a subway train, or strolled the streets of Manhattan. I didn't bridle against it. But I'd taken note. And now, out of the blue, it suddenly popped into my mind— unbidden, unwanted.

Sherrie and I had stepped in it, all right. We were *in* it. But what was *it*? We didn't know. We couldn't know. Whatever it was, this life we were in the process of creating for ourselves—formerly we three, now we four—would take time to play out. Meanwhile there was this Mississippi boy, this new addition to the family who needed to be fed, wiped, and raised right. A St. Patrick's Day baby, we chuckled, three days ahead of schedule. He just couldn't wait to be born.

I slept in Sherrie's hospital room that night, curled up on a small sofa under a spare blanket in the cool dry air. Sherrie, cradling our new son, made a low whispery *sh-sh-sh-sh-sh-sh* sound that I'd never heard before. She was shushing him, she said, amused when I asked. She'd learned how to do that with Myla. I was relieved to have a pro in the room.

I strolled down the hall and back with him slumped over my shoulder, whistling—of all things—the theme song of *Mayberry RFD*. He slept soundly.

In the morning, one of the nurses, a black woman, came in with the birth certificate. She needed signatures.

"I'll be back in a few minutes," she said.

I scanned it quickly. The mother's and son's race were listed as black. The father's, too.

"Hey, hon, check this out," I said.

I thought it was funny, although the nurse was mortified when I pointed out the mistake and rushed off down the hall to have new papers drawn up. I'd been certified as a bluesman by the Mississippi state government, even as our marriage had been adjudged unthinkable. But Sherrie and I were thinking ahead, and we chatted about the future—thoughtfully, not anxiously. What boxes would we be asked to check on our son's behalf? What sort of space would he make for himself in this unsettled new world? We'd floated straight through to this moment on a dream of shared life that exempted us from the claims of history. Now we would see what love could do.

The Mother Goose Years

I t was a delirious moment. When he walked onto that outdoor stage in Chicago with his wife and daughters, it was a fairytale come to life. He was beaming, they were beautiful, everybody was roaring. White people in the huge crowd were clapping, too, when the TV cameras zoomed in; it wasn't just black people. I'd invited a few colleagues over to our new house on Meadowlawn Drive—we'd taken out a mortgage the summer before—to watch the election results. "This is a profoundly important passage," intoned Tom Brokaw on NBC, "out of the deep shadows of our racist past that began with that first slave uploaded on a ship." I felt as though I'd been waiting for this moment my whole life—since 1968, when King and Kennedy were killed two months apart.

That year broke our hearts. The day the music died: Don McLean said it in "American Pie." This day, forty years later, was redemption. This was Etta James singing "At Last." Sherrie and I had chosen that song for our first dance at the wedding four years earlier. But this was the moment for it.

We'd put Shaun to bed before folks came over. He was asleep in his room.

President Obama! Sherrie and I sat hand in hand on the sofa in a living room full of friends, staring at the TV. His wife Michele. Daughters Malia, Sasha. Our new First Family.

The crowd in Grant Park kept roaring, acres and acres of people on a cold November night. He finally quieted them down.

"If there is anyone out there," he said, "who still doubts that America is a place where all things are possible, who still wonders if the dream of our founders is alive in our time, who still questions the power of our democracy, tonight is your answer."

How does it feel to live happily ever after? There's no such thing, except in fairytales. The pursuit of happiness involves pursuit: desire for something you don't yet possess. Men are born restless. They thrill to the hunt. The blues will find you, one way or another. But there are periods in every life, if you're lucky, where you get a taste of that blessed condition.

The first three or four years of Shaun's life were the Mother Goose years. We'd put him into daycare early, when he was only four months old. Mother Goose Day Care, a mile from our house, was run by two Egyptian women in tan housecoats and hijabs. The all-female staff was half black and half white; the infants and kids were the same mix. We noticed such things, as mixed couples do. The Mother Goose years happened to align with President Obama's first term, but that's purely coincidence—although it did amaze us to realize that we were raising a biracial kid at the first moment in American history when a couple like us could point to the TV and say, "Someday that could be you."

I had a wife, a baby, a stepdaughter, a house, a car, and a job. I was fully invested. Myla was a beauty queen: She'd won Junior Miss Most Beautiful Lafayette High School, strutting across the stage, beating out the white girls, some of whom had the sort of professional beauty-queen training pretty white girls get in rural Mississippi. We had more than an acre of land, most of it sun-dappled lawn back behind the house, with a creek flowing down along the edge of the property. We had a Snapper riding mower; I'd get out there on summer weekends and sputter in big loops like Forrest Gump, inhaling the smell of cut grass and small-engine exhaust, happy.

Early on Sunday morning, while my family was asleep, I'd drive out to the crossroads of Molly Barr Road and Old Sardis Road, park just behind B's BBQ, catch a whiff of mesquite smoke, and run miles and miles out and back through the quiet of the country dawn—past cotton fields, forests, peaceful little homesteads with a parked truck or two. Fifteen miles gave me plenty of time to think. New York, the heart attack, my days as a lonely single guy wondering whether my ship would come in, the frantic touring years with Mr. Satan and Miss Macie, six years as a grad student commuting down to Princeton, the bike wreck on Pea Ridge Road: all that was behind me. This was my church. Honoring creation. Observing subtle changes in the seasons. Drinking from water bottles I'd cached behind trees at the five-, six-, and seven-mile point. Melting into the landscape.

On weekday mornings, before Sherrie dressed him and one of us dropped him off at Mother Goose, I'd sit on the back porch with Shaun propped in my lap, chin resting lightly on his sweet-smelling hair. The sun was just coming up over the trees.

"Listen to the birds," I'd tell him. "Hear that?"

I'd hug my son close and we'd listen.

Chirp chirp chirp. Who who whoooo-oooo-ooo. Birdy birdy birdy.

"Birdy!" he'd say triumphantly.

Later in the day, around 5:15, if it was my day to pick up, I'd rumble down the front driveway of Mother Goose, park my car in a visitor's space, and walk inside to claim my kid. The Sandy Hook shooting—twenty six-year-olds slaughtered by Adam Lanza with a Bushmaster assault rifle at an elementary school—hadn't yet happened, so there weren't any security guards. We'd walk back out through the front doors hand in hand, stroll over to daddy's car, and buckle him into the baby seat in back. Then I'd fire up, vroom once or twice, and head out.

Right after Shaun was born I'd purchased *Remember: A Tribute to Wes Montgomery*, a new CD by jazz guitarist Pat Martino. I played it nonstop that first summer, as though it were the soundtrack of my life. It brought back memories of the summer I'd spent at the Berklee College of Music in Boston when I was nineteen, a seven-week course in jazz guitar. Lowell Parker, my next-door buddy back in Congers, had turned me on to Martino and Montgomery, and that was my ambition for a while, to play endless swinging strings of sparkling, popping sixteenth notes. Wes was West Coast cool. Now Daddy and his boy were cruising down the driveway with Mother Goose receding in the rearview mirror and the music percolating through surround sound. It was one more sunny summer afternoon in north Mississippi with daddy in front, baby in back, and sweet baby blues swinging through....

One day, when Shaun was three, for no good reason, I called out "Hey baba rebop!" during our homeward drive.

"Baba *boo*!" he answered.

I glanced up in the rearview mirror, surprised.

"Hey baba rebop!" I repeated.

"Baba *boo*!"

That became our thing. Later I'd throw some variations on him, and he'd come back at me.

Daddy: "Hey samma wee-bop!"

Shaun: "Wabba dabba boo-bop!"

Daddy: "Rinky dinky flop-flop!"

Shaun: "Baba *boo-boo* bop!"

Sometimes when I was running on Old Sardis Road, out around the five-mile point where it dipped down into the woods and crossed a pair of old bridges, I'd see snakes. I'd kept snakes as a kid—garter snakes, green snakes, a corn snake, a pair of boa constrictors—so snakes in the wild didn't bother me. But the rattlesnakes did. There was a bloodied dead rattlesnake with a flattened head in the middle of the road and a live rattlesnake keeping watch not far from it. The live one raised its head as I came into view; I veered to the side. Once you know poison snakes are out there, you make subtle psychological adjustments so you can take evasive action if needed.

Shaun almost stumbled across the copperhead. We'd just come home from Mother Goose; I was following him down the concrete walkway in front of our bay windows. A mottled brown snake with a fat head was curled up in our front entryway. Shaun did a veering little skip around and over it as Sherrie, looking out from inside through the glass storm door, shouted, "Snake! Jump, Shaun!" as she sprung the door open and yanked him inside.

Horrified, I watched it slither into the flower bed next to the walkway, then slow to a stop. Lurking behind a couple of scrawny azaleas, it was masked by the pine straw Sherrie had put down.

"I'll get it!" I shouted.

Keeping an eye on the bulging straw, I heaved open the garage door and grabbed a hoe.

I'd killed a copperhead once, when I was twelve years old. You had to be quick, vicious, and accurate. A wounded copperhead is nasty.

I tried to judge where its head was. Then I hammered downward with both hands, like a man chopping wood. A world of writhing anger boiled out from under the straw. Something primal took hold. I hammered again and again and again, beating and pounding anything that looked like snake. No copperhead was going to mess with my child. The writhing eventually stopped. Trembling, jittery with adrenaline, I felt in the straw with tip of the hoe, hooked the limp body, lifted it out of the messed-up flower bed, and laid it on the concrete driveway. Sherrie and Shaun had been watching from inside, through the bay windows. I heard them come out the front door.

"Daddy killed a big snake," I said, staring at it.

"Daddy killed a *big* snake," Mommy echoed.

"Bisnake," Shaun murmured, toddling up to the edge of the driveway, then stopping. Unsure of whether to come closer.

It wasn't until later, in 2012, near the end of his first term, that it was publicly revealed how deliberately and cynically House and Senate Republicans had plotted, the night before he took office, to void the mandate given to America's first black president by refusing to work with him. That's when news of the four-hour dinner at the Caucus Room, a pricey DC steakhouse, came out. On the evening of Obama's Inaugural Ball, fifteen white men, including former house speaker Newt Gingrich and Fox News pollster Frank Luntz, had convened to eat, drink, and sketch out plans for the all-points blockage required to defeat Obama's triumphant campaign slogan, "Yes we can!" Neither current House speaker John Boehner nor Senate Majority leader Mitch McConnell were there, but they, too, understood what needed to be done.

Sherrie and I knew none of this. But we sensed that the resistance confronted by our new president was founded in something deeper than policy disagreements. Neither of us would have used the word "racism"—that wasn't an explanatory mechanism we regularly invoked—but something weird was going on. The Tea Party protests, which exploded across America only a month after his inauguration, offered posters of Obama-as-witch-doctor with a bone through his nose and caricatures of Michelle Obama as a gorilla with fangs. The Tea Party's "grass roots" displays of popular outrage were funded by the Koch brothers, we found out later.

Aggressive political caricature had always been part of American politics. The *Nation* had mocked George W. Bush ruthlessly with those Alfred E. Neuman *Mad Magazine* covers. But it was harder to explain, now that Obama was in office, a kind of intransigence in which congressional Republicans not only refused the sorts of compromise that are a part of any reasonable legislative process, but voted against policies *that they themselves had vigorously advocated for at some earlier moment*, simply because Obama was now advocating for them.

A bad situation slowly degenerated. It became laughable by the end of his second term. "If Obama is for apple pie," CNN's chief national correspondent John King would say in 2016, "the Republicans are against it. That's part of the world we live in right now."

When does the personality of a young child begin to emerge? Every parent knows that there are things you can train in—traits you can encourage with gentle, repeated guidance—and things that are just *there*, like pre-installed software. Nurture and nature.

When Shaun was a year and a half old, he came up with a game. He'd climb up on a small padded grey storage box, a sort of tuffet, next to Sherrie's big TV. He knew that we liked to watch certain shows in the evening—*American Idol, 24, So You Think You Can Dance*—so it's possible he'd already been shaped by our attentional economy. We tried to be good parents; we'd switch the TV off when he got up there.

"Jump!" he'd say.

Then he'd make the little jump—*boomp!*—down off the box, onto the carpet.

"Clap!" he'd say, looking at us and clapping, milking our response.

"Yaaaaaay!" we'd say, applauding loudly. "Great jump, Boo-boo!"

He had a handful of nicknames. His sister called him Monster; he called her Sissy. Monster wasn't a name I used, but it was apt. You could always tell when sleepytime was approaching because he'd climb up on the back of the sofa, crawl along the ridge next to the wall, and jump down on me—like a kitten, except without the claws. We'd wrestle for a moment; his eyes would get this slightly crazed, unfocused look. Suddenly he wasn't quite there, he was somewhere else, wrestling with somebody, something, that wasn't quite me.

Young kids can be infuriating. I'd heard about the Terrible Twos—"No!" accompanied by a pout and a tantrum—but it sometimes seemed as though the concept were chasing us through the threes, fours, and fives. Shaun could be willful. I thought of myself as a mellow guy. But Shaun knew how to press my buttons. On a handful of occasions, usually when he voiced smirking disrespect, I found myself in a rage that led me to grab him and spank his bottom, hard. I'd yell, too. I never slapped him across the face and would never do that. But one day something happened. It only happened once. It only had to happen once.

We were driving home from Mother Goose. He was in his final year there, five years old, a "big boy." He was riding up front now, in a booster seat. He wanted to be where Dad was.

I can't remember what we were talking about. It wasn't really a conversation. It was him smart-mouthing back at me. Cars in motion are a terrible place for that sort of situation to bubble up.

We were cruising along Woodlawn Drive, rolling down a gentle hill, about to make a left onto Meadowlawn, where our house was. At precisely that moment, he said something that—as Sherrie would put it— got on my last nerve. The fuse melted.

I slammed on the brakes. I wanted to stop the car dead, shake him up, scare him a little, then yell at him.

The car jerked to a stop. His forehead hit the front window with an audible sound, cracking the window.

There are moments we remember for the rest of our lives. Stunned by what I'd just done, I realized instantly that I needed to lie. It would terrify him if he thought I was trying to hurt him—which I wasn't. So I couldn't let him know.

"A…a squirrel," I said, pointing out my window. "I thought I was gonna hit that squirrel. Are you okay? I am so sorry," I murmured as I pulled him towards me to inspect. He had a bruise on his forehead. But the skin wasn't broken. His skull wasn't crushed. Thank you, God. Thank you. Thank you.

He was confused, but he wasn't crying.

"My face hit the window," he said.

I kept rubbing his head, looking at the cracked safety glass, trying not to cry. I kept apologizing and telling the lie about the squirrel, mind racing ahead. I couldn't tell Sherrie. Lying to my wife was something I never wanted to do, but I just couldn't tell her. Once or twice I'd done the same thing in the car with her: hit the brakes hard when I was furious. Not as bad as this, but in a way that had disturbed her. This episode had to be an accident. Otherwise she might decide that I was unfit to be a father to our son. She might take him and leave, as she'd taken Myla years ago out of that failed marriage.

I told Sherrie the lie about the squirrel and made it convincing. I got the front window replaced. Within two weeks Shaun's bruise was gone, and within a month we'd forgotten about the incident. Or at least they'd forgotten.

I took a long jog in the woods the day after it happened. I leaned against a tree and cringed. I knew what had happened. I'd figured it out pretty quick.

I'd suddenly remembered my mom as a young mother with a pair of smart-mouthed brats—that 180-degree turn she'd pulled on the black ice of Massachusetts Avenue one wintry day, heaving the three-cylinder Saab into an uncontrolled skid when Seth and I had pissed her off. Now I'd done exactly the same thing. It was in me—whatever you called that buried rage, that spasm of fury expressed through the car. I couldn't blame my mom for what I'd done. I couldn't blame her for what *she'd* done, because I'd just done the same thing. The only thing that would save me was seeing my action with ruthless clarity for what it was. The buck stopped with me. This couldn't happen again. I promised God it wouldn't. I loved my son. I loved my wife.

A couple of years later I told Sherrie. She wasn't happy, but she'd seen the man I'd become and nothing like that had happened since. She forgave me, and we were okay. The three of us were okay.

Mississippi Band Kid, Part One

I live in an unusual family that is also, in some ways, a typical American family: we've got a band kid in the house.

Although he currently specializes in euphonium and trombone, Shaun has played enough different instruments over the years that it would be fair to call him a utility infielder, or a future band director, or a prodigy. I have my own designated salesman at Amro Music up in Memphis; his eyes twinkle every time Shaun and I walk through the door. We first did that almost twelve years ago, battered pawn-shop trumpet in hand, but I'm getting ahead of my story.

Shaun has perfect pitch and superior sight-reading chops, which means that he can look at almost any piece of sheet music and sing it: not just the lead melody, but any of the parts. As a blues harmonica player who can't sight-read a lick, I find this intimidating. In musical terms, I am the illiterate old Mississippi bluesman and my son, with the blood of Africa and Ashkenazi Jewry running through his veins, is the inheritor of the Western tradition, a kind of North Mississippi Mozart who seems to exude music as effortlessly as he breathes. John Phillip Sousa is a favorite; Shaun has memorized thirty-five of the 136 marches, and he's the kind of nerdy band kid who knows that total-marches figure. But he's also a master of Herb Alpert & the Tijuana Brass's perky, hook-driven melodies ("Tijuana Taxi," "Spanish Flea"), which he first learned on trumpet, and he kills on *Guitar Hero III*, the prime accelerant of this whole process. He knows more amped-up blues-rock from the seventies than I do, and I grew up in the New York suburbs when all that stuff was clotting the radio. Those are my native melodies! But my son owns them. He can play "Brown Sugar" and "Eruption" and "Thunderstruck" on my '75 Telecaster, the one he rescued from its dusty case under the guest bedroom bed and runs through the '54 Tweed Deluxe that he commandeered from my collection of old tube amps. It's got a pedigreed low-end crunch that brings tears to my eyes when I hear it blasting behind the door of his room, running smoking hot as vintage equipment deserves to be run. We are a Fender family. And yes, I know that Mick is singing about the slave trade—cotton fields, a scarred old slave driver, women whipped at midnight—and transforming it into sexual spectacle. But Shaun doesn't care about all that; it's not a song he sings, just a rhythm part he plays, in Keith's open-G tuning.

Shaun disproves every slanderous lie that white male Mississippians of a certain ideological persuasion used to tell about people like him— how they were dangerous mongrels, the degenerate products of "race mixing," weak-willed and conniving, and worse. I used to keep a copy of Theodore Bilbo's ethically odious screed, *Take Your Choice: Separation or Mongrelization* (1947), on the desk of my campus office, hidden under some papers for easy access, just to remind myself of how bad things were in the Before Times, and how exceedingly much better they are now, especially for a family like ours. Yet I'm also reminded almost every day that our time is troubled by its own shibboleths: ideas about race and culture and their presumptive interlinking; about the way in which the anti-blackness that Afropessimists view as foundational to America forecloses all talk of racial progress; about the ever-present threat of microaggressions and trauma requiring the creation of racially distinct "affinity spaces."

To paraphrase James Baldwin, it seems to me that those of us, the relatively conscious race-mixers who are managing to live out the promise of America as it was envisioned by Martin Luther King, Jr., need to do a better job of speaking up for what we know. Bilbo is dead. He's been dead for many decades. I'm the father of a Mississippi band kid. I want to tell you about him: how his remarkable career began, how it developed, and how he has enriched our life beyond measure.

The parents of a gifted child, after the gifts have become apparent, will find themselves thinking back to the moment when they first noticed something unusual. Sherrie and I sometimes laugh about *Little Einsteins*, the Disney-sponsored educational cartoon Shaun glommed onto as a toddler, which wasn't long after President Obama first took office. We remember his response to one particular episode, "Leo and the Musical Families," which was set in a fictive orchestral hall. "Hi, I'm Leo" says the nerdy redhead kid with big owlish glasses, "and I need your help. There's a big concert today, but some of the instruments in the orchestra are lost. Come on! Let's go help find them before the concert starts. Before we start, we need to meet the families. Did you know that instruments have families?"

"Woodwinds!" Shaun would shout, pointing at our desktop PC. "Percussion! Strings! Brass!"

He not only had an unerring ability to sort each wayward instrument into the proper family-quadrant of the stage, based on the instrument's look and the heavily processed, midi-generated simulacrum of appropriate sound it emitted, but he had the born showoff's desire to have us applaud loudly as he engaged in this process. "Clap!" he'd demand, clapping his own hands. "Bassoon! French horn!"

Later, in the evening, he'd jump down off a little stool next to the TV as we were watching *American Idol* in the living room, sticking his landing and beaming. "Clap!"

"Yeaaaaah, Monster!" we'd coo, clapping as we eyed each other. That's our boy. Monster was one of his nicknames, for the way he'd climb up on you and get right in your face. Also Doo-Doo, or just Doo.

One day in the fall of 2011, when Shaun was five, we drove eighty miles up the highway to Memphis and bought him a pawn-shop trumpet. It must have been my idea, although I'd never played trumpet and had only visited a pawn shop once or twice. But it felt like time to add some spice to the mix. That horn was the most beat-ass thing I'd ever seen. Tarnished gold, with a dented bell, missing the finger button on the middle valve. I put that big, battered, shiny, broken-down instrument into Shaun's grasping little hands and it just looked right. He made breathy, spitty, pushing sounds. No actual notes came out, but you could see him engage, intrigued by the challenge. Only fifty bucks. We took it. He walked out of that Memphis pawn shop slinging his horn. No case, just a naked horn, with his black mommy and white daddy trailing behind. It felt right, like something profound had just happened, or could happen.

We drove five minutes to another part of town and walked through the front doors of Amro Music, which we had already sussed out on the internet as the place all the Memphis band kids went. Band supply central. We thought they might be able to give Shaun's new axe a little TLC. Trudging up the steps to the service desk upstairs, we set our acquisition on the counter. Three or four guys were sitting at spotlit workbenches around the cozy little room, quietly working on horns. The guy behind the counter took one look at our pitiful old rescue-dog of a trumpet and tried not to grimace. He picked it up, inspected it briefly.

"There's nothing we can do for this instrument," he said, glancing at me, then Sherrie, then down at Shaun. Our funky modern family. "I'm sorry, man."

"No problem." I smiled gamely. "We knew it was a long shot."

We traipsed back down the steps and out into the showroom, walls festooned with display cases featuring shiny new saxophones, trumpets, trombones, flutes. As we strolled past the front counter, we noticed a young Asian woman testing out a violin.

"Look, Shaun," Sherrie said in the *Wowwwww!* voice that mommies use. "A violin!"

The young violinist tossed off a fast, dazzling run. Shaun, who was trotting out the door ahead of us, turned around and stopped in the open doorway like a mouse-sized superhero, put his trumpet to his lips, raised the dented bell, and blew an astonishingly loud note right at her. *Bwaaaaaahh!*

He'd had the instrument for less than half an hour and he was already doing battle. My son.

That pawn-shop trumpet kicked around the house for a few years, little more than a curiosity. It was good for a big impressive note every now and then. Eventually it was replaced, thanks to Amro, by a new beginner's trumpet and a Hal Leonard instructional book. I was amazed to see my son reading music, since that's something I'd never been able to do. But I could do many things on the harmonica that he couldn't do—and that weren't in the book.

I showed him the blues scale. I put on a recording called "Happy Feet" by alto saxophonist Hank Crawford. It begins with the rising root-to-octave run made famous by Little Walter in "Juke" back in 1952, then descends through the blues scale. He got it pretty quickly. I showed him the difference between the major third and minor third and how to slur the minor third into the blue zone between major and minor, happy and sad. It occurred to me as I was doing this that at some point, if my son got good on his instrument and was being interviewed by a journalist, he would be able truthfully to assert that he had learned how to play the blues from an old white man down in Mississippi. This wasn't how things were supposed to work. But we were living in a brave new millennium, and nothing worked quite the way it used to.

In the spring of 2015, at age nine, Shaun came out onto the streets with my duo, the Blues Doctors, to busk the Double Decker festival in Oxford. Although he had never previously performed or even rehearsed with us, he locked into the groove like a pro and riffed along with "Every Day I Have the Blues." He had the same startlingly loud, raw sound that people describe Buddy Bolden as having had. Mommy filmed the whole thing; Daddy later uploaded it to YouTube as "trumpet blues project."

When the song was over, I encouraged the crowd to tip the young man generously. He made thirty-two dollars for that one song. He was cocky later, back at the house.

"Music is a great career," he said. "It's easy money."

The year 2017 was Shaun's annus mirabilis. In the course of twelve months, he moved from the cello (community orchestra) to electric bass (private lessons) to tuba (sixth grade band) to alto sax (Walmart.com) to trombone (Amro rental) to bass clarinet (mail-order rental) to keyboard (mail-order purchase) to a much better alto sax (Amro rental). I was mortgaged, leveraged, and getting amused looks from my guy at Amro, Leslie York, every time we drove up there. Shaun had perfect pitch, we'd figured out. He could sing any melody he heard and remain perfectly in tune. He hummed and sang around the house. And his refrain was always the same: "Daddy, I want another instrument." At any given moment, he was juggling three or four and clamoring for a fifth.

Supercharging the entire process was a video game called *Guitar Hero III: Legends of Rock*, which required the player holding a controller to duplicate the guitar leads and bass lines from a series of classic blues-rock recordings, while cartoonish Rock God avatars on the screen postured and mugged through a series of fatuous windmill-strum poses. To win required considerable ear-hand and hand-eye coordination, plus the ability to track complicated melodies in your head. Shaun was a gifted gamer. As our Mississippi living room swelled with the cheesy sounds of Mountain, Foghat, and Kiss, the stylized bombastic crap that was all around me as a suburban teen in the 1970s, I suddenly realized that there was indeed a god, and he was laughing at me. No extant theory of cultural transmission could possibly explain why this particular black-and-white boy in rural Mississippi thought that Alice Cooper was cool, or why he even knew about Alice Cooper. Where had these video games come from?

Then I remembered Shaun's year-long campaign for an Xbox, most of which was grounded in a burning desire to join his sixth-grade friends in the playing of more realistic first-person shooter games like *Call of*

Duty: Black Ops, rather than being forced to remain in the little-kid world of *Plants vs. Zombies: Garden Warfare*. The point of all those games was to shoot, blow up, and otherwise annihilate a cadre of enemy beings who were trying to destroy you. The warrior-avatars on your side started off as named vegetable assassinators: Peashooter, for example, who could be versioned as Commando Pea, Toxic Pea, Fire Pea, and so forth. Bit by bit, as kids matured through the ranks, the cartoon-angle faded. By the time you got to Black Ops, your kid was essentially being equipped with all the reflexes and tactical smarts needed to shoot up a school or synagogue, wielding an AK-47 through the finger-operated controller and spraying a shifting array of human figures with great accuracy and grace under pressure.

I'd resisted Shaun's pleas as long as I could. Men with guns had killed Martin Luther King, Jr., and Bobby Kennedy when I was his age. I just didn't want them around. We'd played cowboys and Indians with sticks as six-shooters back in the day, I told Sherrie; we'd made all the machine-gun sounds ourselves. Kids needed to get outside more and use their imaginations.

"It's a different world, babe," she sighed.

I'd finally relented. *Guitar Hero III* wasn't so bad, all things considered, although I could have done without quite so much Kiss. The Xbox could be a force for good, even if it did transform perfectly good vegetables into gun-toting assassins hulking through the streets of a cartoon suburbia.

All this ferment in the matter of instrumental focus led to consternation among Shaun's band directors when it came to the question of what he would play in middle-school band. Kids weren't exactly lining up for tuba, so when he expressed interest in that, Mr. Morse was happy to gift him with a pair of loaners—one for school, one for home—so he wouldn't have to haul the barrel-sized hardshell case on and off the bus. Morse was not delighted when Shaun decided after Christmas to switch to bass clarinet. It's a fantastic instrument with rich, resonant low tones; I had visions of nurturing the next Eric Dolphy. But a band instrument?

Odd man out. Band directors can't let kids play musical chairs, following every instrumental whim, or they'd have chaos. Yet if a band kid happened to start off on tuba, I brooded, that surely couldn't be grounds for chaining him to the instrument for the next six years.

In the summer of 2018, after sixth grade, Shaun did what most Mississippi band kids do for the first time at that age: head off to band camp. Itawamba Community College, where camp took place, looks much as you'd expect a two-year school twenty miles east of Tupelo to look: clean, a bit outdated, lacking in architectural grandeur. But it was on that hot, muggy Sunday afternoon in June, when Shaun and I arrived in an SUV packed with clothes, towels, snacks, and instruments, that I first came to appreciate the moral grandeur, the moral *brilliance*, of Mississippi band camps. A Civil War had been fought, Jim Crow had been installed, the White Citizens Council had been formed, Brown v. Board of Ed had been defied, and the Klan had been reanimated, all for one express purpose, to prevent *this*: the loud, boisterous, egalitarian, gloriously freewheeling fruit of integration.

The campers—roughly equal portions of black and white, with a sprinkling of Asian and Hispanic kids—were anxious, chatty, wholly focused on that afternoon's auditions. They were hyper-aware of color but seemed uninterested in race. Their color consciousness, I learned from Shaun, was about which of six descending color-coded bands their auditions would sort them into. Red Band was the top ensemble: the Olympian heights, an aspirational ideal. Next down was Blue Band. Then White Band. Then the so-called "metal bands": Gold, Silver, and Bronze. Shaun explained this status hierarchy to me as we trudged across campus from his dorm, pulling a hand truck containing his tuba, trumpet, and bass clarinet, each in its own case. Only a handful of kids, it would turn out, audition on more than one instrument, in part because no student is allowed to play in more than one band. No other kid was auditioning on three instruments—or insisting that his dad wheel them through the crowded halls of the multi-winged performance space, keeping guard outside a series of audition rooms while the kid steeled himself for three successive rounds of scales and cold sight-reading on three different instruments. That is how Shaun had chosen to debut.

There were a few tears after the bass clarinet audition, thanks to a flubbed scale. But the final tally, announced later that evening and phoned home from his dorm room, was impressive. As a rising seventh-grader attending his first band camp, Shaun had made Blue Band—second highest—on tuba, plus Gold Band on trumpet and Silver Band on bass clarinet. So tuba was the ticket. He had earned himself a place. What heartened me as we'd made the rounds that afternoon was the serious, self-disciplined, but free-spirited vibe, with hundreds of band kids and their parents flowing through the halls, the wild menagerie of sounds and scales colliding in the auditorium's huge half-darkened staging area, all of it driven by a self-evident faith that every kid would be judged, in the ears of the bandleader/judges, by the content of his or her musical character. This brave new Mississippi was a world in which my son could prevail: a beloved community of quirky, competitive young musicians and their stewards, six bands deep, charged with the mission of getting it together and putting on a good show. An inescapable network of mutuality, King might have called it, tied in a single garment of destiny.

Shaun wasn't interested in the blues, it turned out. He took bass lessons from a pro at the Oxford Music School, learned how to play a walking twelve-bar line, had one public recital, then lost interest and converted his weekly lesson to keyboards until he lost interest in those. As for my thing, blues harmonica: no way. Nor was he interested when I offered to teach him how to play lead guitar—the classic string-snapping blues licks from B. B. King, Albert King, Eric Clapton that I'd used back in my college band. The edgy, yearning microtonal language that moved me left him cold.

Although marching band and orchestral repertoire were Shaun's primary areas of interest, whatever he'd achieved there had come without benefit of a private teacher. Trusting the same intuition that led me to buy that first pawn-shop trumpet, I decided to invest. Trumpet player

Terrell McGowan, a native of Albany, Georgia, was a master's student in music education at Ole Miss who spoke in a way that suggested he might not actually have had a private student before Shaun. He brought some serious jazz attitude to the project, however, along with the technical knowledge and practice routines Shaun had been lacking. We hooked up with him mid-fall of 2018, when Shaun, now in seventh grade, had fully crossed over from tuba to bass clarinet. It was an unusual thing, I knew: to ask a music teacher to instruct a student on an instrument he wasn't currently playing in band. But Terrell was game, as was Shaun, and Terrell's Sunday afternoon ministry proved invaluable.

Week after week, gently but firmly, Terrell gave Shaun the gift of taking him seriously. He showed him the fine points of embouchure and timing, introduced him to the discipline of warmups, scale practice, double- and triple-tonguing, slurs and arpeggios. Shaun hadn't previously had an African American mentor, and here too Terrell, sharply dressed in church wear, imparted essential lessons in craft and commitment, in the way that excellence comported itself.

By the middle of the school year, to his band director's chagrin, Shaun had pivoted from bass clarinet to trumpet; by the end of seventh grade he had risen to first chair, battling his way up through the ranks. Off to Itawamba he went in the summer of 2019. This time he auditioned on trumpet alone, nabbing first chair in Blue Band. "The big kids in band are surprised to see me up there," he reported. "I'm still in junior high, and they've got facial hair."

At some point during this process, Terrell introduced us to the concept of equipment upgrades, starting with Vincent Bach mouthpieces. This conversation morphed with dizzying speed into the need for a step-up trumpet, which meant yet another run up to Memphis for a visit with our mutual friend Leslie York at Amro Music and the holding open of my wallet so that cash could be extracted. I wasn't complaining! But I sometimes felt like a harried band director myself, juggling instrument rentals, rental returns, and purchases—although this would only be the second instrument we'd actually bought there, the first being Shaun's beginner trumpet. (The old pawn-shop trumpet, with its semi-squashed bell and missing middle finger-button, was stowed in the bottom drawer of a filing cabinet, easy to find when nostalgia called.) Terrell felt so proprietary towards Shaun's next big step that he met us at Amro, assayed the instruments Leslie had lined up, and handed Shaun the best. Silver tubing gleamed with an almost pearlescent glow. The smooth spattery sound Shaun produced made the cost easier to swallow.

"Always good to see you, Adam," Leslie said in his soft drawl, smiling as we shook hands after doing our deal.

Drums, to my surprise, caught Shaun's attention. Although he'd happily shouted "Percussion!" as a toddler watching "Little Einsteins" and sorted the lost hi-hat into its proper musical family, he'd never seemed particularly intrigued by the snare drum on a stand that had kicked around our living room since forever. I'd bang on it now and then with a pair of old sticks, do the one primitive *rat-a-tat* rhythm I'd learned. I played foot drums with the Blues Doctors, but Shaun had no interest in that.

Suddenly a switch turned on, a light bulb gleamed. The snare drum disappeared behind his bedroom door and began to make noises. Then Shaun emerged one evening, plopped down on the couch with iPad in hand during a break in Anderson Cooper, and said, "I want to show you something."

I muted the TV. "Sure. What's up?"

"These are the Blue Devils," he said, booting up a video, cueing it with his index finger. "The best in the country."

A long row of young men standing in a twilit parking lot, marching snare drums slung from their shoulders, stood at attention as a small crowd took photos. Then, at exactly the same moment, they kicked into a precision drumming pattern. They were preternaturally, millisecond-perfectly in sync.

"It's called Blue Devils Flams."

"Nice," I said. I listened more closely, trying to find the downbeat. To my surprise, I couldn't—which was rare, since I'd been playing foot drums for almost a decade now and beat-centered music for decades. "What time signature is that in?"

"Twenty-one eight."

"Twenty-one eight? Seriously."

At which point he jumped up, brought the snare and sticks out from his room, and played the same pattern, at the same tempo. Then he clicked on his iPhone's metronome app, as Terrell had taught him to do, slowed it down to 130, and counted it out. For Dad, who was a little slow, apparently.

Thus began a new phase in the life of our resident North Mississippi Mozart. This feeling of being left in the dust by a superior musical intelligence, this Salieri-like wistfulness, was new but not dispiriting. Father and son watched *Drumline* together, cheering hotheaded Nick Cannon as he did battle with his band director and the jealous upperclassman trying to keep him in check. The shoulder-swinging, heavily syncopated choreography of the film's HBCU marching band—the Grambling/Jackson State style—differed from the expressionless precision of the Blue Devils. Shaun preferred the latter, but he loved the taut, spattery, high-pitched *whap!* that both bands extracted from their exquisitely tight snares. Hi-tension marching snares: he wanted one. We bought him one for Christmas, along with a mail-order trombone, which he'd recently been clamoring for. In no other respect did we spoil our son, but yes: Dad had a weak spot. Who knew where this experiment would lead?

We watched *Whiplash* on DVD, enthralled by the struggle between an ambitious young drum student, Andrew Neiman (Miles Teller), and Terence Fletcher (J. K. Simmons), the domineering and manipulative drum teacher at a New York conservatory. I saw the film through the frame of my own short-lived encounter with conservatory training, a summer semester in jazz guitar at the Berklee College of Music decades earlier; Shaun, eager to excel and gifted with a supportive guide in Terrell, surely saw Fletcher as he was intended to be seen: the Evilest Music Teacher in the World. Fletcher's yanking of Neiman's chain, his endless and sadistic inventiveness in the matter of double binds, were something to behold. Yet the film became for both of us a source of high hilarity. To this day, we can crack each other up by barking taglines from the film's best-known scene, where Fletcher's slow burn suddenly erupts into a thrown chair, multiple face slaps, and profanity:

"Not quite my tempo."

"Were you rushing, or were you dragging?"

"So you *do* know the difference!

Supportive as I was of Shaun's musical ambitions, his tendency to jump from instrument to instrument as the spirit moved him made me reluctant to throw down serious cash for a top-notch horn. Sherrie and I had noticed that he tended not to follow up in a conscientious way on the homework Terrell had given him. "Give me fifteen minutes a night," I'd plead. "Give me *five* minutes!" But it was tough. He preferred to emit music, not hone his craft. On any given evening, he'd rather serenade his gaming buddies with an impromptu concert, moving from "Bohemian Rhapsody" (the keyboard overture) to "Tijuana Taxi" (chord changes strummed on electric guitar behind the sung melody) to "Go Team Go!," the all-American fight song (blatted out on trombone). Since my own musical ambitions as a teen had been entirely self-driven rather than overseen by controlling parents, I refused on principle to become a tiger dad. But I continued to hope.

At some point it became apparent that his energies were beginning to coalesce around trombone. He'd been flirting with the bone for a long time; there'd been a rental from Amro early on, then a rental return, then a renewed request leading to the purchase of a two-hundred-dollar mail-order special from Amazon. He'd been wrangling that piece of crap for the past year, until he got to sounding so good, suddenly, that when the hand went up and he said, "Dad, I need a real trombone," I was forced to agree. Up to Amro we went. Leslie was ready. It turns out that if you put a good used step-up Yamaha into the hands of a gifted fourteen-year-old kid and tell the kid to test it out in the acoustically perfect audition room while his dad stands in the corner trying not to grin, the purchase will quickly come to seem so inevitable, the matching of young man with superior horn so fated, that the dad will suddenly intuit, deep in his soul, that free will has its limits. My son taught me the meaning of surrender. Just let go.

Now came the period of trials. Even as Shaun's trombone dreams were suddenly flowering, his journey as a middle- and high-school trumpet player, which had put him in first chair for three straight years, was drawing to a close. Those piercing high notes and the discipline it took to make them no longer called to him. Trading valves for a slide, he'd moved down an octave, using his perfect pitch to dial in notes with wrist and elbow. His weekly trumpet lessons, conducted on Zoom since the advent of COVID-19, morphed into mini-concerts in which he entertained Terrell with the new trombone music he'd just taught himself. Terrell, to his credit, was willing to play along. He was back home in Albany, Georgia, now, an assistant middle-school band director, so shepherding low brass players lay within his wheelhouse. But it was a stretch. Eventually, after postponing the inevitable, it was time to move on. And here I did my best to impart the sort of fatherly lesson that my headstrong son wasn't always eager to hear.

"None of this would have happened without Terrell," I told him. "He changed the game. If you're ready to move on, then you need to do this right. You can't just text him goodbye. You need a final lesson in which you make it clear just how much you appreciate what he's done for you. And you need to keep lines of communication open, so you can touch base from time to time. You're going to need his advice as you move ahead. I can't do this for you," I added. "This is your move."

And he made it. He and Terrell had a really good talk, he said.

HARLEM AWAKENING

Keep On with It

W hen I tell the story of how I met Mr. Satan in Harlem in the fall of 1986 and began playing harmonica with him on the sidewalk next to the Studio Museum, I always begin by pointing out that I was trying to find a faster route to my tutoring job in the South Bronx. That's why I drove through Harlem in the first place. When you lived in Inwood as I did, at the top of Manhattan Island, there were two basic ways of getting to Hostos Community College at 149th and the Grand Concourse: the Harlem River Drive down the East River, or the West Side Highway down to 125th Street and then across. Nobody had GPS back then, so you went with whatever folding map you had on hand, juggling it while you drove. The first route let you avoid Harlem; the second route took you through the middle of it.

Harlem was the beating heart of Black New York. It was black history, black literature, black entertainment: the Harlem Renaissance, the Schomburg Library, the Apollo Theater. It was also the remains of a ghetto, the aftermath of the riots that had scarred the place in the 1960s. It was a place that white people just didn't go. They *used* to go there: you would occasionally run into older white people who would talk about how they'd taken cabs up there in the 1930s and early 1940s to dance and enjoy the nightlife. But they didn't go there anymore. Nobody did, except for occasional tour groups that took a charter bus to Sylvia's Soul Food. Mostly you'd hear whispered asides about junkies, drugs, guns, violence. And, of course, black anger at white people—the long tail of Malcolm X preaching on streetcorners and the whole Black Power period.

My relationship with Harlem at that point was complicated. When my ex-girlfriend Susan and I had first moved to New York six years earlier, in 1980, we'd heard the stories and internalized the warnings. We almost never went near 125th Street, the unofficial boundary, only two blocks north of where we lived in Morningside Heights. Morningside Park, two blocks east across Amsterdam Avenue, was dark, trash-filled, and full of muggers—or so we'd been told—and several notorious murders had recently taken place in or adjacent to it. We'd driven into Harlem precisely once, a warm spring morning when we'd had breakfast at Sylvia's. It was an anxious breakfast, at least for me, at one of many tables in a big side room filled with chattering black customers and bustling black staff. There was no reason for my anxiety, since nobody glared or said anything unfriendly; it was something I'd brought with me, the fruit of inexperience in all-black settings combined with years of whispered warnings. Breakfast was delicious—scrambled eggs, patty sausage, buttery grits, warm biscuits—but the moment we pushed back through the front door and began strolling down the block toward our car, past loitering men who were sipping things from bags, slapping hands, and laughing loudly, I felt weightless with suppressed panic. It was as though something deep inside me was cringing and apologizing for my presence. "Don't mind us!" the voice seemed to plead. "We're not really here! And we'll be gone very soon." This was their world; we were powerless in it. Who knew what they might do to us, just because they could?

I look back at that moment and I'm stunned by the way in which my soul had been cramped by a kind of spiritual sickness. How did I get from there, in my mid-twenties, to where I am now, four decades later—happily married to Sherrie for twenty years, raising our son in a Mississippi college town, looking back in amazement and gratitude at a partnership of more than thirty years with a Mississippi-born bluesman who I hooked up with on 125th Street, only a couple of blocks south of Sylvia's? The music helped lead me out of the dark—that and the people who played it, grooved to it, lived by it.

Harlem wasn't just the scary stories we'd been told. It wasn't just my vague suburban memories—photo essays in *Look* and *Life*—of sweating dark-skinned boys crouching by fire hydrants on sweltering summer days and angry Negroes rioting "down there," in the city. It was Jazz at Grant's Tomb, a series of summer concerts that ran every Wednesday evening in a park only two blocks from where Susan and I lived, across the street from Riverside Church.

The first time I heard the music filtering through our eighteenth-floor window overlooking the subway tracks, I was puzzled but intrigued. Was the Manhattan School of Music hosting a concert? The sound was raucous, tinkling, propulsive, a warm breeze off the river. I walked up the hill from Broadway that first August dusk and found myself in the middle of a huge block party, a thousand people strolling, chattering, mingling, lazing back. The Jazzmobile, a drive-in stage, was parked in the middle of the plaza at the top of the hill, facing the marble steps and high white columns of Grant's Tomb.

I felt my whiteness acutely as I wandered into the all-black crowd, but because this was my neighborhood, not Harlem, I relaxed into the vibe, flowing north with other strollers towards the food vendors and men in colorful robes selling essential oils as sweet incense drifted through the humid summer air. It was darker under the trees, behind the big marble building. I heard every sort of accent—Caribbean, African, hard-edged Bronx. The vibe was peaceful, relaxed, but buoyant with an energy that came from somebody blowing hell out of a trumpet on the front side of the building, mixed with tinkling piano and drums. I bought a plate of curried goat on dirty rice with stewed cabbage and found a place to sit on the side of the building, an open stretch of marble bench. I ate slowly, kept my eyes open without staring at anybody, soaking it all in. So many different kinds of hair and headgear. Dreadlocks, cornrows, Afros; knit skullcaps, trucker's caps, backward-turned baseball caps, cowboy hats. The way people greeted each other—loudly, happily, demonstratively—made it feel like a family reunion.

Later, I eased back around front and squeezed through, getting close to the stage. A sign next to the Jazzmobile said "Dizzy Gillespie and his Orchestra." *The* Dizzy Gillespie? There he was, big-bellied in a blue T-shirt, mopping sweat with a white towel off his jowls and soul-tuft. His trumpet was bent, angling upward towards the darkening sky. He leaned against the front of the piano, relaxed and informal, and sang, "Swing low, sweet Cadillac, comin' for to carry me hoooooooooooome!" as everybody around me, the whole plaza, roared and cracked up.

Half an hour later, at the entrance to the park, I bought a little sweet potato pie for a dollar from a small woman with her hair tied back in a red bandanna. I ate it slowly, savoring the sweet, creamy, cinnamon-tinged orange filling as I strolled downhill towards Broadway. Dizzy and his band played on behind me, the music rippling with good feeling.

That Jazzmobile encounter led to many more. I didn't realize at first that the crowd was Harlem folks descending on Morningside Heights, but I figured that out when I saw the complete schedule with Jazzmobile events on other days of the week, all of them located in Harlem. Summer Wednesdays at Grant's Tomb, in any case, became something I looked forward to. I saw Art Blakey's band up there in 1982 with Wynton and Branford Marsalis; the same band a few years later with Donald Harrison and Terence Blanchard; singer Betty Carter, who swaggered and yelled at her rhythm section; an aging Lou Donaldson playing "Alligator Boogaloo"; Dr. Billy Taylor on piano, lecturing us between songs about the history of jazz.

The PA system was underpowered, the piano was clanky, but the music was bold and soaring with a bittersweet edge, and the vibe, the community feel of the event, was exactly right. People spent more time enjoying themselves in the swirl of activity, hollering and partying, than paying close attention to the musicians on stage. And yet all that energy fed into the music. I knew there was magic at work, but I hadn't yet figured out what it was.

I hadn't yet had the stunningly obvious insight that people just want to be free, and that every single element of those Wednesday evenings at Grant's Tomb—the sputtering high-note solos, the potpourri of smells and tastes from the Caribbean and beyond, the styling and profiling and mutual checking out of young men and women and those who had once been young and were hanging on regardless, the loud greetings, slapped hands, and bumped elbows, the flowing movement of bodies easing gently past each other, the lack of assigned seating, the majesty of white marble and the down-home practicality of the tenting and cooking equipment back behind it, the free-for-all entrepreneurialism, the lack of a cover charge—was part of the whole. The musicians felt that whole for what it was, harmonized and punched it up, and sent it back into the crowd, the soundtrack of free people grooving on freedom.

Harlem broke open for me in the spring of 1986. This was six months before I first jammed with Mr. Satan on 125th Street, but it's the key to that whole period. Without John Spruill, Tippy Larkin, Jimmy "Preacher" Robins, Phil Young, and the other players who welcomed me, without the audiences at La Famille and Showman's, there's no way I would have had the nerve to do what I did later, out on the streets. The experience demolished the way I'd been programmed to think about Harlem. These days politically inclined people use the phrase "cultural appropriation" to cast aspersions on white blues performers; you might assume that a hip place like Harlem would have squinted at me with that sort of jaundiced eye when I first showed up. But that's not what happened—not once I pulled out my harmonicas and blew. I'm not bragging; I feel sheepish about how warmly I was treated, since I was a long way from being a mature player when it happened.

It all started on a cold February night when I drove down from my new apartment up in Inwood and parked on 125th Street in central Harlem, just west of Fifth Avenue. I was there because I had a habit in those years of blowing harp as I walked the streets of New York, no matter what neighborhood I was in. The week before, a young black guy my own age had sidled up next to me when I was doing this down in the West 20s, the flower district. He listened for thirty seconds, grooving, and then we started talking. The sound of harmonica is a universal catalyst. Play it in public—sitting on a park bench, for example—and people will come up and talk to you. They'll tell you stories. This guy told me his name was Kevin Rollins and said he was Sonny's nephew. He told me I ought to go to the Wednesday jam session at La Famille, a restaurant and jazz club up in Harlem where he worked as a dishwasher. He pronounced it La Fah-MILL.

"They'll like what you doin'," he said. "It's a fun time."

That invite was all I needed. I'd paid a lot of dues by that point. I'd been to Europe and back, twice, busking the streets of Paris, Avignon, the French Riviera. The previous summer, 1985, I'd followed and learned from Nat Riddles, the black New Yorker and blues harmonica legend who became a big brother to me, the mentor I hungered for—showing me how to tongue block, handing me study tapes filled with obscure recordings, modeling the busking life with his crowd-stopping performances at the Astor Place Cube. I'd woodshedded incessantly, sat in with a dozen different bands at Dan Lynch, Abilene, and other downtown clubs, haunted the jam sessions down there. I'd played solo on the streets after Nat got shot and fled to Virginia, then hooked up with a manic young guitarist named Bill Taft and busked New York's streets and subways all fall, before he left town. I had lifted myself into a new life, a radical makeover of the young white literary journalist I'd been. Harlem was the next step, a huge step. The size of the step scared me. But you can't end up somewhere new if you don't take that first step and risk failure.

So that's what I do. I park my car on 125th, ask a couple of young guys loitering in front of a bodega where La Famille is, then lock and walk down the block. It's just around the corner on a part of Fifth Avenue that looks like a cozy side street because it dead ends at Marcus Garvey Park. I pause for a moment, then pull open the front door and step in, hesitating on the threshold. There's a tiny stage to my left with drums, a Hammond B-3 organ, a stool, and a mic on a stand. I'm the only white face in an all-black space. No big deal, I tell myself. Just be cool.

I ease forward into the smallish room, smile at a well-dressed couple in a booth on the right. I ask about Kevin Rollins. They haven't heard of him. Nobody has. I hear several people murmuring "white boy." Rollins has warned me not to be put off by Miss Bea—the woman who runs the club. I can't imagine what she might do to me, but I ask around and find her towards the back, near the restrooms. She's light-skinned, austere, not particularly friendly. She has never heard of Kevin Rollins. This shakes me up. My pretext for being here has evaporated. Trying to remain cool, I ease towards the small bar and order a Heineken. (Many years later it would suddenly occur to me that the black leather bomber and blue jeans I was wearing—the Fonz look—might have led people to assume I was an undercover cop.)

My best move, I decide, is to connect with the musicians. I ease back towards the front and end up chatting with a dark-skinned guy in a light blue fedora sitting across from the stage. John Spruill, rhymes with pool. He's Panamanian, mid-forties, an organ player—although he's not on the gig tonight—and for some reason he takes me under his wing. When I tell him I'm a harmonica player looking to sit in, he's cool.

"Talk to Tippy," he says, nodding at the clean-shaven tan trumpet player who has just walked onto the stage. "He'll get you up. Second set, though. Wait until the break."

I notice a little sign in the front corner of the stage: the Tippy Larkin Trio.

I sit with John—he invites me into his booth—and finish my first Heineken, then order another after the waitress comes over, and another after that. Three beers don't begin to counterbalance the adrenaline flooding through my bloodstream. The music, when it starts, is thrillingly alive and propulsive. The drummer, a friendly young guy who will give me his card before the night is over, is Phil Young. Many years later I'll read his bio and discover that he'd won a competition at the Apollo Theater as a teen and toured with Bobby Blue Bland, Stanley Turrentine, George Benson, Aretha Franklin, and Roberta Flack. Tippy is the son of Milton Larkin, a famous Harlem bandleader back in the early 1940s whose lineup included Illinois Jacquet, Arnett Cobb, and

Eddie "Cleanhead" Vinson, all of whom were included on the study tape Nat gave me. I don't know any of this; I just know that the music is swinging in at least four dimensions, not the three I'm used to. The organist, a stooped older man with a ragged greying beard, bad teeth, and tinted red-framed glasses, is playing with both hands and both feet. It's possible that I am in over my head. Without a guitar as anchor, I'm having trouble hearing the chord changes in the organ's huge swirling wash. But they're not playing a blues; I'll be fine if we do that. The *warmth* of the music is what amazes me, the vividness. It's like tasting homemade gumbo made with real roux after spending your whole life eating gumbo prepared from a boxed mix.

Eventually, impossibly, the moment arrives. Tippy Larkin holds up the cocktail napkin on which I've written my name. "Ladies and gentlemen, I'd like to introduce a young man who's going to play some harmonica. Will you please welcome...Adam *Gussow*." He mispronounces the first syllable "Goose."

I take a last sip of beer and walk five feet to the stage as the scattered applause dies.

"Don't touch the mic," Tippy warns.

I turn towards the drummer and organist as I pat the pockets of my black leather jacket and tell them I'd like a B-flat blues, medium shuffle. They chuckle when I pull out a harp.

"Okay, man," grunts the organist. And the drummer counts it off, and they hit it. And we're swinging.

There's a hush. People are listening for something. I lock into the groove—it's hard to miss—and run some basic changes, boogie-woogie style, the way you'd show a dance teacher that you know how to count off the steps, but swinging hard at the same time, pushing against the groove without forcing the tempo. A couple of people start clapping along. Then a guy in back, a young trumpet player I'd chatted briefly with at the bar, calls out "Don't stop!"

Provoked, I wail like a lost child on the four-hole draw, the basic power move that every harp player knows and that Nat had down stone cold. It's nothing special, but *his* way was special, dirtying it up with the five hole like Howlin' Wolf, and I've paid attention, woodshedded the hell out of it, and know how to throw it down with my own little yelping twist. That breaks things loose. People are shouting "Blow!" and "All right now!" The energy level soars in a way that almost knocks me off my feet, but I've paid just enough dues to recognize what's happening and hold on. I'm suspended in a force field—drums kicking me from behind, organ washing over me, John Spruill shouting on my right, a huge wave of hungry attention pouring down over the bow as I stand in the spotlight, feeling it in my throat, my throat's suddenly aching, I'm suddenly almost desperate because I've wanted this for a long time, it's like coming home into the music, walking through a door into the place where the music lives. I reach down into my throat with tongue and lips and wrench out the bluest blue third I've got, halfway between major and minor with a rising edge—wrestling it into place, struggling to hold it—and then I cut them hard with that knife-edge, the whole room. And they feel it. They feel *me*. They're shouting at me, happy. On and on and on we go.

We finally swing to a close—I glance over my shoulder—and the place explodes. I stand there, stunned. Relieved. My whole life people have been warning me to stay out of Harlem. White people. Now this.

I glance at the organ player. He smiles behind his tinted glasses, gestures at the mic. "Play another one," he croaks.

When I step down off the bandstand five minutes later after a jumped-up instrumental version of "Pontiac Blues," with organ and drum solos and a second full-house explosion, John Spruill is beside himself. Over the next five hours, as we drink vodka, snort coke, and club-hop the streets of Harlem in my old Datsun wagon, looking for additional venues in which he can showcase his white phenom, John will embroider and enlarge what I've done so that it takes on the status of urban legend. "My man Adam is a *harmonica* player!" he will tell the doorman at Sutton's and other uptown watering holes. "He just took the place *apart* down at La Famille. Women were tossing him their undies. I was wondering if maybe he and I could play a few tunes." Right now he's just warming up.

"You stole the *show!*" he hisses, grabbing my hand, his Panamanian accent throbbing as Tippy and the band play on. "You see what those folks were doing? They *loved* you, man. Ain't nobody come in and play like that for a *long* goddamn time." He pulls me close. "Sometimes we get white boys who come in, you know. Blow a little trumpet or something, and they are hor-ri-*bull*, man. And somebody has to go up and say, '*Do not play any more*.' But you? No, man. People want something new, and you just threw it down."

As I make my way towards the back to use the bathroom and get a beer, it seems as though everybody wants a piece. Musicians come up and thump me on the back. A gorgeous young woman in a tight black dress with tumbling brown hair reaches out from a booth to touch my hand; her dazzling grin presses buttons I didn't know I had. While waiting my turn at the men's room, an older man in a dark blazer exits, spies me, and clasps my hand with both of his.

"That was you up there?" he says.

"Yes sir, it was."

He beams. "I ain't heard nothing like that since Jimmy Reed."

"Stevie Wonder," murmurs somebody behind me. I turn to see a smiling woman, fortyish, in an orange pantsuit. "Do you have a manager?"

"Not yet."

She reaches into her purse. "Here's my card."

Four days later my Harlem education kicked back into high gear at a club called Showman's, half a block south of 125th Street on Frederick Douglass Boulevard. I'd seen a little ad in the back of the *Voice* for a Sunday jam session starting at four; I jumped in my car, drove down from Inwood, and walked in at six. Nothing was going on. There were maybe a dozen people scattered across the room—relaxing at tables, nursing drinks at the three-sided bar. Tippy Larkin was there, wearing the same blue blazer and tan slacks. Phil Young was assembling his drums on the big low bandstand. Tippy looked up and smiled.

"Maurice, right?"

"Adam."

He laughed. "You know you all look alike."

I asked about the jam session.

"Chill out, brother," he said in a friendly, jaunty way. "We'll get there."

I ordered a Heineken. Beers were served with a white cocktail napkin wrapped around the neck and a wine glass on the side. When bar patrons got up to use the bathroom, the bartender put a fresh cocktail napkin across the top of your glass. I'd never seen that in the downtown clubs.

Bit by bit the evening assembled itself as I sat there drinking—the crowd filling in, everybody well-dressed and most of the men wearing sharp hats; John Spruill coming through the door, missing me as he skirted the tables and sat down at the organ, fingering a few chords, then spying me and hopping up to grab my hand; John and Phil kicking the groove into motion; Tippy leaning back on his stool, trumpet flashing as he quietly spattered the head for "Take the A-Train." By mid-set the house was full, a percussionist had heaved his conga onstage and was slapping and bopping away, and there were a pair of sax players up there, a black guy and a white guy. (Lonnie Youngblood and Jim Holibaugh, I found out later.) Then the band was kicking into "Tenor Madness," a hard-charging jazz-blues I'd jammed on a few times down at Dan Lynch. I checked my harps and found the right key. After the full ensemble played the head, Tippy stepped off the bandstand and I saw my chance. I got up off my bar chair, leaned over, and asked him if I could get up and blow after the sax players had done their thing.

"It's in B-flat," he said.

I patted my pocket. "I'm ready."

"Your move, baby."

I walked up onto the stage from the side and squeezed in behind the white sax player as the black sax guy blew a heavy solo. I shouted in his ear that Tippy had given me the go-ahead to blow third, after him.

"Cool," he said.

Then he bit down on his reed and started wailing as the black guy tailed off, coming in right behind him without missing a beat, accelerating into a ferocious streaming blast—he was no white pretender but the real thing—and I suddenly thought, Oh shit. You're gonna stand up here and play blues harmonica after Dexter Gordon and Phil Woods have blown their faces out? What were you thinking? The beer and adrenaline were boiling through me, wrestling for dominance, combining and recombining like epoxy starting to smoke and fume. I took a deep breath and dug deep. What was my strategy? Then it came to me: differentiate. There were a zillion things these guys could do that I couldn't match, but there was one thing I could do that they couldn't match, which was play harmonica. I had that sound. If I did my thing, I could take people all the way back down South.

I took a step towards the mic as the white sax guy finished up, raised it to face level, and let things die down. It was risky leaving that much space, because the rhythm section kept cooking along regardless. I had to keep an ear out for the chord changes, stay locked into the twelve-bar cycle as I was surveying the room, keep breathing and take it all in as the riff came to me, whatever needed to happen in this moment, right now. Don't overthink it. Just feel it. Hit the two-hole draw, the tonic note, five times, softly: *bum bum bah-bah BAH.* I could feel things shifting around behind me, I heard Phil give a little rim-tap, a "Yeah, buddy," and I did it again…

Bum bum bah-bah BAH…

…and he hit the last three accents, with a *pow!* on the last one so perfectly propulsive and well calibrated you'd have thought we'd been playing together for years. I heard John call out "That's right!" and I did it again, Phil kicked me even harder from behind…

Bum bum bah-bah BAH!…

…and then, as calls and shouts filtered into the mix from around the room, the two saxes suddenly swooped in from the side on a little improvised riff that fit *between* my riffs, like a Kansas City horn section from the 1930s.

Before I know what's happening, I'm perched on the shoulders of a thundering herd, I'm sitting in the cockpit of a turbocharged Lamborghini and we're roaring down the road, I'm feeling the explosive power as we shift and throttle up, I've never come close to commanding this sort of pedigreed excellence, but somebody has handed me the keys, thrown me into the bucket seat, put my hands on the wheel, and said "Go ahead." And I do.

I was sitting at the bar much later, around midnight, working on my sixth Heineken of the evening. The last three beers had been bought for me—two by older men in suits, one of whom had tears in his eyes as he shook my hand, the final one by the bartender, a sexy lady in a clingy yellow dress who kept chuckling "I sure do love that harmonica" as she put liquor bottles away. I'd tried to leave and people wouldn't let me. It was all Tippy's fault. He'd found me at the bar between sets, leaned down—I could smell the cognac on his breath—and hissed in my ear with a kind of happy brotherly exasperation, "When you hear something you can motherfucking *blow* on, man, you get up there and motherfucking *blow*."

How could I argue? So when a female singer in a tight gold dress got up with the band later as they kicked into a slow blues with a triplet-feel groove and said, "You mind if I sing some *blues*, y'all?," and a collective shout went up, I paid attention—especially when a couple of people sitting near me leaned over to ask if I was going to get up there with her.

"I'd love to," I said.

But I watched and listened first. I wanted to appreciate where she was coming from. Not every blues needs harmonica.

She took her time. She left space between phrases and hit the bittersweet pitches with husky, tossed-off precision. (In this she was the opposite of bad white female blues singers, who rush the beat, fill every moment with self-consciously roughened timbre and disinhibited high-end shrieks, and have a sloppy, imprecise understanding of blues tonality.) She didn't just sing, she sang *to* people. Her stage persona mixed bruised laughter with a self-preserving hardness that said, "Don't you dare fuck with my heart unless you mean it."

I waited until what felt like the right moment, then approached the stage gently, from the side, and caught her eye. She nodded and smiled without missing a beat, giving her energy to the audience as she finished the phrase and let the band play on—accepting their applause, handing me the mic, then turning away from the audience and, as I played something soft and plaintive, raising her arms above her head and shimmying her golden backside, dropping her head slightly, doing a slow one-two dance step and giving it to us that way, too, making love to the room. An electrical charge crackled through; people pounded tables, rose partway in their chairs, hollered her on. "Take me down in the alley!" somebody shouted. She moved sinuously, pridefully, as my harmonica moaned, feeling its way towards the best notes, the right notes, for this, all of this.

By midnight I was starting to feel embarrassed by the stroking I'd received, the several dozen hands I'd shaken as people exited the premises. It was thrilling, obviously, to be received this warmly, exhilarating to be graced with the chance to make music with heavyweights who were far above my level. But I wasn't a jazz cat, just a blues player with open ears, and I was leery of incurring the resentment of the other musicians. Surely they saw what I'd quickly figured out, which is that Harlem loved a novelty act and I was this week's flash in the pan.

That's when one of the older men who'd bought me a beer earlier, the one who didn't have tears in his eyes, paused by my chair on his way out.

"Young man," he said, "I really enjoyed what you did up there tonight."

I started to put myself down. He put his hand on my forearm and stopped me.

"I play ten instruments," he said. "I've been playing keyboard as long as I can remember. I've been all over. I've seen all the greats play; I've worked with a few of them. I've seen white people try to play our music. I watched when you bent down. And when you came back up, people were watching. They were *listening*. We know when you're playing from the heart."

"Thanks," I said, astonished. "Thank you. I don't know what to say."

"No need, no need." He took his hand off my arm and reached into his shirt, pulling out a thin gold chain and showing me a set of tarnished silver wings. "See that? That's the Triple Nickels paratroopers. Five Hundred and Fifty-Fifth Parachute Infantry Battalion. I fought for my country in World War Two. I risked my life for my country. I'd do it again, too. I'm *proud* of my country. But then—when I got home, when God had let me live and I got home to Georgia, I *still* had to sit at the back of the bus."

"I'm sorry."

He smiled. "Things are different now. Anyway, I really enjoyed that harmonica. Keep on with it." He patted my arm again and limped slowly towards the front door.

Getting It Together

In 1991, when my blues duo Satan and Adam first began to break into the national market with the release of our debut album, *Harlem Blues*, journalists and DJs were curious about how we'd met. What they were really trying to say was, "He's an older black bluesman from Mississippi by way of Harlem; you're a younger white guy with degrees from Princeton and Columbia. You've got nothing in common."

Sometimes they said that in so many words; sometimes they just hinted at it. The music spoke for itself, but the union-of-opposites theme was high in everybody's framing. It was the tension between the visual tableau we presented and the music we produced that provoked conceptual unease in those who were determined to parse America's racial terrain in familiar ways. And of course they were curious about his name. So I told the same story I'd told many times—one I eventually polished into a set piece in my 1998 memoir, *Mister Satan's Apprentice*. Sometimes I added more detail, sometimes less. But the basic outlines were the same.

I'd been driving through Harlem in late October of 1986, trying to find a faster way to the job I'd recently started as a writing tutor at Hostos Community College in the South Bronx. I had put busking aside by that point, determined to get a straight job and ease into an as-yet-undetermined career. But as I cruised across 125th Street, shortly after passing the Apollo Theater, a faint bluesy roar caught my ear. I crossed Seventh Avenue with the State Office Building rising on my left, eased slowly past the bus stop, then glanced right and saw him in front of the New York Telephone office.

It's *that guy*, I thought. And almost without thinking, I pulled the Honda to the curb, parked, and got out.

An older black man with a greyish beard and greying cornrows was playing electric guitar through a pair of Mouses—the same battery-powered amp I'd been using—and keeping the beat on a hi-hat cymbal. He was singing hoarsely through another amp, almost shouting, his words partially drowned out by the guitar.

Awkward and exposed as I felt standing on the Harlem sidewalk, intensely conscious of my own whiteness, I was even more thrilled to have stumbled into this particular musician again.

Two and a half years earlier, strolling with Susan in our Columbia neighborhood on a mellow spring evening, I'd paused to watch a trio of blues musicians on the corner of 113th Street and Broadway: two guitarists backed by a drummer. The guy with the grey beard was the front man. He was drinking heavily—upending a paper-bagged forty-ounce and draining it as he rocked back on his heels, shuddering in a comically exaggerated way as though the booze was ripping down through him, then strumming a shuffle groove with an incredibly catchy backbeat.

"Oh baby," he sang, "You don't have to gooooooooo...." I'd been so blown away by his music, so intimidated by his power and presence, that I'd gone up to the other guitar player when they took a break and asked him about his amp. This was a month before Susan moved out; I was already feeling the busker's call.

"This thing?" the second guitarist said with a nasal twang. "That's a Mouse. You know Manny's Music downtown?"

"On Forty-Eighth Street?"

He cocked his finger at me, tapped it against the edge of his black trucker's cap. "There you go. They'll hook you up."

77

I'd paid a lot of dues since then. Breaking into the busking life during my first trip to Europe with a grad-school buddy; chasing Nat Riddles around the Village; working Manhattan's streets and subways with Bill Taft and Bill Collins; debuting at La Famille and Showman's; two months in Paris and Avignon with Bill Collins this past summer. I could barely remember the guy I'd been in the spring of '84. And here he was: the man whose call had provoked that response. Playing solo now, without the band.

I leaned back against my parked car, watching him go, astonished once again by his deathless groove, his rasping voice. He was two steps lower down than Tippy Larkin, Preacher Robins, the jazz cats and soul men I'd been jamming with in the clubs. His take on the blues was closer to my own guitar-driven sweet spot, but with a wild-eyed funk edge propelled by complex inner voicings.

Glancing at the half dozen people who were watching, I leaned towards a guy standing on my right—he had the slightly angular, tilted look of somebody with a prosthetic leg—and asked who the musician was.

"Who, him?" he said. "That's Satan. Everybody in Harlem knows Satan. Uh huh. That's his spot, right there."

Satan? I thought.

Although we wouldn't end up calling ourselves Satan and Adam until we recorded our demo in 1990, the seeds of our duo-name were planted in that moment. The union-of-opposites theme was baked in. It hadn't happened yet, but if it did: Satan and Adam would be jamming on the streets of Harlem.

"Do you think he'd let me sit in?" I asked. "I play harmonica."

"Harmonica?" He chuckled. "Stevie Wonder, my man." He extended his hand and we slapped five. "Sure, he'll let you play. *Can* you play?"

"I can play," I said, surprised at my own boldness.

"Yeah, I think Satan will do that."

His name was Duke. He called me Adams. I told him I'd be back the next day with my stuff.

That's how things started. I'd driven back to Inwood after work and walked out into Inwood Hill Park, up around the crumbling macadam path under the trees. I'd woodshedded fiercely below the Henry Hudson Bridge as dusk fell— ripping off long echoey strings of notes, hammering my groove into shape.

The next day at noon I spun out the door with a daypack over my shoulder and Mouse dangling from my hand. I jumped in my Honda and flew down the West Side Highway, exiting at 125th Street and pushing into the heart of Harlem.

Satan was playing the same spot, just east of Seventh Avenue. The weather was lukewarm and calm, one of those Indian summer days New York sometimes gifts you with.

I pulled to the curb. Duke was there; I jumped out and grabbed hands, then leaned back as Satan roared on. My heart was thrumming, my whole body. It was La Famille all over again.

Satan finished the song and leaned forward to adjust his hi-hat, which was sitting on a big dirty square of cardboard. He'd kicked it so hard that the cardboard had slid forward, away from his hi-chair. He tugged it closer.

I eased toward him, leaned down, and thanked him for the music. He smiled distractedly as he glanced up at me.

"Thank you, sir."

"Do you...think I might be able to sit in on a song or two? I'm a harmonica player."

He continued to adjust. "Where are your instruments?"

I jerked my head. "My Mouse and harmonicas are in the trunk of my car. I won't embarrass you," I added.

A few seconds went by. Then he made a big beckoning motion, like he was tossing a tennis ball back over his shoulder. "Come on up!"

A crowd began to form the moment I set my Mouse on the sidewalk and began plugging things together: mic, digital delay pedal, cable. When I was ready to go, Satan kicked into gear, a fast groove in E. I did my best to hold on. People were shouting from all sides as I wailed. We played for what seemed like forever but must only have been six or seven minutes. Satan brought the song to a close with a withering flurry of guitar and cymbals as I screamed on a bent ten-hole blow. Sidewalk traffic had frozen. The intensity of the response was hard to believe. Several guys grabbed my hand, asked me where I was from. Dollar bills and change tumbled into the blue plastic bucket between Satan's legs, where the mic stand was planted.

That was the beginning of a lifelong musical partnership, one that would endure for thirty-four years until Sterling's death of COVID-19 in September 2020. Neither of us knew that at the time. But the feeling was there from the start.

My journal tells me that we first played together on Thursday, October 23, 1986. At noon on that day, according to the *New York Times*, a group of eight hundred peace activists in the Great Peace March for Global Nuclear Disarmament walked across the George Washington Bridge and continued south to Grant's Tomb. Half of them had walked all the way from Los Angeles. Straight through the desert, the heartland, in seventh months. Judy Jones, a participant from Coronado, California, sent home the following account to her local newspaper:

> After leaving Grant's Tomb, we march through Harlem toward our campsite at Randalls Island. Looking up at the decaying buildings, I see children peering out of broken glass windows covered with burglar bars. I am surrounded by Harlem's colors, spirits, smells and yells. A spiritual band follows us down the street, and a man playing and singing blues on the sidewalk gives several marchers a chance to unwind and boogie.

That bluesman was Sterling—Mr. Satan, as I quickly came to call him. He told me about it two days later as we were standing next to his old white Chevy step van out on Seventh Avenue after playing a couple of sets three blocks north in front of Mart 125, a discount emporium. I'd just pulled my Honda even with his van and raised the hood so he could get a jump from my battery.

"I could have kicked you in the butt!" he chuckled. "That whole damn march came by right after you left the other day."

"On 125th Street?"

"You darn right. Thousands of 'em, right after you packed up."

"Oh shit," I groaned. "I had a job to get to! I was late for my tutoring gig."

"I was mentally putting my foot in your *behind!*" he roared.

That's how we talked, in full public view on one of Harlem's big boulevards, after knowing each other for only two days: a fifty-year-old black guy and a twenty-eight-year-old white guy. There's something about grooving with another musician that tends to break down barriers, but I'd never experienced this sort of immediate connection. Harlem, it turned out, was about to gift me with the chance not just to shed my residual racial anxieties, but to blow them sky-high.

I first became aware of the phrase "beloved community" a year or two after that debut. I was reading Baldwin, Ellison, Malcolm X, Albert Murray, W. E. B. Du Bois, whatever I could get my hands on, trying to make sense of the experiences I was having down in Harlem. I picked up Stephen B. Oates's biography of Martin Luther King, Jr., and was struck by a statement of King's that gave shape to the partnership that Sterling and I were in the process of forging.

"We are caught in an inescapable network of mutuality," King had written in his "Letter From Birmingham Jail" (1963), "tied in a single garment of destiny." Later, after I'd moved to Mississippi, gotten engaged to Sherrie, and begun collecting notes for a book on racial reconciliation, I read a study by religious studies scholars Kenneth L. Smith and Ira G. Zepp, Jr., entitled *The Search for Beloved Community: The Thinking of Martin Luther King, Jr.* "The ultimate aim," King had written in 1957, speaking of the Southern Christian Leadership Conference, "is to foster and create the 'beloved community' in America where brotherhood is a reality...Our ultimate goal is genuine intergroup and interpersonal living—*integration.*"

"Getting it together," a phrase I heard a lot in Harlem, is the musical equivalent of working towards beloved community. Like beloved community, it has an individual and collective dimension. You get your own thing together—you woodshed specific songs and techniques, you and your axe, striving for a soulful sound—but musicians who work side by side also seek common ground, especially with regard to volume, pitch, and groove, in a way that isn't obvious to outsiders but that makes a huge difference to the players themselves.

Early in our relationship, as Sterling and I were getting things together in that fashion, a third musician was part of the group: a washtub bass player named Bobby Bennett, a.k.a. Professor Six Million. A slim, acerbic, bronze-skinned man with a hoarse voice and a harsh laugh, Professor—as Satan called him—was an unlikely agent of beloved community. But there he was, sitting next to me in my Honda on my second day in Harlem as we followed Satan's step van across 125th Street and over the Triborough Bridge to Randall's Island to play for the anti-nuclear activists who were camped out there. WBGO was playing on the radio; he scatted along, then turned and stared at me.

"Things has lightened up in Harlem a lot since the last six or seven years. Six or seven years ago, they'd *kill* me if they saw me in this car with you."

"They?"

"*Them*. All of 'em. They don't like it one bit."

He paused, turned stiffly away, then fixed me in his eye. "I killed three men. Three." Another pause. "Satan killed two."

I assumed I was being hazed but wasn't sure. "Three men?"

"Can't let nobody mess with your shit," he said. "This is *Harlem*." He rubbed his eyes hard with the heels of his hands. "Somebody fuck with your shit, ain't but one thing you can do."

Professor was the guy, Sterling told me much later, who had broken him out onto the streets back in the early 1980s when he was easing back into music after losing his third wife to cancer and taking on his new name. The two men had an uneven relationship—bickering like brothers one moment, laughing uproariously the next. Both men said "shut up" a lot, in a fond way that meant "hush your mouth." I quickly took that sort of incoming fire from both men—and was happy for it. I was part of the team.

Even as Sterling and I made our separate peace, first with Professor and then as a duo, we were aware that race relations in the city were toxic—at least to judge from the headlines and the way in which they skewed the feeling in the neighborhood. There was a trilogy of low points during our half-decade on 125th Street, a murderer's row of troubled locations in which black men and boys died at the hands of white men and boys: Howard Beach, Bensonhurst, Crown Heights.

§On the night of December 19, 1986, four black men were driving Cross Bay Boulevard in Queens when their car broke down. Seeking help, three of the men walked several miles to Howard Beach, an Italian community—home to mob boss John Gotti—where, after stopping at a pizzeria, they were chased by a mob of white teens with baseball bats. One of the black men, Michael Griffith, twenty-three, ran onto the Belt Parkway to escape his attackers and was struck and killed by a car. Mayor Ed Koch compared Griffith's death to "the kind of lynching party that took place in the Deep South."

§On the evening of August 23, 1989, a sixteen-year-old black boy named Yusef Hawkins and three of his friends traveled to Bensonhurst, an Italian community in Brooklyn, to look at a used 1982 Pontiac that had been advertised in the local paper. They were met by a large group of white teens, most of them carrying baseball bats, who had staked out the house of a local girl named Gina Feliciano who was reputed to be dating black guys. Mistaken about Hawkins's motives, the infuriated mob chased him and his friends; one of the white teens, Joey Fama, pulled out a pistol and shot Hawkins twice in the heart, killing him. Mayoral candidate David Dinkins, who would beat Koch three months later to become New York's first black mayor, termed Hawkins's death a lynching.

§On the evening of August 19, 1991, a young Hasidic Jew named Yosef Lifsh was driving a station wagon in Crown Heights, Brooklyn, bringing up the rear in a three-car motorcade for his spiritual leader, Rabbi Menachem Schneerson. Struggling to catch up, Lifsh raced through a red light, hit another car, veered onto the sidewalk, and struck seven-year-old Gavin Cato, the son of Guyanese immigrants, killing him instantly. Long-simmering tensions between the neighborhood's Caribbean and Jewish communities boiled over. Angry black residents began rioting; one, Charles Price, shouted "Kill the Jews!" Twenty young black men surrounded Yankel Rosenbaum, a Jewish grad student from Australia, stabbing and beating him, fracturing his skull. He later died. The riotings continued for several days. Jewish homes, businesses, and cars were the principal targets. Mayoral candidate Rudy Giuliani, who would beat Dinkins three months later, characterized the riots as a pogrom.

1987 was one week old. I'd spent Christmas out in California with my family, visiting my grandmother. When I got back to New York, the city was still aching from what had happened in Howard Beach. The *New York Times* and the tabloids had garish front-page headlines, day after day. I hadn't seen Satan in a while; it was just warm enough, about forty-five degrees, that I thought he might be out there. So I drove down to Harlem one afternoon and rolled to a stop in front of the New York Telephone store where we'd first jammed several months earlier. That spot would be our home for the next five years, although we didn't know it at the time.

He and Professor had just finished packing up. Satan's amps and percussion were loaded into his shopping cart with the hand-lettered sign "The One Man Blues Band, by Satan"; Professor had tossed his broomstick and clothesline into his old metal washtub. They were bickering at each other, scowling.

"Well, now," sneered Professor, eyeing me as I came up. "Motherfucker. I know that word, Satan. I know *lots* of goddamned words. Piss and shit too."

Wincing, Satan held up his hand for silence. "Stop. Stop. Just—"

"And monkeyshines, don't forget about them."

"I'm getting ready to dismiss you from my sight, Mister Bobby."

"Hey, Mister Satan, you're packing up?" I said.

He glanced up. "Hey, Mister Gus."

"We just talkin'," Professor said, spitting toward the curb. "Me and Satan. Ain't no big thing."

"Let's play over by Columbia," I said.

Satan stroked his beard and thought. We'd done this once back in November and made good money. I could see the idea percolating.

"You have your Mouse with you?"

"It's in the car."

Suddenly he broke into a grin. "Hell yes! Let's drive on over and collect some of that good green money they've been holding for us."

Professor leaned in on me. "You in the group now, motherfucker," he whispered hoarsely in my ear, behind his hand. "Shut up."

I popped the Honda's hatchback. We folded down one of the split rear seats and Satan off-loaded his shopping cart, carefully placing Professor's washtub face down over his Mouses. Then he slammed the hatchback—carefully, not hard—and Professor and I got in and drove slowly down the block while Satan hiked the empty shopping cart around the corner of 125th onto Seventh Avenue and three blocks down to Shakespeare Flats, the building where he had a first-floor studio apartment. Professor had folded himself into the back seat so Satan would have the front.

"Well," he declaimed as I paused at the light.

85

"Yes indeed," I countered.

"No it ain't."

"That's what *you* said."

"Hah!" he laughed harshly, slapping the back of the seat. "You doin' Satan now."

I'd already begun to learn that life with these two men proceeded by a kind of antic surrealism, a ceaseless back-and-forth conducted on multiple dimensions with a few basic rules subject to on-the-spot variants. I hadn't yet consciously recognized that the music we were making drew on the same sources.

After picking Satan up, we drove five crosstown blocks on 123rd Street, passing by the Morningside Gardens apartment complex where Susan and I first lived when we'd moved to the city back in 1980. I swung right on Broadway, then made a quick left on LaSalle and a second left onto Broadway, heading south to the Broadway Presbyterian Church on the corner of 114th Street, just across the street from the Chemical Bank where I'd first seen Satan and his trio several years earlier.

We set up on the sidewalk in front of the church steps and ended up staying until dusk: two older black men and one younger white man making music together on a cool January day, two weeks after Michael Griffith's death out at Howard Beach. There was something uncanny about the smiles on people's faces as they pitched dollar bills into Satan's open guitar case; you could almost feel them feeling *themselves* contributing to a righteous cause.

"Kicking ass and stomping dick" was the phrase Satan and Professor had used to describe our playing. Was blues performance a kind of symbolic violence—a recapitulation of the violence that circulated out there, in the social world? (I'd heard Harlem musicians talk about cutting somebody at a jam session.) Or was it a healing spell against such violence? Or was it both things at the same time? I didn't know. But I knew that we were doing something useful just by being there, making the racket we made as people strolled by and paused to watch.

We were crowing as we drove back to Harlem after packing up. Money and music will do that.

"I got so *goddamned* much money I don't know what to do with it," Professor shouted from the back seat.

"Ain't it the truth?" Satan said loudly, reaching forward to push in the dashboard cigarette lighter.

"Whooo! I'm gonna lay it on my bed and roll in it."

"We killed," I said. "I can't believe the cops left us alone."

"They *had* to," said Satan. "I'm very serious. The Earth knows what we're about."

Professor laughed harshly. "You talkin' crazy now, baby."

Satan slapped my thigh as he lit up a cigarette and rolled down the window. "You can *blow* that harmonica, young man. I was talking about you over Christmas. My people be coming up, talking all this mess about 'Hey, Mister Satan, we see you got you a white boy who can blow.' And I said, 'He's *got* to be good if he's playing with me!'"

A few minutes later I rolled up in front of Shakespeare Flats and popped the trunk as we all got out. The guy I'd been only a year ago would have had alarms going off in his head. Harlem! Dark streets! Men sitting on stoops sipping from paper-bagged bottles! Except for the faint flickering recognition that those voices would have been there a year ago, there was nothing in my head now but music and the singular fellowship that seemed to have sprung out of nowhere, binding us into a band of brothers. The money didn't hurt.

"I love you, man," Professor chuckled. "Don't worry about Satan."

"I love you guys, too," I said.

Satan came up and took my right hand in both of his. "I shouldn't say this," he laughed, "because it goes against correctness of speech, but you played *hell* out of that thing, Mister!"

"Aw shit," Professor sneered, grinning tightly. "Here we go."

Two days later we played out on 125th Street, another cool grey January day. Satan was scowling when I arrived—he'd been there since eleven, Professor had shown up at one—but the moment I plugged in, we were kicking and stomping, the music was flowing, and the bills were fluttering into the tip bucket. I was filled with jumping energy, hungry to blow. I'd already learned how to discipline that feeling, falling into formation behind the others, weaving my riffs between the vocal lines, waiting for Satan's call. "Blow on, Mister Adam!" he'd shout into the mic. And I'd blow.

Letting my eyes drift towards the big vertical sign for the Apollo Theater, a block down on the left, I'd gaze at the endless parade of bundled-up Harlemites: puffy goosedown coats, black leather coats and brown suede coats, cheap navy watch caps and spiffy Kangols and fedoras, big white high-top sneakers like the rappers wore on MTV, lots of blue jeans and black jeans and Timberland boots, men in suits—politicians? ministers?—with mufflers flapping around necks. Women, too: groups of schoolgirls giggling and shouting, elderly church ladies glancing sideways at me through spectacles, drop-dead beauties my own age and ten, twenty, thirty years older, full-figured women with heartbreaking curves that declared themselves through every sort of clothing.

The older men hovering near us, some holding paper-bagged bottles and cans, would turn to watch a particularly stunning goddess stroll by. They'd shake their heads in amazement, then glance at each other and crack up, slap hands. Sometimes they'd call out: "Hey baby!" or "God *damn* you look good!" Most of the women ignored them but occasionally one would turn and flash such a devastatingly cute grin that they'd almost fall down, or pretend to.

Out beyond the sidewalk was the usual mix of Transit Authority buses with whooshing diesel engines, bright yellow taxis, freshly washed Lincoln Town Cars sporting livery plates, older beaters grimed with winter dirt, plus a steady stream of gold-trimmed, pimped-out white Lexuses and Benzes with fancy chrome rims, sound systems thumping like pile drivers as sullen black male voices talked trash over hip-hop beats.

This particular day, with the troubles at Howard Beach still dominating headlines, was charmed. "We are the Creators!" Satan roared into his mic. "We are a *threesome*! And while you're at it, put your hands together for the young man! He's been blowing that thing!"

Satisfying as the music was, big as the crowds were, most of the action took place between sets as Sterling and I hung out near our amps, gabbing with whomever came up. I kept assuming that somebody was going to give me grief for what had happened to Michael Griffith, but nobody did. Just the reverse: when I mentioned "that bullshit out in Queens," the person I was talking to made it clear that *we*, all of us up in here, were on the same side. One young black guy came up to me—he had horn-rimmed glasses and was holding a paper-bagged pint—he grabbed my hand and shouted, "I love you man. I *love* you. Do you know what I'm saying?" He was almost weeping.

That was one encounter out of many. "I slapped hands at least two hundred times this afternoon," I wrote that evening in my journal. I was an avid journal-keeper back in those days, because so much was happening and I wanted to remember it all.

Much later, after we'd packed up and Professor had disappeared, after I'd driven around the corner and down three blocks to Shakespeare Flats while Satan pushed his shopping cart along the same route, we leaned against the side of my car as winter dusk fell in Harlem, tossed back a couple of half pints of Romanoff vodka, and began to make plans: huge plans, staggering plans, plans that had us playing the streets all spring and hitting the road when summer came. Healing the soul of America. That's when he first called me son.

"I'm calling you son," he said, "because that's how I feel about you."

Driving Miss Macie

T he International BuskerFest in Halifax, Nova Scotia, was a test for Mr. Satan and me. Apart from one weekend in May 1989 when we'd driven across the George Washington Bridge and down to Liberty State Park in Jersey City two days in a row to play a street fair, we'd never actually left the island of Manhattan. The healing-the-soul-of-America dream had been put on hold as we worked our same old spot on 125th Street, honing our sound and harvesting tips. So the idea of loading up my car in Harlem and driving 350 miles north to Portland, Maine, driving onto the *Scotia Prince* ocean liner, traveling overnight to Yarmouth, Nova Scotia, driving off the boat and another 135 miles to Halifax along the rocky coastline, busking for ten days straight in front of large crowds as part of an international cohort of the world's best street performers, cashing in our Canadian dollars for American dollars, then turning around and traveling all the way back to Harlem—it was a big step. Satan and Adam hit the road! I'd wanted this to happen for a while. But it was a lot of ground to cover.

I was very curious, which is to say anxious, about whether Mr. Satan could sustain his identity out in the larger world. That identity worked beautifully in Harlem. Everybody there—absolutely everybody—called him Mr. Satan. (The Mr. got added not long after I came along; he called me Mr. Adam, not Adam, and I returned the favor. Everybody else followed suit.) His "real" name, I'd discovered early on, was Sterling Magee. Over the years people had filled in bits and pieces of his back-story: his band-work as a guitarist with King Curtis, Etta James, Little Anthony and the Imperials; his singles as a solo artist in the sixties and the album he'd made with George Benson and the Harlem Underground in 1976, including the song "Funky Sterling"; his time as a Brill Building songwriter with partner Jessie Stone. But although his driver's license bore that birth-name, he never used it and didn't want it used. So what would happen when we met people out in the real world, they asked him what his name was, and he said, "I am Satan"? How would that go over in Canada?

My other big anxiety concerned the third member of the team, Miss Macie. Professor Six Million was no longer around; Mr. Satan had kicked him out of the band when he got drunk out on 125th Street one after-noon and cursed up a storm. But Miss Macie had been around almost as long as I had. She was Mr. Satan's girlfriend—"my wife," he called her matter-of-factly—but theirs was a common-law marriage, not one certified by a minister or court. She'd shown up in March 1987 during a ten-day period when I had the flu and stayed home. Next time I drove down to 125th Street, Mr. Satan had added a second hi-hat cymbal for a much bigger percussion sound, and she was there: a smallish woman, medium brown, with very large tinted glasses and a bulky handbag, sit-ting cross-legged in a folding chair on the sidewalk, watching us play. He'd give her most of his bills when he counted shares out of the mon-ey-bucket. She'd occasionally hand him a white towel so he could mop his face. She chain-smoked in an aggressive way, crossing and uncrossing her legs, shifting on the chair, giggling to herself. She was friendly to me at first, but when she took off her glasses, her eyes darted in all directions in a way that I should have taken as the warning it was.

Her name was Macie Mabins: "Macie *Ophelia* Mabins," she was fond of declaring. I didn't really understand her, but she had a down-to-earth orientation, a jeans-and-T-shirts vibe, that seemed like a good match for

Mr. Satan. She had an unerring ability to punch through his high and mighty talk, refusing to take him as seriously as he took himself, and he was tickled by this. If he was standing tall and pontificating—"I am Satan! I am the Earth! My little people gonna be very surprised by the outcome of my wrathful judgments," and so on—she'd sometimes get angry. "Nowwww, Satan," she'd huff, "you can just stop all that nonsense right now. Because I *will* go off." Sometimes she'd just snap, "Shut up, Satan." And instead of taking offense, he'd pause, like a cartoon character suspended in midair—and then crack up!

"You see what I'm dealing with?" he'd laugh, eyes mirthful. Later he'd call her "Miss Crab" and complain fondly about his "evil little crabby."

I was vaguely familiar with the psychological concept of a *folie à deux*: a madness of two. Two unbalanced people who create their own crazy little world. There was some of that going on. But the truth is, she was the crazy one. It took me a while to realize just how bad things were. It started when we began to go on road trips—Sterling and me up front, her in the right rear seat—and she began to complain about the things my car was saying to her through the stereo speakers back there.

"Now, Gussow," she'd call out from the back seat, "you *know* what's going on."

"What's that?" I'd say, glancing up in the rearview mirror.

"Don't pretend you don't know. I'm not your fool."

Mr. Satan would turn and try to calm her down; he'd ask her for a cigarette, light his off of the glowing tip of hers, make idle chit-chat. But she'd just simmer.

"The smells, Gussow. You know you put them in the sound system back here."

"*Smells?* Miss Macie, I have no idea—"

"Tell him, Mister Say-tan. Tell him about the voices saying 'Nigger!' That's all we are anyway. You know all about that, Gussow. You may think we're fools, but we're not."

Her mood, as she talked, would veer from angrily self-righteous to softer and more plaintive, but the possibility of a serious explosion was always there. This behavior started on that very first road trip to Halifax.

At a certain point in the mid-1990s, after many such episodes, I used Lycos or WebCrawler to look up "paranoia" and "paranoid schizophrenia," and it became clear to me that she was suffering from some version of one or both of those mental illnesses. She was unmedicated, as far as I knew. When I wrote *Mister Satan's Apprentice*, in the middle of my graduate studies at Princeton, I hinted at this behavior but muted the full extent of it, because Macie was alive at the time and because it would be fatal to my hoped-for future as a professor of African American literature to represent my partner's wife, a black woman, as what she was for much of the time we spent on the road: furious, troublemaking, and psychologically deranged. Sterling loved and needed her; she was, for better or worse, the third member of the duo. One reason she resented me, it became clear, was because of the pleasure that he and I took in each other's company—the joy we shared onstage every night, making our big raucous sound, and the way we cackled and crowed about it during the following day's long drive. She was jealous.

Back in 1980, a pair of feminist literary critics, Sandra Gilbert and Susan Gubar, published an influential study, *The Madwoman in the Attic: The Woman Writer and the Nineteenth-Century Literary Imagination*. They argued that female novelists in Victorian England—with Charlotte Brontë's *Jane Eyre* as the paradigmatic example—had created outwardly "crazy" characters and stowed them in tight fictional places as a way of expressing their own sublimated rage at the way that they, as women writers in a patriarchal society, had been damaged, wounded, by the constricted space they'd been forced to inhabit. As a thoroughgoing feminist at the time, I'd embraced this concept. I knew it was a bad idea to simply write off the crazy person in your midst. Paranoid people aren't necessarily making everything up, projecting their own sickness onto an otherwise benign world. Sometimes they're just more sensitive than the rest of us to the sickness that's actually present in the world. Sometimes they blurt out inconvenient truths at inconvenient moments—moments when more "sane" people silence themselves to keep the peace. Which means they have something to teach us.

What brought this point home was what happened when, after finishing up in Halifax, driving back to Yarmouth, boarding the *Scotia Prince*, and steaming slowly through the night, gently rocking in our beds, we drove our car up out of the boat's belly the following afternoon and down into the immigration holding area in Portland, Maine. My stomach was a wreck. Seasickness was mostly to blame, but it felt worse than that. I asked Mr. Satan to take the wheel and drive us off the boat while I swooned in the passenger seat and tried not to vomit.

We were one of a hundred cars on the ship, a steady outpour of vehicles that spiderwebbed across the tarmac and sorted themselves into half a dozen lines. Our car had a U-Haul clamshell up top, something I'd rented in the Bronx the day before we left New York. We'd filled out our immigration cards on the boat; Mr. Satan had placed all three cards plus our driver's licenses right on the dash, ready to go. When we finally pulled even with the guard booth, the US Customs agent bent down and Mr. Satan handed him our cards and licenses with his usual beaming smile and a cheerful "Hello, sir!" He also handed the agent a copy of our demo cassette, which had a diptych composed of two photos, Sterling playing guitar and me blowing harmonica, plus the headline "Satan and Adam." It was, we'd agreed, the best way of making clear that we were a musical act on the road. Mr. Satan told the customs agent that we were on our way home to Harlem after playing the International BuskerFest in Halifax.

The agent, leaning down, saw a black man with a gold tooth and spiky, Brother-from-another-planet hair; a black woman in the back seat with the same kind of spiky hair, smoking and muttering to herself; and a younger white guy—I was thirty-two at the time—with unkempt reddish blond hair, holding his belly and looking ill.

I didn't realize we were being profiled until all the other cars had disappeared and it was just our car, alone on the tarmac, and we had been asked to step out and sit on a nearby curb. But then, as the three customs agents began opening the car doors and hatchback, heaving out amps and suitcases, pulling off amp covers and springing suitcase latches, and rifling through our stuff, I suddenly got it. They were looking for drugs. We fit the template. We'd pegged the needle. Harlem. Ghetto hair. Blues musicians. A white kid on drugs. Rooftop carrier. Bulky equipment. Lots of places to hide drugs.

I sat on the curb, holding myself, slowly rocking back and forth, trying not to puke as I had my big revelation. I wanted to smile at the agents and groan, "No, man! Naaaaaawww." Because we didn't have any drugs. We'd drunk a lot of Molson and Labatt's up in Halifax, but we didn't do, or carry, drugs.

But they didn't know that. And I didn't say anything—although it wouldn't have mattered if I had. They went to work. Ten minutes. Twenty minutes. Half an hour. The longer they searched without finding drugs, the more determined they became. You could see them thinking, "These guys are *good*," as though we were professional drug runners.

Meanwhile, as all this was happening, Miss Macie was doing a slow burn out on the tarmac. "We're just niggers," she sneered under her breath, fidgeting with matches, lighting another cigarette. "Ain't that right, Gussow. You know all about that."

"Hush, Miss Baby," Mr. Satan murmured. "It ain't no big—"

"*Now*, Satan, what *are* you going to do about it? That's what I want to know."

She was right. For once Miss Macie and I were on exactly the same wavelength. There was nothing we could do except submit. But we saw what was going on, and we didn't have to pretend that we didn't.

The agents popped the hood. They unscrewed the wing nut, took off the air cleaner, poked metal rods down into the carburetor. They lay on mats and shone flashlights up under the front and rear suspension. They flipped open the rooftop carrier and felt around under Mr. Satan's old hi-chair and the scuffed wooden board he'd built to anchor his hi-hat cymbals. Bad as my stomach felt, I was fascinated by the approaching paradigm shift. At some point, unable to find any drugs, they were going to realize that we didn't, in fact, have any drugs.

That moment arrived. After retreating to the guard booth and conferring briefly, the agents returned and put everything back in the car. Nobody apologized. But one of the agents asked us to follow him; he told us he'd lead us out to a nearby motel, and he did. We drove home to Harlem the next day. That was our first out-of-town trip.

"You'll live through it." That was Mr. Satan's favorite saying.

It didn't matter what sort of complaint I was sharing with him, or where: on 125th Street in Harlem, or in the car now that we'd become a national touring act. He refused to coddle me. Girlfriends, fever blisters, car troubles. The man would not indulge. *Healthy* complaining, full-throated, soul-powered blues declarations, were okay. He did a lot of that. Sing your song, baby. Get it out.

"I had so many wives die on me," he once declared, "I was thinking of opening a funeral parlor." I knew for a fact that he'd been so devastated by his third wife's death that he'd had a breakdown and renamed himself Satan. Now he was joking about it!

But whining—anything that smacked of serious weakness, depressive capitulation, loss of soul force—was a no-no.

"You'll live through it," he'd say, brushing me off. "That's for damn sure."

And I always did. He was batting a thousand.

Sometimes, when something went wrong on the road—a missed connecting flight the first time we flew to Finland, for example—he'd take a deep breath and sigh, "We'll live through it," as though some trials just had to be endured.

Later on, I thought about the life he'd lived as a boy coming up in Mississippi in the 1930s and 1940s, and the phrase made more sense. He'd seen much worse than anything I was going through. He was trying to toughen me up.

When Satan and Adam hit the road, things weren't always a feuding, bickering mess. Sometimes they were fun, even idyllic, like Huck and Jim on the raft. Sometimes Miss Macie was asleep in the back seat, or lost in her own thoughts, and Mr. Satan and I would sit up front, trade cigarettes from the general-use pack, and tell stories as one or the other of us logged our hundred-mile shift. We'd crack windows to let out the smoke. Everything we needed was on board, carefully stowed in back and up in the rooftop clamshell—four amps, Ampeg Superstud guitar and pair of hi-hat stands, cymbal bag, wooden sounding board and fold-up hi-chair, jigsaw-puzzle artwork with the squared circles and circled squares in case he felt like preaching, my harp bag, our suitcases, CDs for sale. We had load-in and load-out down to a science. I'd hand him one piece of equipment at a time as he stood behind the Honda, and he'd find just the right spot for it. "I am the packing master!" he'd roar proudly. After a couple of years out there, we knew our car. Road life wasn't just about the music; we'd gotten to the point where we could take that part of the show for granted. It was about making the gig. The car was our magic carpet, front porch, U-Hall truck, lifeline.

Because he'd spent lots of time on these roads, back in the day, Mr. Satan had a story to go with virtually every highway we drove. Heading out of Harlem towards Philadelphia and points south, we always hooked a quick north up the West Side Highway and over the George Washington Bridge before shooting south on the New Jersey Turnpike. Fifteen miles down, in the smelly part of north Jersey near Newark Airport and the Meadowlands, a long narrow girdered bridge called the Pulaski Skyway arced over our heads, heading east toward the Holland Tunnel. Every time we passed it, Mr. Satan would tell the same story about the night King Curtis careened across it in a Cadillac at a hundred miles an hour. Back in the late 1960s, he'd played guitar for Curtis; that's where he and bassist Jerry Jemmott had first crossed paths.

"The damned fool was *crazy* about that car, mister," he chuckled. "Wasn't nothing we could do except tumble around in the back seat, cursing and praying."

King Curtis, in his view, was an object lesson in the wages of disrespect. "The fool got himself killed on his own damn stoop, telling some junkie to get a move-on," he'd say, making a sour face. "The man *played* beautiful, I ain't got no complaint about that. But he had ugly ways—with women, too. Licking his lips, wiggling his tongue. I can't abide that mess."

Many years later, when I'd drive past that skyway after the two-day drive up from Mississippi to see my mom, or when heading home after visiting her, I'd think, "There's the King Curtis Memorial Bridge."

Mr. Satan was a great driver: alert, focused, aware of his surroundings. It amazed me that a guy with such an outsized personality would drive in such a controlled way, but it meant that I could relax and doze when he was at the wheel. He had incredible endurance, very much in line with how he played. He locked into the groove and held it. Sometimes he'd pull a double shift—two hundred miles—just for kicks. On our way down to Miami one time, he told me how he'd once driven from Harlem to St. Petersburg, Florida, where his parents lived, in seventeen hours straight.

"I was drinking liquor, too," he laughed.

"Seriously?" He sometimes teetotaled, sometimes drank on the gigs, but I'd never seen him drive under the influence.

"Hell yes. You'll be a *very* good driver, too, when you pull some mess like that, because you can't afford to get stopped by no police."

I think of myself as a good driver. I don't get speeding tickets or have accidents. But every now and then, out on tour, I'd get fired up when some idiot behaved aggressively or did something truly stupid in my vicinity. The moment I engaged—speeding up to give chase, riding somebody's bumper—Mr. Satan cracked the whip.

"Mr. Adam," he'd say, exasperated, "*please* let that trouble get on away from you. More musicians than you'll ever know been killed out on these highways."

My touring years with Mr. Satan, 1991 to 1998, were my finishing school as a road warrior. They taught me how to walk fearlessly through any door, anywhere, with a smile on my face and a friendly greeting ready to go. Because that's how Mr. Satan presented himself to the world, even as he and I were accompanied by the ever-present possibility of disaster represented by Miss Macie. She didn't always act out, but when she was in a huff—when she thought white folks were giving her funny looks; when she sensed, or imagined, something that today might be called a racial microaggression; or when she was furious at Mr. Satan for no good reason—she could go off.

I remember one tour where we ended up in Valdosta, Georgia, after a two-day, thousand-mile drive from New York. We had a college gig that night and a half dozen Florida shows after that. By this point, any self-consciousness I might initially have had about the figure we cut as a threesome at large in America's unevenly racialized public space had faded to the vanishing point. We were a family—a somewhat dysfunctional one, thanks to Miss Macie's temperament, but a family nonetheless. Father and son were tight, self-reliant, quick on our feet. We spent our time on the bandstand dancing with each other's sounds and the rest of the time, apart from motel stays, sharing driving, navigation, and auto upkeep. We had more in common with each other, on a daily basis, than we had with anybody we encountered on the road, white or black. I kept waiting for somebody, anybody, to loft a racist comment in his direction. I would have jumped the motherfucker in a heartbeat. But it never happened. And we went everywhere in America east of the Mississippi: Maine to Miami, Chicago to New Orleans.

But I remember getting out of the car at a Shoney's in Valdosta, Georgia, late one afternoon with some apprehension. We were about to walk through the front doors of a restaurant in the Deep South and Miss Macie was in a bad mood. She and Mr. Satan had been bickering in the car; she was implacable, he was trying to calm her. He'd gone beyond the usual diminutives revolving around crabbiness. "I got my own private lobster," he sighed as she raged on. As we pushed through the door into the waiting area where the greeter stood behind a podium, Miss Macie had finally had enough.

"Shut up, Satan!" she snarled.

A room full of white folks in pastel cardigans went silent, locked and rigid, staring up at us.

I put on my best white-guy smile. "Three for dinner."

During an earlier Florida trip, Mr. Satan's brother-in-law Bufus Gammons told me that Sterling—he used Mr. Satan's birth name; everybody down there did—was a master mechanic. High achievement seemed to run in the family; Sterling's sister Janet, Bufus's wife, was a computer programmer at NASA. There were Magees scattered across Florida and Mississippi, and they were all incredibly friendly to me. Sterling was the eccentric brother, I gathered—"I'm the prodigal son," he told me—but they were happy to see him, and a whole crew, including his parents, drove over from the Tampa Bay area to catch our show when we played The Junkyard, a fabricated juke joint for tourists in Casselberry, near Disney World, with chicken wire and old hubcaps nailed to the walls.

That's when I met his parents. His mother was a small, shy woman with large round glasses, a mouthful of gold-capped teeth, and an unexpectedly girlish voice. He called her Miss Mama. His father, tall and stooped, looked like a minister in his black coat and tie. Sterling, who had mocked him more than once back in New York as "the super deacon," called him Mister Magee. They both called him Sterling. It was the first time they had ever seen him perform. It was the first time his mother had ever set foot in a bar. It was the first time I'd heard anybody call him Sterling to his face.

His father approached the stage several times while we played, as though taking the measure of the music. It was blues, after all, and he was an upright Christian elder. He shook my hand later, after the set. "I like the way you blow that harmonica. You two gonna go all the *way*." He leaned towards me. "How long you been playing with Sterling?"

"Six and a half years," I said. This was in 1993.

He shook his head. "Must be doing something right. Sterling never stayed with anybody else half that long."

There was an impromptu dinner party the following evening at the Gammons' big, expensive new house in Clearwater. That afternoon, Mr. Satan showed me some photos at his parents' house in St. Petersburg, the place where he'd grown up after they'd moved down from Mississippi. One was on the wall: him at age twenty, clean shaven and chipmunk-cheeked, smiling and confident in his serviceman's jacket and cap, a US Army paratrooper over in Germany. Another, in an album of his mother's: him in his early forties with a wispy black goatee, arm around a busty, big-legged woman in a short skirt and tight sweater.

"That's Mr. Parker's daughter. The wife who died. I didn't know Mama had that." He chuckled. "Don't let Miss Macie see it." He pointed at a snazzy guitar. "That's my Fender Jaguar, leaning against that amp."

Mr. Parker was the super of Shakespeare Flats, where Mr. Satan lived when I first met him. A stout, genial man dressed in janitorial green, always puttering around.

Dinner was fried chicken, niblet corn, rice, cans of beer. His younger brother, Junior, and twin sisters, Mary and Martha, were there, along with his older sister, Ollie, painfully thin-limbed in her black tights, with an addict's sad distracted smile. Janet's three boys, Anton, Benton, and Carlton, ages seven to twelve, who ran track at local schools, were playing video games in the den. (Twenty-three years later I would meet the sons again when they came to Sterling's eightieth birthday party gig at a club in Gulfport, Florida. Two were members of the Florida bar—an assistant US attorney, a family attorney—and the third was a military officer. The US attorney had brought along his wife, a tall pretty white woman.) The party was loud and fun; everybody except Ollie was in a great mood. Sterling's father got up from his chair at one point, shuffled over to me, and bent down.

"Tell me one thing: do you feel at home here?"

"Yes sir," I said.

"Good." He patted my arm.

"He'd better!" Sterling called out. "He's danged sure part of the family now!"

Mister Satan's Apprentice

When I sat down in the fall of 1995 to write the memoir that would become *Mister Satan's Apprentice*, I felt the pressures of what journalists were fond of calling "America's racial divisions" weighing on me like a clear and present danger. O. J. Simpson had just been acquitted in the killing of his wife, Nicole, and her friend Ron Goldman. Many African Americans had responded with glee, viewing O. J. as a latter-day Staggolee who had beaten the (white) system at its own game thanks to the brilliant forensics of his black lead attorney, Johnnie Cochran, and the overt racism of Los Angeles cop Mark Fuhrman. Most white Americans had viewed the same acquittal with incredulity and rage. *Not guilty?* Were blacks crazy? Or were whites simply beginning to taste the crestfallen disillusionment in a so-called justice system that black folk had known for far too long? "Whites V. Blacks" proclaimed *Newsweek*. "Were We Watching The Same Trial? After The Verdict, The Two Communities Talked Past Each Other, With Passionate Misunderstanding."

I was a second-year English grad student at Princeton when the verdict came in. Less than an hour after it arrived, in fact, I was sitting in Nell Painter's seminar on African American Intellectual History, one of two white students in an otherwise all-black class, filled with the same anxieties that always filled me in such race-conscious academic settings. Those anxieties certainly weren't Professor Painter's fault. A brilliant, probing, and contrarian scholar, interracially married, a fan—she once confessed to me—of country music, she repeatedly challenged us to ask unsettling questions, counterintuitive questions, the questions nobody else was brave enough to ask. If I'd had the nerve, I would have asked the question that preoccupied me in those days, the same question a black man named Rodney King asked despairingly when another jury verdict three years earlier had led to what were referred to as either the LA Riots or—if you were a hip leftist—the LA Uprising: "Can we all get along?" But I didn't have the nerve. Demoralized by an academic culture that seemed determined to see me as white, to reify whiteness as what psychologist Aaron David Gresson has termed a "spoiled racial identity," and to transform those who shared my race, class, and gender—straight white middle-class males—into emblems of racial bad faith, I'd lost my public voice, or whatever voice I possessed in the racially mixed classroom.

But I had a book contract in hand and a story to tell. And it was here, I swore to myself, that I would do what Nell Painter had insisted we do: go for broke. I'd write a book about the black men and women I'd known and loved, the *people* I'd known and loved and hated and learned from and gotten my heart broken by and made music with—black, white, all of them. I'd strive to represent both Uptown and Downtown as I'd experienced them, the full catastrophe of a race-maddened New York that was also, and simultaneously, bubbling with transracial alliances that couldn't wholly be accounted for by the rhetorics of suspicion then fashionable in the academy. And I'd start exactly where I'd started out on my own blues journey: with the smart, naïve, lonely, and wild-hearted suburban kid I'd been back in my hometown of Congers, New York. To imagine that such a white boy—a prep-school townie, off to the Ivy League—would ultimately transform himself into a blues performer with any legitimate claim on the music was counterintuitive, to put it mildly. But here I was: Mister Satan's sideman, a touring pro with a Harlem pedigree and the respect of my peers. How had that happened? *Did* I, in fact, have a legitimate claim on the blues? Or was I one more cultural thief, a ravenous and suspect racial adventurer of the sort eviscerated by bell hooks in her well-known essay in *Black Looks: Race and Representation*, "Eating the Other"? All I could do was tell my story and trust the answers to emerge.

I wrote *Mister Satan's Apprentice* in fifteen months, most of it in two-, three-, and four-hour blocks sandwiched between graduate seminars. The writing process was facilitated by the fact that I'd kept a daily journal from 1984 onward, more than thirty volumes. Although many pages were taken up with notes for a novel about the European busking scene that I'd been laboring on for the past decade, I'd also managed to document my emergent life as a New York City blues musician. My unlikely debut at La Famille in Harlem was there to be harvested, as were other uptown and downtown episodes. Mister Satan, one-man-bluesband extraordinaire and streetside Harlem's prophetic scourge, was a large and vital presence. I'd accumulated a bag of cassette tapes over the years, too—recordings of our performances on 125th Street, but also recordings made in Sterling's apartment on 116th Street and the first couple of harmonica lessons that my soon-to-be-mentor, a black New Yorker named Nat Riddles, gave me in Morningside Heights. And of course my two stints on the road with the bus-and-truck company of a Broadway musical called *Big River*, each day a new town and a fresh drama, were made for journaling and ripe for transmutation into something more substantial.

In stylistic terms, what guided my writing was a desire to find middle ground between the onrushing confessional frankness of Kerouac and the signifying terseness of Hemingway, between spilling it all out and holding some of it back. That synthesis had been a conscious goal for years; one way of reading *Mister Satan's Apprentice* is as the protagonist's gradual emergence out of Kerouackian innocence—alternately buoyant and shattered—into something like a bluesman's ability to reconcile euphoria with despair and accept life's paradoxes with good humor. But two other literary precursors shine through when I reread my book now, a decade later: James Baldwin and Ralph Ellison.

Baldwin, especially as the author of *Another Country*, gave me the courage to write about interracial desire as though it were, in fact, at the heart of our American experience, and not to confine my gaze solely to members of the opposite sex. The youthful white blues apprentice takes notice of the bodies of his two older black masters at various points in ways that deserve to be called erotic. I didn't expect that dynamic to surface when I sat down to write, but I allowed it and I'm okay with it. Desire refuses to be contained; a yearning for musical communion and transracial connection sometimes expresses itself as heightened attention to the embodiment of musical wisdom. As for the half-dozen women I wrote of: the blues they inspired me to feel, sing, and play would have made far less sense had I tried to silence their voices, or mute the various registers in which they thrilled, disillusioned, wrecked, challenged, and educated me.

Ellison stands squarely in the path of any author who would do justice to the blues paradoxes of American experience. As I meditated on my Harlem sojourn and thought about the challenge of representing my daily musical odyssey with Mister Satan, I found myself drawn repeatedly to the prologue of *Invisible Man*. Ellison's protagonist smokes a joint while listening to Louis Armstrong's trumpet; the melodic question, "What did I do to be so black and blue?" precipitates a spatio-historical reverie, a Dantean descent in which the ground of consciousness gives way and the protagonist sinks down through the generations, back through black history, until he finds himself in dialogue with a maternal ancestral figure, a slave who loved and hated her white master. This tableau resonated profoundly with several transformative musical experiences I'd had, and its influence hovers over my narrative: that first night in La Famille, when I grab hold of the groove and find myself dragged downward into a far more challenging confrontation with black music than I'd anticipated; the first afternoon I play with Mister Satan and Professor out on Randall's Island and suddenly sense the possibility of a deeper musical communion; and the day that Nat Riddles supplants me at Mister Satan's side on 125th Street, signifying powerfully on my still-shallow soundings and thrusting me into a series of fresh insights about what the blues are and where they come from.

"Sweet Harlem Summer," which follows Nat's blow-down, is one of the book's pivots. It represents not just a turning away from the melo-drama of romantic despair—the principal source of my white boy's blues to that point—and towards a deeper commitment to my craft, but an acknowledgment that death haunts the blues and must be confronted and transcended with the help of the community. I listen for the first time, as that chapter begins, to the silence behind my notes. I hear a dance with death in the stylings of a half-dozen sax players. I encoun-ter Death himself in the form of a comically terrifying Harlem specter named Mr. Sims who threatens repeatedly to slit my throat—until I confront him one day, find my voice, and make peace.

Death is everywhere in *Mister Satan's Apprentice*. Death shadows Nat Riddles. Every "bastard" who has ever worked with Mister Satan or taken his handouts eventually gets himself killed, it would seem. Sterling's wives prior to Miss Macie have all died. Our street-partnership is shadowed by New York's sensationalized racial violence: the beatings and death of Michael Griffith in Howard Beach, the murder of Yusuf Hawkins in Bensonhurst. The lesson I begin to absorb in "Sweet Harlem Summer" comes home to roost—a blues line repeated, with emphasis— on the day that I'm threatened by two men who view my presence in the neighborhood as a political affront. Death waits for me, too. It's no longer just a black thing, a regrettable but containable threat that has profoundly shaped the Harlem blues people with whom I've cast my fate while leaving me exempt. My ass is on the line, too, if I choose to continue my journey. That I have a choice at all is a mark of my racial privilege, but the choice I make is not trivial.

An alert reader will notice moments where I am signifying with subver-sive intent on the African American literary and intellectual tradition. At the beginning of Chapter 8 I speak about the "vague cringing empathic defensive stab—a kind of quadruple consciousness" that I feel as I walk through the Village with my black lover Robyn. I was trying to up the ante on W. E. B. Du Bois and his celebrated claim about the "double consciousness" that marked African American life, much as I strove musically to go beyond Little Walter, James Cotton, Magic Dick, and my other musical precursors on the harmonica. There's an edge to my writing in such passages, a defiance of political correctness bred by frustration. An admirer of Du Bois, a child of the Civil Rights movement, I found myself painfully and unwillingly at odds with the black cultural nationalism that had emerged in the late 1960s with Larry Neal's call for "the destruction of the white thing" and that had persisted in various forms through my college years and beyond. I was happy to see the white thing destroyed, god knows, but not if it included my harmonica and me! The most deliberate affront I could offer to fundamentalist ideologies of blackness and whiteness, particularly when they sought to render my experience invalid or invisible, was to write of the creole blues culture I knew.

The white-boy-lost-in-the-blues story was familiar, but certain complications had been left out. Both Nat Riddles and Sterling Magee are African American bluesmen animated, in part, by white musical exemplars—Kim Wilson in Nat's case, Elvis Presley in Sterling's. I give blues harmonica lessons to an older black man who pays me for my services. "Thunky Fing," an original composition dating from my Harlem years, begins as another flipped script: an unconscious inversion of the *Sanford and Son* theme song that I recast on the harp in an innovative way and then bring down to 125th Street to test out. Sterling matches me with backing chords, then flips the script again by renaming my—now our—song. Where, precisely, is "black music" in all this? Or "white blues"? *Mister Satan's Apprentice* rises to a climax in which a representative musical text, our first album *Harlem Blues*, is produced against all odds: black-and-white music, I call it. That choice of words, and hyphens, is deliberate. As author, I felt as though I were committing an act of gentle vengeance against black cultural nationalism and white racism alike. We *can* get along, I thought, as I finished up my manuscript. Modern blues life is exhausting, exhilarating, unlikely. But this is what it looks like. This is what it sounds like. Power to the people!

In retrospect, the racial discord that frames both the events narrated in *Mister Satan's Apprentice* and the writing of the text itself has come to seem like news from a peculiarly dark and distressing time. Our own moment seems charmed by comparison, although only a fool who knew nothing about the blues would presume a definitive pronouncement. As I write these words, Barack Obama has just been sworn in: America's first black president—and first black-and-white president, for that matter. The underlying commitment to transracialism that drove me to write my memoir seems uncannily aligned, ten years down the line, with the American national purpose in 2008. I make no claim to prophetic intent, but I'm delighted at where we've arrived.

Shoot Myself a Cop

When I entered the English PhD program at Princeton in the fall of 1994, *Mister Satan's Apprentice* hadn't yet materialized, although my apprenticeship itself and the weekend-warrior career it had led to was ongoing. More importantly, I had no intention of becoming a traditional blues scholar, a discographer-cum-ethnomusicologist, nor would the Princeton English Department have been the right route for that. But the eight years I'd spent at Sterling's side, helping hammer our distinctive sound into shape, had made me eager to explore ideas about transracial musical collaboration—or so I'd insisted on the personal statement that helped earn me admission. I was looking to push back hard against the prevailing racial essentialist view that saw all white investments in black music as invidious—exploitative, diluted, pervaded by minstrelsy. Greg Tate, *Village Voice* columnist and founding member of the Black Rock Coalition, would later epitomize this prosecutorial approach in *Everything But the Burden: What White People Are Taking from Black Culture* (2003). Some white blues *was* bad-faith burlesque, to be sure, and the whole cover phenomenon of the 1950s—Pat Boone's insipid, profiteering remake of Little Richard's "Tutti Frutti"—was a problem. But what Sterling and I were about couldn't be so easily dismissed. So that was my intended academic work: to drink deeply from the firehose of higher learning in a way that would enable me to craft a convincing response to the doubters.

All this changed a few weeks into the term when I began working on a report for Arnold Rampersad's seminar on the Harlem Renaissance. Rampersad, who would become a key mentor, was a legend: a MacArthur Fellow best known for his two-volume biography of Langston Hughes, he was our generation's Alain Locke, a mandarin man-of-letters. Born in Trinidad, educated at Harvard, he had a broad mouth, slightly down-turned, and a resonant yet austere voice with a vaguely Caribbean lilt. I'd heard him speak at Columbia literary events a couple of times over the years, always in the same dark suit; now he was sitting at the head of our Princeton seminar table, presiding with dry gravitas and occasional terrifying flickers of incredulity when one of us said something he adjudged to be stupid. "Oh, I don't think so," he'd say mildly. I was awed, intimidated, but thrilled to be in the room. Our syllabus was a feast: *When Harlem Was in Vogue* by David Levering Lewis; *The New Negro* anthology, with an introduction by Rampersad himself; *Home to Harlem* by Claude McKay. This was Harlem in a new key, exactly what I'd hoped for.

Given my other life as a blues harmonica player, which Rampersad viewed with bemusement, and given his expertise in the matter of Hughes's blues poetry, he was pleased when I volunteered to report on blues music's role in the Harlem Renaissance. J. A. Rogers's essay in *The New Negro* said a fair bit about jazz and the spirituals but little about the blues. Levering Lewis's cultural history, though, had a long chapter titled "Nigger Heaven"—we would read Carl Van Vechten's novel by that name later in the term—that offered a road map to the subject, including a brief but tantalizing description of the sensation caused by Mamie Smith's "Crazy Blues," the recording that inaugurated the race-records craze in 1920. I went looking for the song and discovered that it had been reissued the previous year, 1993, as the lead track on a Rhino Blues Masters compilation disc, *Classic Blues Women*. Every history of the blues I consulted referenced the song and its explosive sales: seventy-five thousand copies in Harlem in the first month of release, more than a million copies by the end of the year. But nobody reprinted or wrote about the lyrics, authored by black songwriter Perry Bradford, just the fact that it was the first blues recording by a black female singer with an all-black band and had become sensationally popular almost overnight.

Nothing prepared me for what I heard in the final ten seconds of the recording. I plugged headphones into my boom box and turned it up. I played the ending half a dozen times. What the hell? In 1920?

I visited Rampersad in his office during office hours, boom box in hand.

"Hello, Adam," he said, glancing at my hardware. "You've come prepared."

"I need to play you something. You have a minute?"

"By all means."

He came around the side of his desk. We sat across from each other.

"Have you ever actually heard a recording of Mamie Smith's 'Crazy Blues'?"

"No."

"I'd like to play you the whole thing. It's three and a half minutes long. Something very strange happens at the end."

I pressed Play. For most of its length the song is an unexceptional vaudeville blues about a woman whose man mistreats her by leaving her, driving her crazy with grief. Smith is a decent singer, but she's no match for Bessie Smith. Then comes the final chorus:

> Now I've got the crazy blues
> Since my baby went away
> I ain't had no time to lose
> I must find him today
> I'm gonna do like a Chinaman, go and get some hop
> Get myself a gun, and shoot myself a cop
> I ain't had nothin' but bad news
> Now I've got the crazy blues.

Rampersad stared at me as the final notes died away. He'd almost fallen off his chair. He looked as close to shocked as I'd ever seen him.

"Did we just hear that?"

"Yes we did." I slowly repeated the hop/cop couplet.

"That's remarkable."

"Drugs, guns, and cop-killing in the first recorded blues. You think that might help account for why it was so popular?"

"Who else has written about this?"

"Nobody. These lyrics aren't in print anywhere. It's like they don't exist."

He smiled. "Surely they're in print somewhere. What about the sheet music?"

"Aha! Great lead. Thanks, Professor."

"Arnold. Please call me Arnold."

That's how it all started—the seminar presentation that became the seminar paper that became the nucleus of the dissertation that became my first scholarly monograph, *Seems Like Murder Here: Southern Violence and the Blues Tradition.*

My next stop after Rampersad was the New York Public Library for the Performing Arts at Lincoln Center, where I found two different versions of Perry Bradford's sheet music. One version contained the astonishing couplet; one did not. So we *had* heard correctly. And I had a legit scholarly scoop—a discovery that would, with additional research, enable me to contextualize the song in multiple dimensions. On one hand "Crazy Blues" looked back to a late-nineteenth-century tradition of black badman ballads like "Staggolee" and "Railroad Bill" and, in the year 1900, the so-called "Robert Charles song" referenced by Jelly Roll Morton, about a black laborer and civil rights activist in New Orleans who, after being disrespected by a white police officer, got into a struggle with him, shot him, and ended up killing a total of five lawmen before he was shot to death and dragged through the streets. On the other hand, Bradford's composition offered an unexpected precedent for the gangsta rap and hardcore punk of the early 1990s and the furious response those recordings had leveled at overaggressive policing in the aftermath of Rodney King's beating, especially NWA's "Fuck tha Police" and Ice-T's "Cop Killer."

Harlem circa 1920 was the primary context. A black metropolis in transition, it had swelled over the previous five years with an influx of migrant black southerners: blues-loving folk who had fled the Jim Crow South and a scourge of lynching in which local sheriffs—southern cops—sometimes took part. Jazz Age Harlem was the city of refuge, in the words of Rudolf Fisher; his short story by that name was featured in *The New Negro*. Harlem was a brave new world in which a blues-woman like Mamie Smith could sing a song that shouts insurrection without fear of violent reprisal. It was a world where a black consumer with two dollars in hand could purchase Smith's voice and blast it over the rooftops to their heart's content. Which was exactly what people had done, according to historian Jervis Anderson in *This Was Harlem: A Cultural Portrait, 1900–1950*. Not long after "Crazy Blues" was released, he wrote, the record "was being played in almost every household of Harlem that owned a Victrola."

That's how it all started—my unexpected career as a blues scholar. But that's not quite true. And the way in which it's not quite true requires an explanation.

I've been asked more than once how a white guy from a small town in downstate New York, twenty miles north of New York City, ended up becoming not just a professional blues harmonica player but a scholar of African American literature and culture with a focus on the Deep South. My basic inclination is to offer complex, multivariate responses to good questions. Here, for once, I'll be direct.

One of the downsides of having a high IQ as a six-year-old and skipping a grade, as I skipped from kindergarten to second grade with only two months as a first-grader, is that you end up a year younger than your peers, straight through the end of high school. Younger translates early on into smaller and more vulnerable; the smart, runty kid is easier to mock, stigmatize, and beat up. All he's got is his brains, his fears, his loneliness—and his heart, which in my case always sided with the underdog, since I knew how that felt. Some of my instinctive feeling for black people, such as it was, began as the purest sort of underdog sentimentalism grounded in a handful of journalistic images from the civil rights movement that had made their way into my childhood world. Black people, including kids, being blasted off their feet with fire hoses in Birmingham's Kelly Ingram Park as snarling German shepherds and batons were wielded by mean white policemen. Martin Luther King, Jr., in all his sonorous and stentorian nobility, speaking truth to power and offering us, all of us, a way out of the racial mess.

I knew very few actual black people growing up. My mom worked for a man named Ed Gordon in the early 1960s, a famous black psychologist at Teacher's College down in the city, and we were friends with him and his family that whole decade: his white wife Susan and their four tan kids, who had bigger hair than my brother and I did. They were richer than we were; we'd occasionally drive to their place, a few towns over, for a pool party and cocktails. There was another couple down in Tappan, Joe Fiorello and his wife Barbara; she had an English accent and a shaggy dog named Beast. They had two brown kids, older than us, and we'd play with them when my parents drove us over there for drinks and conversation. Later, when I asked, my parents told me that Joe was a communist who had been married to a black woman; she had died at some point and the boys were the kids they'd had back then, although Barbara was their mother now. Both families seemed happy.

The one black adult with whom I had anything like a significant relationship in those days was a man I wrote about in *Mister Satan's Apprentice*. Mr. Foreman was my bossman, in a manner of speaking, although he never bossed me; I was his boy. Everything about him bespoke southern origins, although I had no capacity to recognize or verbalize that at the time. I was a smart, lonely fifteen-year-old, the Rockland Country Day School's resident valedictorian-townie, and there was something about him—he was the school's caretaker—that made me feel less alone:

He lived with his wife and foster kids in a small house next to the basketball court. He smiled a lot, talked in a slow lazy way, limped around the school, kept things clean and fixed. His skull was brown and shiny when he took off his porkpie hat. One of his thumbs had been half cut off; he'd use it to nub through the hundred keys in his quadruple key-ring until he found the right one. I liked Mr. Foreman. I'd been his janitorial assistant during the fall of junior year. I'd bicycle up to the school on Saturday mornings and help him mop dirty floors and fix sticking locks. His favorite word was "mash." We'd be crouched next to a door, squirting 3-in-1 oil into the keyhole.

"Mash on it," he'd say, nodding at the frozen handle, smiling a little. "She'll open."

Same thing if I was mopping. "Mash it into the corner," he'd tell me. "We gonna *get* that dirt."

He was the gentlest person I'd ever met. He was a minister on Sundays, people said, at a church down in Nyack. I always wondered if my biblical name made him treat me extra nice. His house, when his wife opened the door, always smelled like warm delicious food: pork chops, buttered sweet potatoes, juicy long-cooked things. His foster kids would hang back, eyeing me.

Even as I crafted this sketch, a couple of years into my graduate education, I was well aware of how viciously my peers and I could disembowel such a sentimentalized portrait. Mr. Foreman is the Negro Mr. Rogers, the folksy Uncle Remus of downstate New York welcoming the innocent white boy into his world. Plantation paternalism! Got it. But his gentleness and my innocence—as in naïveté—were the point, as was the fact that I was working for him, learning from him, *joining* him, however fleetingly. Education has to begin somewhere. I had a long road to travel and a great deal to learn. But the interracial fellowship thing was there from early on.

My early exposure to African American literature was effectively nil. I can remember being entranced by Twain's *Adventures of Huckleberry Finn* as a kid, especially the endless idyllic days that Huck and Jim spent drifting down the Mississippi on their raft; many years later, reading Shelly Fisher Fishkin's *Was Huck Black? Mark Twain and African American Voices*, I'd learn the extent to which Huck's voice had black roots, even as Jim's gosh-a-mighty affect was shaped by Twain's fondness for blackface minstrelsy. But black lit? It barely registered—not at the Rockland Country Day School, not at Princeton during my undergrad years in the late 1970s, although Ellison's *Invisible Man* did show up on a Twentieth-Century American lit syllabus. There was a copy of Eldridge Cleaver's *Soul on Ice* kicking around our house in the late sixties, and I have vague memories of seeing Angela Davis on TV, with her huge Afro and finger upraised, like she was lecturing, or snarling. Black people were angry about everything: that was the basic lesson. And then it faded into Nixon, Watergate, and Jimmy Carter.

Working at The Viking Press for a couple of years in the early 1980s, I was an editorial assistant for a guy named Rich Barber, who knew lots of writers, including black writers. Wole Soyinka, a Nigerian writer, came by the office one day; on another day, Claude Brown stopped in. I'd heard of *Manchild in the Promised Land*, although I'd never read it. But I knew he was, or had been, famous. "Hey, man," he said in a friendly way, shaking my hand after Rich introduced us. He was wearing a brown corduroy suit and tan desert boots. When I wasn't assisting Rich, my chief duty as the so-called slush reader was to plow through stacks of unsolicited manuscripts. One day I came across a proposal for a cookbook called *Barbecue'n with Bobby*, authored by Bobby Seale, the former Black Panther. I showed it to Rich. We both chuckled. Quite a comedown from Burn, baby, burn! Viking didn't publish cookbooks, so I sent it back in the stamped, self-addressed envelope.

In the summer of 1982, Alice Walker's novel *The Color Purple* was published and got a lot of attention, beginning with Mel Watkins's review in the *New York Times Book Review*. By that point I'd written a handful of short reviews for *Saturday Review* at fifty bucks a pop and, at age twenty-four, with two years at Viking and a brief stint at the Curtis Brown agency behind me and Columbia's MA program ahead of me that fall, fancied myself a literary journalist on the rise—a latter-day Edmund Wilson or Malcolm Cowley, calling them as I saw them in clear, unfussy prose. Walker's novel was the hot new thing. So I bought a copy, wrote a review, and sent it off to *Chicago Review*, which published it the following summer as the novel was being awarded the Pulitzer Prize and National Book Award, a watershed in the world of black women's writing.

The novel fed a hunger I hadn't yet consciously realized I had: to lose myself in an underdog's story of being beaten down, as those black people in Birmingham had been beaten down by Sheriff Bull Connor's men, then find myself made whole by the underdog's fierce and principled resistance, a refusal to submit. The mean mistreaters in Walker's novel were black men, not white men, but I wasn't invested in them and unconcerned with the problematics this substitution created. "The Color Purple," I wrote in my first full-length book review,

> is the story of five women—black, battered, and ultimately triumphant over a world that seems to have been designed to drive a black woman mad. Walker's language is incandescent, heated with love and rage, and her vision is clear and hard as cut glass.

> Celie is a 14-year old girl in the Jazz Age South: spunky, vulnerable, and almost illiterate. Raped repeatedly by the man who may or may not be her father, robbed of the two children that result, bereft of her beloved sister Nettie—who fled to seek a better life—she picks up a pen and pours out her soul to God. Her letters to Him make up the first half of the novel. Like Huckleberry

Finn, Celie is a naif, able to describe her emotional trauma with an innocent's clear sight, even as she is unable to understand the full horror of it. Like Huck, her language—a broken deep South vernacular—is a supple and expressive idiom, charged with native poetry.

Many years later, after repeated rereadings, I would decide that couldn't stand Walker's novel, mostly because I could hear the author's heavy ideological hand inscribing every abject, pity-producing word Celie writes to God. And I'd discover that I wasn't alone. One of my heroes, Trudier Harris, a plain-speaking scholar of lynching and African American literature, had savaged the novel in 1984, even while confessing her ambivalence, as Walker's fellow black woman, about criticizing such a universally lauded work:

> My dilemma started in Alabama in July of 1982 when I completed the novel and went into a fit of cursing for several days. Here, I felt, was a novel that had done a great disservice through its treatment of black women and a disservice as well to the Southern black communities in which such treatment was set. I couldn't imagine a Celie existing in any black community I knew or any that I could conceive of. What sane black woman, I asked, would sit around and take that crock of shit from all those folks? How long would it take her before she reached the stage of stabbing somebody to death, blowing somebody's head off, or at least going upside somebody's head? But the woman just sat there, like a bale of cotton with a vagina, taking stuff from kids even and waiting for someone to come along and rescue her. I had problems with that. And so did other black women. By contrast, most of the white women with whom I talked loved the novel.

A bale of cotton with a vagina! But stumbling across this review in the mid-2010s merely confirmed something I'd known for a long time, which is that there isn't and hasn't ever been a unitary "black perspective" on anything, except perhaps the genius of Willie Mays, and that white folks who view black folks through a sentimental lens, for political reasons or merely out of ignorance, are always diminishing black humanity rather than acknowledging it.

What began to wake me up was the course I took with Amiri Baraka at Columbia in the spring of 1983, "Black Women and Their Fictions." The edge conveyed by that word, *fictions*, was intended; he made that clear on Day One. I had read nothing by Baraka at that point—not *Blues People*, not *Dutchman*, not *Black Music*, not "Black Art," none of the texts that I would later come to know, use, teach. I just knew that he was a famous, loud, angry guy from the Black Power period, a rabble-rousing poet who was unafraid to speak his mind. There were thirty-five of us at our desks, loosely semicircled, when he walked in. He was a small, trim, bearded man in a brown tweed sport coat with a strong voice and bright, piercing eyes that were lidded with cynicism. They flicked around the room, appraising. I had never been in the presence, much less the sustained presence, of a revolutionary black intellectual. He was a marvel of improvisatory riffing—changing tonal registers, dipping in and out of Marxist dialectics. He used the word "bourgeois" a lot, in disparagement. He had that judgmental vocabulary: "petty bourgeois intellectuals," "assimilationist," "middle-class Negroes." He wasn't raging but soulfully irritated, pushing us.

Everything we read, except *The Color Purple*, was new to me. *Incidents in the Life of a Slave Girl, Jubilee, Their Eyes Were Watching God, I Know Why the Caged Bird Sings, Sula*. Two-thirds of the class was female. He'd take questions, comments. I was intimidated early on, but I loosened up. When we read *Jubilee*, I raised my hand and said that some of Margaret Walker's white characters weren't believable—the dialogue was stilted—and that she seemed to care more about large historical movements and socioeconomic processes than character development. His eyes showed irritation. "It's an epic," he said. "That's what they do." Then he went off in her defense, as he did in a 1999 eulogy in the *Nation*:

> Margaret was the human speech itself, raised like Du Bois or Langston to reach past itself. To be itself, simple and open and daring to be paraphrased. She needed no hocus pocus, no abstractions, save language, full open, itself. For Margaret, like those others in the tradition, the language itself was the monster. The sounds we make everyday, stirred up, rolled around, these are the what-nots and what-it-is-es of what we slur as literature.
>
> Margaret took the highest of the oral tradition: the oracular divinity of high religious speech. The Preacher. But not just the preacher, like Jimmy B. for instance, she reaches past the preacher to where the preacher spose to be getting his stuff from, the all-the-way-out, past the Waygonesphere. At that point, just before your eyes roll up in yr head and you screaming hallelujah, or death to slavery, there is that place, it's moving—of high-up sequential reasoning. Where Perception have took us to meet Rationale and we have persisted past that to Use and that use has rose us up from On to reach Dig, before we see Serious. As the Dogon would say.

That's what Baraka was like: a whirlwind ninja, slicing and dicing in five dimensions. But one day his mouth got him in trouble.

We were discussing *The Color Purple*, which was the novel of the moment and which he clearly didn't like for the way it depicted black men as violent abusers. The room was full of feminists at a slow boil, black and white. When the subject turned to Celie's fling with Shug, he just couldn't hold back. "If you think that two sisters getting it on with each other is the best way of bringing about the black revolution," he said disdainfully, "you've swallowed the white man's Kool-Aid." The room erupted. It was awesome.

I wrote my paper on *Their Eyes Were Watching God*, which I labored mightily to understand, although I had a hard time with Hurston's black southern dialect. He graded all the papers. When I got mine back, he'd written two words on the last page: "too abstract."

Anchored in the discovery of "Crazy Blues" and the cop-killing lyric uproar it had imaged, my intellectual trajectory as a doctoral student at Princeton in the second half of the 1990s forced me into a confrontation with one of the darkest chapters of American history, the scourge of spectacle lynching that had erupted across the South a hundred years earlier. Nothing in my previous educational track—a BA at Princeton, an MA at Columbia, almost a decade with Mr. Satan—had even hinted that this history was there to be read. Yet there it was. And Trudier Harris, it turned out, was far ahead of the curve: the first literary scholar to take the measure of the scourge and the way African American writers, especially Richard Wright in "Between the World and Me," had addressed it. The flap copy of her *Exorcising Blackness: Historical and Literary Lynching and Burning Rituals* (1984) neatly summarized her project:

> By lynching, burning, castrating, raping, and mutilating black people, contends Trudier Harris, white Americans were performing a rite of exorcism designed to eradicate the "black beast" from their midst, or, at the very least, to render him powerless and emasculated. Black writers have graphically portrayed such tragic incidents in their writings. In doing so, they seem to be acting out a communal role—a perpetuation of an oral tradition bent on the survival of the race.

I modeled my own approach on Harris's brutally direct confrontation with the facts, but the compulsions that drove me were complex. I was filled with a hunger to disillusion myself and everybody in my vicinity, to take vengeance on the lies of omission that had shaped my vision of American history. Dismantling those lies made those brave black souls who had violently resisted abjection and fought back against Evil

Whiteness a subject of particular interest to me. (At no point did I pause to wonder, as I would later, whether the lyric celebration of cop-killing might have negative downstream effects in the real world. I was a cultural historian, not a social scientist.) Even as I was overwhelmed by descriptions of lynching that let me view black southerners as both sacrificial victims and, when they engaged in retributive violence, revolutionary heroes, I was determined not to sentimentalize them—which led me, before I knew it, into a third and politically problematic arena of subcultural history, the "cutting and shooting" that went on in all-black blues spaces, especially southern juke joints, as furious black folks, their hunger for justice mocked and dismissed by the white law, took matters into their own hands and wreaked bodily vengeance on each other. Every black southern blues musician spoke about this particular occupational hazard. Politically progressive black intellectuals, especially Robin D. G. Kelley, preferred to elide such things from their evocations of the People's Culture; I found Kelley's vision of the blues' reparative dynamic tinged with sentimentality and did my best to demolish it.

All of this inter- and intra-racial violence stood at the farthest remove from the hunger for transracial fellowship, for beloved community, that had long served as my North Star, shaping my deepest yearnings, including the relationship Sterling and I had forged on the streets of Harlem. Yet I felt compelled to push onward—spurred, I suspect, by a fascinated dread connected with the scene of mobbing that lay deep in my own schoolboy past, a dim but bone-deep memory of feeling stigmatized, surrounded, imperiled, unwanted. Alone and afraid.

Whatever was driving me to wrangle with the history of lynching was part of a broader cultural awakening, it turned out. An extraordinary quartet of books dropped like a gift into my dissertation research, one per year between 1995 and 1998: *A Festival of Violence: An Analysis of Southern Lynchings, 1882–1930*, by Stewart E. Tolnay and E. M. Beck; *Race, Rape, and Lynching: The Red Record of American Literature, 1890–1912*, by Sandra Gunning; *Under Sentence of Death: Lynching in the South*, edited by W. Fitzhugh Brundage; and *Trouble in Mind: Black Southerners in the Age of Jim Crow*, by Leon Litwack. Suddenly, in

January 2000 as the new millennium began, lynching was everywhere—on the *Today Show*, in the *New York Times* and *New York* magazine—as "Witness," an exhibit of seventy-eight lynching photographs and postcards opened at the tiny Roth Horowitz gallery in New York in conjunction with the publication of *Without Sanctuary: Lynching Photography in America*, a coffee-table book designed to ravage racial innocence and snuff out conversation.

I went to the Roth Horowitz. I waited in a long line on the cold sidewalk outside, then stepped down into the small space. I heard shocked whispers as I slowly made my way around the room. Having spent the previous half-decade grappling with this material, I was underwhelmed, or just numbed. The postcards featuring charred black bodies and leering white crowds were surprisingly small, the images tiny; you had to lean in and squint. Although none of the reviews or scholarship acknowledged this, a fair number of the postcards featured whites lynching whites, mostly cattle rustlers out West. It was good to know that my fellow citizens were finally being forced to reckon with this stuff. The truth was, I found the narrative descriptions in the "Hellhounds" chapter of Litwack's book far more affecting than these images.

The 1996 Modern Language Association convention in Washington, DC, was a chance not to workshop my work-in-progress—I'd already done that at the American Studies Association meeting in Pittsburgh and the Delta Symposium in Jonesboro, Arkansas—but to shadow Rampersad and attend a once-in-a-lifetime event: a gala celebration for the just-published *Norton Anthology of African American Literature*. Having finished all my coursework, passed my qualifying exams, and defended my dissertation proposal, I knew that at some future moment I'd be going on the market as an African American lit specialist with a project on the blues—a tough hand for a white guy to play in an age of political correctness, even with a side gig as a legit blues player, but not impossible, I'd been told. Every bit of on-the-job training counted. This was a chance to see the top-tier black intelligentsia at work: not just co-editors Henry Louis Gates, Jr., and Nellie McKay, but Albert Murray,

Sherley Anne Williams, Rita Dove, Hortense Spillers, Robert O'Meally, Frances Smith Foster, plus Rampersad—he'd edited a section or two of the anthology—and the man he was there to introduce, Amiri Baraka.

The fact that the anthology existed at all, that a working canon of this particular tradition had been birthed as a big, thick volume with Norton's imprimatur, seemed to float the assembled company on a cloud of joy. *We've won!* That was the vibe. *This has finally been done. It can't be undone.* The people in the room, on the dais, were literally the people who had, over the previous thirty years, engaged in the epic unearthing, recuperating, reassembling, and theorizing required to create the tradition *as* a tradition. I was awed to be present at this birth. An earnest and determined tiller in the field, no longer young at thirty-eight, I yearned to further the cause and, with luck, make my own mark someday.

After Gates and McKay sketched the work that had been accomplished, Foster introduced Williams, who read her poems. But it was Baraka who took us out to sea. Thirteen years after that spring at Columbia, there was more grey in his beard, but he was relaxed and pinpoint sharp, a comic with honed timing as he leaned into the mic.

"In the funk world," he said, "if Elvis Presley is King, who is James Brown? God?" He slipped on his reading glasses and said nothing as people chuckled, then slipped them off. "Literary Q&A. Critics are always asking me how I have been influenced by white people. Bringing us here, I guess."

He said nothing for twenty seconds, just looked around the room, deadpan, letting the chuckles ripen and flow.

He read three or four poems from *Wise, Why's, Y's*. "Read" is the wrong word. He began each poem by humming a bluesy riff from a jazz player like Coltrane or Monk or Sun Ra, then eased into the words, repeating words and phrases, conjuring a spell, letting it take on weight. The scene of the crime varied from poem to poem, but the spirits he conjured sought to warn us, like the blues god invoked by Black Arts poet/theorist Larry Neal, of what was ahead—the Middle Passage, all that death, trails of bones, desolation. He eased an unseen dagger into his hand as he moved into the latter portion of his final poem. "A people flattened chained / bathed & degraded / in their own hysterical waste," the stolen Africans had been thrust weeping into a subterranean grave, a blue-black hole beneath the skyscrapers of modern America, a holocaust beyond imagining—

"Slavery!" he shouted. "We were SLAVES!" He shouted the word again and again—slowly, urgently, thirteen times. Sounding the alarm. Trying in vain to warn us against the depredations of the steam-driven cannibals.

Baraka shook me, floored me, put tears in my eyes before I knew what had hit me. He helped anchor my vision of black history as the story of a people's comprehensive ravaging, an Afropessimist perspective I would argue with for the rest of my career. It wasn't wrong, yet it wasn't the whole truth—as Baraka himself showed with his portrait of insurgent black creativity in *Blues People*—and discounted the power to be found within the blues' tragicomic dialectic.

Rampersad, too, was a critically important guide. Arnold and I didn't have a particularly close relationship. He didn't copyedit my prose or dispense much praise. But he presided over three of the twelve graduate seminars I took—Harlem Renaissance, Modern Southern Literature, and, shortly after returning from MLA, African American Autobiography—and he asked me to TA for him in Introduction to the African American Literary Tradition, an undergrad survey. It sometimes seemed as though he'd written introductions to most of the canonical black texts in print. His prose voice, like his speaking voice, was measured and direct. He shaped his critical appreciations the way a master carpenter frames a house. He was Apollonian, his clean, classic lines purged of dark excess. He could be edgy; he could say shocking things with a flat affect. But he kept his politics close to the vest. His studiously non-ideological posture was grounded in a kind of intellectual arrogance, a dislike of theory and a biographer's fondness for the resonant, or inconvenient, fact. "Teaching to liberate," the scholar-activist's creed, was the furthest thing from his mind.

For a man of such achievement, he was disarmingly modest. "I write bubblegum biography," he joked several times, referring to *Arthur*

Ashe: Days of Grace (1993) and his soon-to-be-published life of Jackie Robinson. But he could also improvise, as he sometimes did when lecturing from the new *Norton Anthology* in the survey—executing an on-the-spot exegesis of Hughes's "The Weary Blues" or McKay's "If We Must Die," blending cultural history, biography, and prosody into a bravura close reading.

The black autobiography seminar was memorable. I was the only white student. There were seven of us, all men. What should have been an anxiety-inducing situation, given my earlier experience in Nell Painter's African American Intellectual History seminar, was the opposite of that: an open, free-swinging, and incredibly dynamic exchange of ideas. The brilliance of my classmates, all of whom went on to have notable careers, was evident. You had Sam (Samuel K. Roberts), Ken (Kenneth W. Mack), and Jeff (Jeffrey Allen Tucker), each with a different intellectual toolkit and approach, everybody freed from the burden of racial representation and thus able to simply show up and throw down. Differential placement along the tragicomic continuum—dark and brooding, cool and composed, chucklingly sanguine—created sparks; accent and dress bespoke diversity. Mychel Namphy, with his pale angled-up face and wisp of a mustache, made the commute down from New York and had an urban vibe: a hipster engagé in clean threads.

My presence seemed to trouble nobody; I was one more brother at the table, trying to get a word in edgewise as the dialogic energies swelled and careened. Nerved but game by the end of week one, I volunteered to report on *The Life of Olaudah Equiano* in week two, then came in and proposed that when Equiano, a seafaring British slave born in Benin, spoke in a stock-taking midlife poem of how, in earlier days, he had "assay'd to stifle guilt with sin" and decried his own "lust, anger, blasphemy, and pride," he was signifying on the handful of passionate same-sex relationships he'd had with white sailors and sea captains—including a "young lad" named Richard Baker. "We at length became inseparable," he'd written of Baker, five years his elder,

> and, for the space of two years, he was of great use to
> me, and was my constant companion and instructor.

Although this dear youth had many slaves of his own,
yet he and I have gone through many sufferings together
on shipboard; and have many nights lain in each other's
bosoms, when in great distress.

My claim about Equiano's sexuality caused a ruckus, but it wasn't a racial ruckus. The guys who thought I was crazy said so, but not everybody thought I was crazy. Malcolm X, too, Rampersad noted, had had same-sex encounters when he was a younger man, according to biographer Bruce Perry, although his autobiography was of course silent on that issue.

The seminar was on. I'd found my voice.

WOKENESS, HETERODOXY, AND DREAMS DEFERRED

Of Dissent and its Discontents

> That brings me to the second mode of civil
> disobedience. There's a time when the operation of
> the machine becomes so odious, makes you so sick at
> heart that you can't take part! You can't even passively
> take part! And you've got to put your bodies upon
> the gears and upon the wheels, upon the levers, upon
> all the apparatus—and you've got to make it stop!
> And you've got to indicate to the people who run it,
> to the people who own it—that unless you're free the
> machine will be prevented from working at all!!
>
> —Mario Savio, Mississippi Freedom Summer
> volunteer and founder of the Free Speech
> Movement (December 2, 1964)

For the past forty years I've given faithfully to Princeton's Annual
Giving campaign. My contribution has been laughably modest—one hundred dollars most years, $250 when major reunions
come up—but consistent. My rationale has been mixed: grounded in
deep gratitude for the ten years I spent on campus between 1975 and
2000 and the two degrees in English, undergrad and grad, I obtained
there, but animated by the farfetched hope that small but consistent
annual gifting would grace whatever children I someday produced with

an incrementally better chance of gaining admission to the university that changed my life.

A couple of weeks ago I decided to suspend my annual gift for the foreseeable future and redirect it towards Princetonians for Free Speech. I'm aware that I may be hurting my teenaged son's chances of admission by sharing this news publicly, and that saddens me. A Mississippi native and gifted musician, Shaun would have carved his own line across campus, wreaking wondrous havoc in the process. But the Princeton I've been hoping he'd attend has been supplanted, over the past five years, by a troubled, wounded institution, one that no longer aligns with its own highest ideals—or mine. So we'll move on and look elsewhere—perhaps to the University of Mississippi, where I've been teaching for the past two decades. And he'll flourish regardless, even as this regretful decision, one I couldn't have imagined half a decade ago, now seems urgently important, a matter of conscience.

The proximate cause for my change of heart is the recent firing, this summer of 2022, of Joshua Katz, a tenured professor of Classics. Those who have been following the fraught progress of his case on the PFS website will be unsurprised to know that an academic like me, graced with a humanities PhD but located at a safe remove from Princeton's disciplinary shenanigans, has finally had enough. But many who know me—my career as a scholar of blues and African American literature, my thirty-year musical partnership with Harlem bluesman Sterling "Mr. Satan" Magee, and of course my interracial family circle—will be surprised that Katz, of all people, is the metaphorical hill I'm prepared to die on. Isn't he the noted racist? some will ask—the one who showed his true colors in a *Quillette* essay by deriding the Black Justice League, a student activist group, as "a small local terrorist organization" and reaped the ignominy he deserved, his name and words embedded into an illustrated polemical history of white supremacist bad behavior at Princeton offered by "To Be Known and Heard," a website on the Princeton.edu domain underwritten by The Trustees of Princeton University?

I'll have more to say in a moment about that specific characterization of the BJL. For now I'll simply say yes, this *is* that hill. And no, I haven't suddenly taken leave of my senses. I was gifted during my doctoral studies with the chance to work with (and in two cases TA for) Professors Arnold Rampersad, Claudia Tate, and Nell Painter: a trio of inspiring black mentors. I've taught a course on Mississippi's Freedom Summer of 1964 several times at my university and regularly assign works by Frederick Douglass, Richard Wright, Melba Pattillo Beals, and Jesmyn Ward as a way of helping my students come to grips with slavery, segregation, the struggle for civil rights, and racialized precarity in the modern South. My personal and professional life, both musical and academic, has been an attempt to live out the promise of beloved community, a vision of transracial brotherhood and sisterhood put forward by Martin Luther King, Jr., and John Lewis.

And yet I'm willing to say that Joshua Katz, for all his flaws, is my hero—one of a double handful of heterodox public intellectuals, including John McWhorter, Glenn Loury, Coleman Hughes, Chloé Valdary, Wesley Yang, Bari Weiss, Andrew Sullivan, Thomas Chatterton Williams, Sam Harris, Charlie Sykes, and Princeton's own Sean Wilentz, who have managed over the past two years not just to maintain critical consciousness in the face of a would-be revolution and its illiberal tendencies, but to speak and write freely. In ideological terms, these thinkers are all over the map, although they tend to occupy the territory that runs from center left (McWhorter, Williams, Harris, Wilentz) to center right (Weiss, Sykes). Several (Hughes, Valdary, Yang) don't easily slot into that schema; Loury and Sullivan call themselves conservatives, although both are the antithesis of reactionary. All, however, would agree with one of classic liberalism's foundational tenets, which is the importance of free speech, especially in a time of pronounced ideological narrowing.

Some free speakers—the late Christopher Hitchens, for example—are more aggressive than others. They speak irritably and raise hackles. Katz's aggressively irritable comments about the Black Justice League, although they drew censure from pretty much every corner of the Princeton campus, including his colleagues in the Department of Classics, President Eisgruber, and most of the 350-odd signatories to the July 4, 2020, manifesto that Katz had critiqued in his *Quillette* article, were not, as we know, the reason he was fired. He was fired, or so it is claimed, because the re-investigation of a case of sexual misbehavior—a consensual affair with a twenty-one-year-old undergraduate, in violation of university policy—for which he had been investigated and punished with a year's unpaid leave in 2018, a re-investigation prompted by extensive investigative reporting in the *Daily Princetonian*, had disclosed new evidence of such gravity as to merit termination. The evidence that Eisgruber, Vice Provost for Institutional Equity and Diversity Michele Minter, Dean of the Faculty Gene Andrew Jarrett, and pretty much every other right-thinking administrator, faculty member, and campus activist had viewed Katz as an embarrassing gadfly if not outright ideological enemy for the past two years is, we are to understand, utterly immaterial to this outcome.

Dear reader, were you born yesterday?

Many years ago, in the summer of 1983, I interned for editor Victor Navasky at the *Nation*. His long-lived and celebrated journal of opinion, he explained to me, conceived of itself as a staging ground for dialogue between liberals and the left. I was so politically naïve at that point that I wasn't entirely clear on the difference between those two entities. "Liberals think that social change can be effected inside the system," he explained, always happy to educate, "through rational debate, the passage of laws, normal governmental process. The left knows that you sometimes need to take it to the streets. We help them talk to each other."

Victor's bugaboo was McCarthyism. Three years earlier he'd published *Naming Names*, a history of the Hollywood blacklist. His favorite word, almost a mantra, was "dissent." The measure of a democracy's health, he kept repeating, is its willingness not just to tolerate dissent but to value it, to make a space for it. America during the McCarthy years, captured by anticommunist hysteria, had quashed dissent and ruined lives in a way that Victor viewed as evil—a quintessentially American mania, with roots in the Puritan witch hunts of the 1690s, that should be studied, unpacked, memorialized as a negative ideal, the better to be warded off in the future.

McCarthyism engendered fear to foreclose dissent: fear of being labeled a subversive and losing one's job; fear of being outed—if one were homosexual—as a sexual deviant. Princeton's campus these days is wonderfully hospitable to every possible gender and sexual orientation, with a signal exception recently noted by Joshua Katz's wife, alumna Solveig Gold '17: relationships between older male faculty members and female undergraduates, at least when the older male faculty member is considered an ideological enemy of the powers that be. Every Princetonian of conscience should be concerned by the uncanny parallel between the way that McCarthyism mobilized sexuality to silence dissent and banish undesirables, and the way that Princeton's current administration, underwritten by a continually expanding Title IX regime and assisted by the *Prince*, has found it both necessary and expedient to re-investigate Katz with a fervor that just *happens*, miracle of miracles, to have disclosed actionable new forms of sex-adjacent misbehavior. Foucault was right. This is how power works, when it sees the need to punish heresy:

> The exercise of power can produce as much acceptance as may be wished for: it can pile up the dead and shelter itself behind whatever threats it can imagine.... It is a total structure of actions brought to bear upon possible actions; it incites, it induces, it seduces, it makes easier or more difficult; in the extreme it constrains or forbids absolutely.

Or perhaps Foucault is the wrong touchstone here. Perhaps *The Matrix* offers a better analogy: that horrifying moment when Neo, having chosen to take the red pill, wakes to discover himself alive but barely, immured in a gelatinous pod with a thick electrical cable clamped into the back of his head and a dozen others plugged into his back, chest, shoulders, and arms, suspended high over a dark, dystopian metropolis—a contemporary reimagining of the all-encompassing, death-dealing American Moloch against which Allen Ginsberg rages in "Howl." Conscious now, if barely, aware of his own existence as a potentially autonomous human subject rather than a colonized and exploited meat-envelope, Neo is of no use to the Matrix. So the Matrix's presiding enforcer, a monstrous ant-like *Alien*-jawed machine, appears out of nowhere and swivels into place, yanks out all his cables, and flushes him down the drain—extruding him, but also, paradoxically, liberating him.

After readily admitting to the consensual affair late in 2017 and serving a one-year suspension without pay, Katz returned to active duty on the Princeton faculty in the fall of 2019. The young woman with whom he'd dallied had refused to participate in Princeton's investigation. "Indeed," as Gold has written, "she had repeatedly by email expressed her dismay that the school would even consider punishing him." Then, in February 2021, the *Daily Princetonian* published a five-thousand-word hit piece. Although the young woman in question, given the pseudonym "Jane," refused to be interviewed by the *Prince*, the article, which included interviews with eight of Jane's classmates, rehearsed the affair in depth—the affair that Katz had already acknowledged and been punished for. And it did something more: it added to the pile-on by telling the stories of "Clara" and "Bella," pseudonymous alumnae with whom, more than a decade earlier, Katz, a widely-acknowledged master teacher on campus, had…not had sex:

> Clara, who attended Princeton after Jane graduated, told the 'Prince' that Katz pursued her while she was a student. For over a year, she alleges, he brought her gifts, commented on her appearance, and paid for expensive off-campus dinners.
>
> "I would say that in my own experience, 'repeated boundary violations' characterizes the relationship I had with him," Clara said.
>
> The third student, Bella, said that Katz asked her on what she understood to be a date while she was a student in his class, and paid for their dinner and wine at an

upscale restaurant in Princeton during that semester's exam period.

Expensive off-campus dinners and focused attention? *Gifts?* The horror! And here I really do need to make a confession. I do so in the hope that I may teach the young—including sensitive young women like Clara and Bella—just how much they missed of the wild frontier life at Old Nassau.

When I was a Princeton undergrad in the late 1970s, my thesis advisor was a man named Thomas McFarland. He was a tall, big-bellied man with a jowly face and piercing eyes, a famous Coleridge scholar who wore grey tweed sportscoats and incongruously slim-hipped black jeans a size or two too small. He tottered slightly when he walked, his belly curving over his belt. Sometimes he'd sport a Kangol cap, like Mr. Toad from *The Wind and the Willows*, whom he eerily resembled. Professor McFarland never laid a hand on me while he was my advisor. But on graduation weekend, when my then-girlfriend Susan and I attended a small cocktail party at his house, I ended up alone with him in an upstairs bedroom lined with bookshelves. And then, to my surprise, he propositioned me. His voice changed—lowered, deepened, became more intimate.

"I'd like to get close to you," he growled. "It would take years off my life."

Shocked, I smiled nervously. I was flattered by his attentions. Who wouldn't be? But I was also straight as an arrow, madly in love with Susan, and not the slightest bit attracted to him.

"I'm heterosexual," I said.

"I wouldn't be interested in you if you weren't."

Flustered but not scared—he never did touch me; we could hear party chatter downstairs—I temporized, made excuses, found the right words to put him off. But his attention, his ardent words, his *hunger*, produced a buzz. It conferred on me a new, unfamiliar, almost feminine power that I hadn't realized I had.

That episode in the spring of 1979 ended without incident. You might have thought, given how flustered and sexually uninterested I was, that I would have resolved never, ever, under any circumstances to have anything to do with Professor McFarland. But a couple of years later, when I was thinking about applying to the English graduate program at Columbia, I needed three letters of recommendation. I knew what a powerful and celebrated scholar McFarland was. His new book, *Romanticism and the Forms of Ruin*, had just been published. I'd bought it. I was awed by his erudition, the way he wielded words like "reticulated." So I wrote him, told him of my plans, and he invited me to the Century Club for dinner—an astonishing honor for the twenty-three-year-old literary-critical ephebe that I was.

I wanted something from him. And we did have that curious track record. So I could hardly plead ignorance or dismay when, somewhere mid-dinner at our cozy mid-dining-room table, he leaned forward into the candlelight, face florid after the wine we'd consumed, and reiterated his pitch. He wanted to get close to me, it would take years off his life, etc.

"Call me Tom, please," he insisted, when I addressed him as Professor McFarland, as I always had.

Once again, nothing actionable occurred. I coyly put him off, trying not to hurt his feelings even while allowing the evening, and his keen attentions, to roll onward. We shook hands later as I thanked him warmly for dinner, outside the club's front door, and I subwayed home to the apartment I shared with Susan. Several weeks later, his letter of recommendation arrived in the mail, sealed in its envelope with his signature carefully scrawled across the flap.

And that was the end of that—until 1989, when *New York* magazine ran a big tabloidy story, "Arms and the Man: A Sex Scandal Rocks Princeton." I learned much about McFarland that I didn't know, but nothing that I couldn't believe. An unnamed Princeton English grad student, new to the department, was offered a ride home from the beginning-of-the-year party by McFarland, who then invited him back to his house for a drink. After a glass of wine and twenty-minute conversation about Wordsworth, the student asked to be taken home. What followed, in the student's words, was a night of terror. McFarland twisted his arm behind his back, released it, twisted it again. He pushed the student onto his sofa and climbed on top of him, pushing his face into the sofa. He dragged him into the bedroom, twisting his arm as he asked him questions. The student was crying at this point. "If I did not answer them in the way I wanted," he told the reporter, "he would twist my arm harder. I soon learned what answers I should give."

"Who do you love?" McFarland whispered.

"You."

"Where's the sir?"

"You, sir."

According to the student, "the professor spent the rest of the night fondling him...but there was no attempt to go further." McFarland finally drove the student home around dawn. The student slept for four hours, then woke and called Elaine Showalter, feminist scholar and head of graduate studies. The rest was history: a huge, sensational scandal, one that rocked the Princeton campus and blew up the English department. Four faculty members soon left for other campuses, several of them openly incensed about the way that the administration had soft-pedaled the disciplinary response to what appears, if the student is to be trusted—and I trust him—a case of criminal assault by a Princeton faculty member against a Princeton grad student. McFarland had been allowed to take early retirement; no criminal charges were ever brought. The administration had made a calculated choice about what was in its best interests, as university administrations always do.

Which brings us back to the subject at hand: Joshua Katz, a hatchet-job in the *Daily Princetonian*, and the question of what had changed between 2018, when Katz was punished by the administration with a year of unpaid leave for the consensual relationship he had had with "Jane" fifteen years earlier, and 2021, when the administration reopened that same case, their hand conveniently forced by the *Prince's* expose.

What had changed, of course, was Katz's status in the woke hierarchy of virtue, thanks to the irritable missive he had published in *Quillette* in July 2020. He was now a reviled campus heretic, not a celebrated, if slightly quirky, undergraduate instructor, one of a handful of Princeton faculty whose letters of recommendation were considered the gold standard among those applying for prestigious fellowships. The means had to be found for flushing him from the Matrix. That outcome has now been achieved.

The Joshua Katz affair is no localized campus kerfuffle, no "personnel matter," or at least it hasn't been since the *Prince* and a broad array of administrative functionaries went to work in the weeks and months following Katz's *Quillette* essay. The world is watching. And the world doesn't like what it sees. Princeton ranks dead-last among the Ivies in a recent assessment of free-speech protections on campus conducted by the Foundation for Individual Rights in Education (FIRE) and #134 out of 159 American colleges and universities: an astonishing, almost incomprehensible fall from grace for an institution that has long prided itself for #1 rankings of all kinds. My own University of Mississippi, by contrast, ranks #11: a free-speech oasis! Where is the closed society now? PEN America, a blue-chip defender of liberal values and intellectual freedom around the world, understands precisely what is at stake here:

> The question unavoidably arises as to whether Katz's speech [i.e., the *Quillette* essay], made in the period between the two investigations of his behavior and deeply offensive to many, contributed to his firing. When speech has been a precipitating trigger leading to the reopening of an inquiry into conduct, the consequences of such a probe unavoidably redound back to the expression that set the inquiry in motion.

> Without clear indications that offensive speech forms part of a pattern of harassing conduct, the expression of controversial or even offensive views should not be the impetus for the university to dissect unrelated behavior going back decades or to reopen formal investigations of previously adjudicated conduct. If that becomes the norm, institutions risk becoming environments wherein speech is technically protected, but objectionable

speech becomes a catalyst for reprisals for other conduct that would otherwise have gone unpunished. In such circumstances the protection of speech is significantly weakened, and there exists a powerful disincentive for expressing views that may give rise to reproach.

What's at stake, in a word, is the right to dissent: freedom of thought and freedom of speech for members of Princeton's on-campus community, especially when what is being questioned is the reigning—or incoming, or rapidly consolidating—orthodoxy.

That orthodoxy, in the aftermath of George Floyd's death in Minneapolis on May 25, 2020, and the heartfelt protests and outrage and, yes, riots and looting that swirled across America in the weeks that followed, was the new religion of antiracism, one accompanied by an exquisitely heightened consciousness of racial difference, strident invocations of privilege and "allyship," and a still-in-process set of radical demands. In Victor Navasky's terms, liberalism and its gradualist, meliorative horizons had been routed by the left, which had taken to the streets and *owned* the streets. On July 4, a sizeable subset of Princeton's faculty bodied forth this new orthodoxy in a lengthy, forty-eight-point manifesto, a "Faculty Letter" addressed to President Eisgruber and his administration demanding—the word "demand" and its variants showed up seven times—that Princeton "become, for the first time in its history, an anti-racist institution."

When I first set eyes on the letter, perhaps a week after it was issued, I was unaware that Katz had just published his explosively controversial reply. But my initial response as I worked down through the itemized list—apart from his singling out of the Black Justice League, a group I knew of only vaguely—was, I would discover later, quite similar to his: a mix of qualified support ("Sure, seems like a reasonable idea") and incredulity bordering on alarm at the way in which several specific demands, if actualized, threatened to transform Princeton into the academic equivalent of China during the Cultural Revolution, a place where each faculty member's words and actions would be subject to stringent review in a way that struck me as ripe for overreach and potential abuse:

11. Constitute a committee composed entirely of faculty that would oversee the investigation and discipline of racist behaviors, incidents, research, and publication on the part of faculty, following a protocol for grievance and appeal to be spelled out in Rules and Procedures of the Faculty. Guidelines on what counts as racist behavior, incidents, research, and publication will be authored by a faculty committee for incorporation into the same set of rules and procedures.

Several weeks before encountering the Faculty Letter, even while striving to make sense of what that letter would call the "massive global uprising in the name of racial justice" that Floyd's death had precipitated, I'd come across Sam Harris's podcast, "Can We Pull Back From the Brink?," with its scrupulous, data-based, point-by-point questioning of the emergent narrative around supposedly endemic police violence against unarmed black men. Harris had, almost inadvertently, introduced me to an array of heterodox black thinkers whose writings and podcasts I had begun to explore with great interest: Glenn Loury, John McWhorter, Thomas Chatterton Williams, Coleman Hughes, Kmele Foster.

I devoured Williams's memoir, *Self-Portrait in Black and White: Unlearning Race*, in two sittings, then immediately read it a second time, transfixed by its evocation of his interracial marriage and the problematics of self-identification confronted by blended children, thrilled by his urging that we reject race altogether, withdrawing our investment in racial marking. McWhorter, working through the idea-set that would later become *Woke Racism*, saw social justice activism in its current incarnation as a new American religion driven by fundamentalist intolerance. Hughes was a data-based contrarian best known for having had the nerve, as an undergrad philosophy major at Columbia, to argue against reparations—head-to-head with Ta-Nehisi Coates—at a congressional hearing in 2019. The perspectives these thinkers offered and the ethos they modeled—calm, fearless, inquisitive, discerning—inspired me. Their ability to think through the moment we were in and speak it freely helped me cope with the fact that, pervaded by an unfamiliar fear, the fear of one too cowed to dissent publicly or even ask reasonable questions, I'd temporarily lost my own voice. I researched and wrote an essay about the death of Trayvon Martin just to maintain my sanity, knowing it could never see print without torpedoing my career, then pushed on and wrestled with what happened to Michael Brown in Ferguson, Missouri.

Later, with the help of Loury, McWhorter, and Hughes, my fear would ebb and I'd regain my voice, publishing an essay about the problematics of an antiracism workshop I'd attended as an academic researcher, long before DEI administrations at corporations, universities, and government offices across America had begun to demand that you and your fellow citizens submit to "training" of a sort that only two decades earlier had been the province of a tiny activist vanguard. And then, long after the fact, I came across Katz's July 8, 2020, essay in *Quillette*, "A Declaration of Independence by a Princeton Professor," and began to follow the progress of his case.

Katz's essay strikes me now, two years after the summer of our discontent, as an astonishingly brave and needed—and, yes, foolhardy and intemperate—act of dissent, issued at a moment and in a context where no other professor I know would have had the chutzpah to take a stand. His willing embrace of certain line items in the July 4 Faculty Letter and his forthright critiques of others together offer a model of critical thinking, as does the mischievous schema in which he offers four reasons why he presumes people signed the letter:

(1) They believe in every word. I suppose this is true for a few, including, presumably those members of the faculty who were the initial drafters.

(2) They signed it without reading it. I would not ordinarily believe this, but I am aware of a similar petition, not at Princeton, that people were asked to sign—and did so!—before knowing what they were putting their name to.

(3) They felt peer pressure to sign. This is entirely believable.

(4) They agree with some of the demands and felt it was good to act as "allies" and bring up the numbers even though they do not assent to everything themselves.

"I imagine that the majority fall into this last category," Katz argues. "Indeed, plenty of ideas in the letter are ones I support."

One doesn't have to try hard to imagine how many faculty feathers were ruffled by this breezy deconstruction of "solidarity." Katz isn't presuming bad faith among his peers, exactly, but then again: what do you call a lack of due diligence and a willingness to be cowed by the political exigencies of the moment into signing a document one disagrees with in significant ways? After quickly enumerating the "plenty of ideas" he supports, including "substantial expansion" of the Mellon Mays Undergraduate Fellowship Program that "encourages underrepresented minorities to enter PhD programs and strive to join the professoriate," he scrolls through "dozens of proposals that, if implemented, would lead to civil war on campus and erode even further public confidence in how elite institutions of higher education operate." These include explicit preferences for Princeton faculty of color ("Faculty of color hired at the junior-level should be guaranteed one additional semester of sabbatical"), alterations to the required undergraduate curriculum ("Establish a core distribution requirement focused on the history and legacy of racism in the country and on the campus"), and alterations to campus architecture ("Commit fully to anti-racist campus iconography, beginning with the removal of the John Witherspoon statue").

One doesn't have to agree with every single critique Katz offers to agree that these proposals should, in fact, be debated. As I've noted, I share his profound dismay with the proposed creation of a faculty committee charged with investigating and disciplining "racist behaviors, incidents, research, and publication":

> This scares me more than anything else: For colleagues to police one another's research and publications in this way would be outrageous. Let me be clear: Racist slurs and clear and documentable bias against someone

because of skin color are reprehensible and should lead to disciplinary action, for which there is already a process. But is there anyone who doesn't believe that this committee would be a star chamber with a low bar for cancellation, punishment, suspension, even dismissal?

To which I respond: Right on, Brother Joshua! This is why you are my hero: because you had the bravery and sheer gall to speak truth to power—power, at this particular historical pivot, being wielded by an earnest but wildly overreaching activist cadre within Princeton's faculty ranks.

Yet all of this critical pushback, plain-spoken and forceful as it was, is not what got Katz into trouble. Here I want to speak directly to his most reviled and picked-over paragraph, which concerns the Black Justice League.

The BJL, when Katz wrote of it, was a defunct student organization, no longer active on campus—which is to say that his critique was directed at alumni, not students currently enrolled at the university, and was an acerbic response to one specific demand in the faculty letter: "Acknowledge, credit, and incentivize anti-racist student activism. Such acknowledgment should, at a minimum, take the form of reparative action, beginning with a formal public University apology to the members of the Black Justice League and their allies." To which he responded:

> The Black Justice League, which was active on campus from 2014 until 2016, was a small local terrorist organization that made life miserable for the many (including the many black students) who did not agree with its members' demands. Recently I watched an "Instagram Live" of one of its alumni leaders, who—emboldened by recent events and egged on by over 200 supporters who were baying for blood—presided over what was effectively a Struggle Session against one of his former classmates. It was one of the most evil things I have ever witnessed, and I do not say this lightly.

When I first read this passage in *Quillette*, and knowing little of the Black Justice League except the fact that they'd once staged an overnight sit-in in President Eisgruber's office and handed him a list of demands, I took Katz's "terrorist organization" slur as I presumed he intended it to be taken: as the hyperbole of a man fed up with the way that social justice activists sometimes force the issue, discomfiting the rest of us in the process. A needless provocation, I thought—one that devalued the word "terrorist," much as leftists have diminished the potency of the word "Nazis," by applying it imprecisely, over-broadly. As for the Instagram Live struggle session claim: having been subjected myself in 2003, in an all-white context, to a smaller-scale version of this social ritual, silenced by two facilitators before being showered with criticism by a circle of activists-in-training, I had no trouble taking Katz at his word. I had seen that sort of evil in action.

One point that became apparent as I began to seek out more information about the BJL was that they had responded with particular vindictiveness to black students who disagreed with them, viewing that dissent as a kind of racial treason. The *Daily Princetonian*'s 2020 two-part history of the BJL hints at this dynamic, quoting former BJL members Joanna Anyanwu, Trust Kupupika, and Destiny Crockett:

> Anyanwu said that while she could bear criticism and hatred from non-Black students and faculty, dissent from Black students who did not agree with the BJL's methods or demands hurt much more.

> "Friendships were falling apart," said Kupupika. "A lot of Black students would say stuff like, 'How dare you speak for me?' 'How dare you call yourselves the Black Justice League?'"

> Crockett echoed this sentiment.

> "I think the most painful backlash and the most frustrating backlash has not been from white students

and not been from administrators; it has always been from Black students," she told the 'Prince' in 2017.

But as Professor Robert George clarified while moderating an alumni panel, "The Fight For Free Speech at Princeton and Beyond," held during Reunions this past May, members of the BJL responded to the pain engendered by that perceived betrayal by lashing out in ways that substantiate Katz's basic claims:

> [Katz, in his *Quillette* essay,] was referring specifically to the…persecution of black students by people in the Black Justice League because those black students wouldn't go along. They were dissenting. I marched a young woman, a young black woman who was a dissenter from the Black Justice League program, and a critic, who came under ferocious attack, I marched her over to [Vice President for Campus Life] Rochelle Calhoun's office…to explain to Rochelle how she was being treated. The smears that she was enduring; the threats—"We will make sure you never get a job anywhere"; the intimidation. Being referred to by them as Aunt Jemima. She laid the whole case out in front of Vice President Calhoun, and to her very great credit, Vice President Calhoun made it stop. But it's a special burden on our minority students who *do* dissent to speak up.

The 350-odd members of Princeton's faculty who signed the July 4, 2020, letter find it far easier to indict "anti-Black racism" on the Princeton campus and beyond than to acknowledge this sort of inhumane and anti-democratic behavior within BJL's own ranks—behavior that stands at an unimaginable remove from the compassion and soulforce that animated Martin Luther King, Jr., Fannie Lou Hamer, Bob Moses, and the BJL's own patron saint, Ella Baker. Lift as you climb? This is tearing down your own sister with the backing of a mob. And these Princeton faculty, along with the university's current administration, would have us condemn and excommunicate Joshua Katz for calling such illiberal behavior to account.

Does calling a black female undergrad "Aunt Jemima" and threatening her with "We will make sure you never get a job anywhere" qualify as terrorism? The former slur is an odious reminder that old-school bigotry still occasionally rears its head on Princeton's campus; the latter threat, as any student of the civil rights movement knows, was one of the prime tactics used by the White Citizens' Councils in the late 1950s and early 1960s to intimidate and punish black Mississippians who tried to register to vote. Both behaviors are something Princetonians concerned with racial justice should be decrying, not engaging in—or, for that matter, eliding from the tendentious, activist-approved history of racism at Princeton conveyed by the "To Be Known and Heard" website.

Here's the question I'm ultimately forced to wrestle with: Why would I want my son, a Mississippian who wears his mixed-race identity with grace and a palpable lightness of spirit, to attend the Princeton that Princeton has become? Would he truly thrive there? Would he think for himself? Would he be *allowed* to think for himself? Or, stepping afoul of those who keep racial score, would he be insulted, hounded, excommunicated—criticized for his "proximity to whiteness" and abrogation of a compelled "allyship"? What values, ultimately, would those he encountered on campus, including his professors and the administrators who oversee them, encourage him—or pressure him—to uphold?

Your Trayvon,
My Trayvon, Our Trayvon

Life is not about good vs. evil, but about
good and evil eaten off the same plate.

—Kalamu ya Salaam, *What Is Life:*
Reclaiming the Black Blues Self

I.

Given the perils that haunt young American men of color, I want to give my son accurate information about the social world in which he's coming of age. Fathers are supposed to be wise elders. Sensible guidance, as much as food, clothing, and shelter, *is* what we owe to our sons. Our ability to offer that guidance depends on our ability to see and think clearly. I'm a more emotional man than some might assume, and I take pride in that; you shouldn't play blues if the fire's not burning. But intellectual clarity—lucidity—is also a paramount value. I've spent my whole life striving to see clearly. And it's suddenly gotten much harder to do that, this summer of 2020, or to find others willing to help me do that, although I keep looking.

My dad used to say, "Everything in moderation, including moderation." He was a moderate guy, and I always thought he meant it as a joke. But maybe it's worth a revisit. Although *lack* of moderation is hardly what we need right now.

The test of a first-rate intelligence, F. Scott Fitzgerald once wrote, "is the ability to hold two opposed ideas in the mind at the same time and still retain the ability to function." Nobody seems interested in that concept these days. You can't organize Twitter mobs or cable news networks around it.

According to Ibram X. Kendi, author of *How to Be an Antiracist*, "we are all either racists or antiracists." There is no middle ground. I've read and taught Jonathan Edwards's "Sinners in the Hands of an Angry God"; I recognize in Kendi's stringent fundamentalism the language of sin and salvation deployed by Edwards, the prime mover of the Great Awakening. "There are black clouds of God's wrath now hanging directly over your heads," he preached to a Connecticut congregation in 1741, "full of the dreadful storm, and big with thunder; and were it not for the restraining hand of God, it would immediately burst forth upon you."

The awakening is upon us. I don't dispute that. But what is it that we are being asked to awaken into? And is there really no middle ground?

I know I can never publish what I'm about to write. But I'll write it anyway and put it away, so that I'll remember how it felt to be where we are now, in the summer of 2020: the fear that showed up as the racial reckoning caught fire.

It was the death of Trayvon Martin back in 2012 that lit the first match, followed, later in Obama's second term, by Michael Brown, Laquan McDonald, Tamir Rice, and Philando Castile. Why were so many young black men getting shot to death by the cops? Mostly white cops, but not all, and George Zimmerman wasn't a cop, just a neighborhood watch captain with a gun. But still: the pattern was scary, and the video of Castile, who calmly and politely informed Officer Jeronimo Yanez during a routine traffic stop that he was carrying a firearm before Yanez panicked and blew him away, was heartbreaking. Shaun was only a boy back then, but I remember thinking: I need to understand what's going on or my kid's in trouble. He might be in trouble anyway, but at least I'd be able to give him thoughtful advice when it came time for the Talk.

Now he's fourteen, and big—more than two hundred pounds—and light brown, with lots of dark curly hair and broad shoulders, and he's a happy and voluble young man, a trumpet player. He loves pedaling his bicycle at night around the lake at Wellsgate, a nearby upscale development, with his unruly Afro haloing as he pushes back through the front door. Sherrie isn't a worrier, but she's aware of the problematics, as am I. George Floyd, a large black man, was killed by four cops up in Minnesota last month and America exploded. Shaun walked into the living room as I was watching impassioned demonstrators and violent rioters clash with militarized police on TV. I was trying to maintain my usual wait-and-see attitude, since I'd been stung before by these sorts of racial melodramas when the rest of the story finally came out. But it was tough. CNN and MSNBC kept showing the same eight-and-a-half minute loop of officer Derek Chauvin kneeling on Floyd's neck with three other officers holding him down as he said "I can't breathe!" and called for his mama, then stopped moving. It looked bad. It was terrible, in fact.

"How would you like it," Sherrie called from the kitchen, "if that was a member of your family?"

"I wouldn't."

We were both upset. Stuck in the house during the pandemic, working from home, trapped with the TV. Now people were protesting and rioting as our big son eased through the living room, blotting out CNN as he passed me. Breaking the spell.

"People are very angry," I said.

"Racism is stupid," he snorted. "I can't believe anybody still believes in that stuff."

I thought for a moment.

"Have you ever heard of Trayvon Martin?" I said.

"No."

I was surprised. Shaun knows everything about everything, or thinks he does, thanks to YouTube and TikTok. He loves to dispense slightly skewed factoids about the decades before he was born—the eighties, the nineties—because he's seen the videos. How could he not have heard about Trayvon Martin and George Zimmerman? I took a deep breath. He was only five when it happened.

As a scholar who had written about the shaping effect of lynching on black southern blues people, as an instructor at the University of Mississippi who had lectured on Emmett Till's murder more than once, I was primed to view Martin's death in Sanford, Florida, as the latest outrage in a long history of racist vigilantism on Southern soil. But since my profession was grounded in—or used to be grounded in—the ability to think critically, I had forced myself to do that. Mob justice, whenever it showed up in American history, was a failure of procedural justice. Mobs thrived on rumor, inflamed emotions, one-sided interpretations of incomplete evidence. Even as I'd gathered information and absorbed the narrative offered by mainstream and progressive sources, even as I'd spurned the inanities of Fox News, I'd refused to give in to outrage before all the relevant facts had come to light.

By 2012 I had already become dimly aware of the term "social justice warrior" and understood that many progressives with whom I shared a basic philosophical orientation had taken to jumping the gun in matters of procedural justice: quickly folding the latest racist outrage, as they understood it, into a continuing narrative of white racial prejudice, structural racism (especially, as Radley Balko and Bryan Stevenson have argued, a criminal justice system critically compromised by anti-black bias), economic inequality, and white privilege manifesting itself as the vigilante's perceived right to police black bodies in public space.

The continuing narrative wasn't wrong. Anybody who'd taken the time to study African American history knew that; any black person who had come of age in America, especially older black southerners, carried this knowledge in their bones. But it was a bad idea to allow this baseline truth to override the particulars of any given event. Do that and you were tossing procedural justice into the bonfire for the sake of a claimed commitment to social justice, or for the sake of payback, or for an unstable mixture of both motives. If "only justice can stop a curse," as Alice Walker had famously claimed, then both procedural justice and social justice were required. Cooler heads were a vital part of the conversation. Swinging slightly behind the beat was a good idea.

The continuing narrative wasn't wrong, but it wasn't the whole truth. It could give us insight, as Ta-Nehisi Coates would later argue in *We Were Eight Years in Power: An American Tragedy* (2017), into the counterrevolution that sought to delegitimize, caricature, and disempower our first black president, a process Coates framed as the second coming of Redemption, a multi-decade power-grab beginning in 1875 through which white southerners travestied Reconstruction as a festival of black incompetence and rewrote state constitutions to disenfranchise black voters. I agreed with Coates's framing of Obama's presidency as a period of "Good Negro Government," much like Black Reconstruction; I agreed that Obama's status as a "caretaker and measured architect," not a revolutionary, someone who had "steered clear of major scandal, corruption, and bribery," made him and his all-American family "a walking advertisement for the ease with which black people could be fully integrated into the unthreatening mainstream of American culture, politics, and myth." Coates and I agreed that it was precisely these accomplishments and atmospherics, not policy disagreements, that had panicked a substantial subset of white Americans on a deep, unconscious level, giving energy to the birther movement and a yearning to configure Obama as illegitimate. (Later I would come to understand, thanks to heterodox thinkers, that Obama had greatly expanded Title IX administrative powers in a way that had invidious results, tamping down some of the admiration I'd felt for him.)

But Coates's schema, powerful as it was, couldn't account for the multiracial coalition, sustained by immoderate hope, that had brought Obama to power in the first place — including many working-class whites, seven to nine million, who would later vote for Donald Trump. At worst, in an age of social media flash mobs and audience-seeking cable news hosts, a continuing narrative that cried "Racism!" and "White supremacy!" at the drop of a hat could become a prosecutor's brief that airbrushed away the bad facts, a fundamentalist orthodoxy that demanded ritual assent and excommunicated skeptics who asked hard questions.

As the Trayvon Martin/George Zimmerman story caught fire and exploded into the American media universe, I thought back to the Duke lacrosse rape case of 2006 and how so many, leaping to conclusions, had gotten the particulars of that case wrong, and slanderously so. Houston A. Baker, Jr., a celebrated black literature professor there and somebody I'd once admired, characterized what happened as "abhorrent sexual assault," promulgated by rapacious athletes who, "safe under the cover of silent whiteness," had been given "license to rape, maraud, deploy hate speech and feel proud of themselves in the bargain." I couldn't blame him for his failure of judgment, just how nasty and public it was. I'd been fooled, too, instantly presuming that righteousness lay with the black female stripper who cried rape, not only because I was constitutionally inclined to take the black woman's word about such things, but because I'd retained a chip on my shoulder against privileged white prep-school jocks—the sort of guys back at Princeton who'd grinned off the porch of Cottage Club at freshman losers like me.

Yet the truth, as Peter Applebome noted in the *New York Times* after the case had fallen apart, is that "all three [of the accused players] were totally innocent of the charges against them." They were men of character, in fact. It took a remarkable investigative study by Stuart Taylor, Jr., and K. C. Johnson, *Until Proven Innocent: Political Correctness and the Shameful Injustices of the Duke Lacrosse Case*, to make clear just how badly Baker, Wahneema Lubiano, and other progressive faculty, black and white, had erred by presuming guilt and innocence through an intersectional lens before they'd aggregated all the facts. The lesson stung, but it taught me something. When racial melodrama unfolded on cable news, Americans seemed to forget the point of *A Time to Kill* and every other Hollywood picture in that vein, which is that apparently simple and straightforward stories involving a rush to judgment always have second acts.

The Trayvon Martin case, as it first emerged, was a morality play: the life of a youthful black innocent snuffed out by a hulking white vigilante within the confines of a gated, whites-only space: the Retreat at Twin Lakes. As many commentators would soon observe and later analyze ad infinitum, the initial coverage was galvanized by the juxtaposition of two iconic and misleading images: smiling, fresh-faced Trayvon in a red Hollister T-shirt, the picture of lighthearted fun; and surly, overweight Zimmerman, an unshaven menace in what appeared to be an orange prison jumpsuit. (The photo of Martin had been taken at least one year before his encounter with Zimmerman and, according to the Poynter Institute, as much as three or four years earlier; the photo of Zimmerman, in what turned out to be an orange polo shirt, had been taken seven years earlier. Neither photo met the most-recent-available standard prescribed in journalistic ethics classes.)

Travyon, we were told, was visiting the gated community to stay with his father and his father's fiancée; he had left the townhouse during a basketball game, visited a local convenience store, purchased Skittles and a can of Arizona Iced Tea, and was walking back home when he was racially profiled and followed by Zimmerman, a wannabe cop and hyper-vigilant neighborhood watch volunteer, then accosted and, after a struggle in which he repeatedly cried out for help, shot dead by the much bigger and heavier man.

Helping solidify this narrative were excerpts from the recording of an extended conversation that Zimmerman had had with the police dispatcher when he had called to report the youth's "suspicious" presence. As reported by Lilia Luciano and, a few days later, Ron Allen at NBC News, Zimmerman had volunteered of Martin, "This guy looks like he's up to no good. He looks black," then, when asked what the black youth was wearing, added, "A dark hoodie." Here was plain evidence of aggressive racial profiling of a sort that would alarm and infuriate the parent of any black teen—or any black man of any age who had ever been pro-filed, or anybody, including me, who cared about such issues.

In an early portrait of Zimmerman as arch-racist, Gary Tuchman at CNN, piggybacking on a claim made by Cenk Uygur at *The Young Turks* and with the help of an "audio design specialist," reported that Zimmerman, at a slightly later moment in the tape, had expressed frus-tration with the siege of youthful black male criminals that his over-heated imagination was leading him to invent by uttering the phrase "fucking coons." That second word, poisonous and archaic, twisted in the air for at least a week, dominating the daily news cycle and inflaming outrage, even as Jon Stewart and several other dissenting voices expressed doubts. (Sanford PD investigator Chris Serino told the FBI that local gangs, who typically dressed in black and wore hoodies, were referred to as "goons" in the community. When interviewed shortly after the inci-dent, Zimmerman himself had told the Sanford Police Department that the word he'd uttered was "punks," and that was the word the prosecu-tion ultimately used in the opening argument of Zimmerman's trial as the by-then-discredited "coons" fell by the wayside.)

Another week of outrage was ginned up by a new video, released by ABC and picked over by *The Young Turks*, of Zimmerman's initial appearance at the SPD on the night of the incident. This video turned out to be a slightly zoomed-in, one-generation-removed copy of the closed-circuit TV video as it appeared on a police station monitor, filmed surreptitiously (it would appear) with an unsteady smartphone. It seemed to show no abrasions or other injuries to Zimmerman's skull, contravening his claim that Martin was the aggressor, jumping on top of him and beating him so badly that, after crying out in vain for assistance, Zimmerman felt he had no choice but to shoot the seventeen-year-old in self-defense.

The moment I realized that I had been lied to by the sum total of media coverage to date was the moment, roughly two months after Martin's death, when a pair of bloody iPhone photos of Zimmerman, taken three minutes after the shooting, were finally released. These photos, it would turn out, were consistent both with Zimmerman's statements to police and with an examination performed the day after the shooting by a physician's assistant at a local clinic, which found that he had a broken nose, two black eyes, and lacerations on the back of his head.

Whatever else had happened, Zimmerman had taken a beating during the encounter. The closest eyewitness and the one with the best view of the fight, John Good, asserted as much when interviewed by police investigator Chris Serino on the night of the incident. He'd seen "a black man with a black hoodie on top of the other…just throwing down blows on the guy kind of MMA style," and he later reiterated that claim at the trial. At bare minimum, these two photos should have placed a momentary check on those, including participants in the many "Justice for Trayvon" protests and vigils, who were determined to interpret Martin's death as the martyrdom of an innocent, framed within the fierce certainties of a racial morality play.

The recordings of Zimmerman's calls to the police dispatcher had been doctored so misleadingly by NBC News and its Miami affiliate, it turned out, that Luciano, local reporter Jeff Burnside, and the line producer would all be fired. Zimmerman had specified the suspect's race to the SPD dispatcher only when specifically asked whether "this guy" was "white, black, or Hispanic," and he'd mentioned Martin's hoodie, too, along with "jeans or sweatpants" and "white tennis shoes," only in response to a direct question. But there were many other relevant facts that had been left out of the emergent narrative—facts that didn't just complicate the deadly encounter, but that undercut the depictions of Zimmerman and Martin as white racist aggressor and innocent black victim of racial profiling, respectively.

The idea that Zimmerman was white, the function of an initial police misidentification that was repeated by Reuters and other early news sources, was quickly deconstructed, although the mark of evil whiteness lingered in the label "white Hispanic." Zimmerman was, and is, biracial, or tri-racial, in a way that would have allowed him to self-identify on the 2010 US Census as white and black, or white, Hispanic, and black, although he put Hispanic on his voter registration form. His father was an American of German descent; his mother was a Spanish-speaking Peruvian immigrant whose grandfather was black. (If he'd been alive during the Jim Crow era, when Florida's black codes, instituted in 1865 and updated in 1892, stipulated that "every person [in the state] who shall have one-eighth or more of negro blood shall be deemed and held to be a person of color," Zimmerman, like Homer Plessy in New Orleans, would have been termed an octaroon and restricted to the colored railroad car.) He was raised Catholic and spoke Spanish fluently, a byproduct of his multicultural upbringing.

As his defense attorney Mark O'Mara noted later, long after Zimmerman's acquittal at trial and shortly before Obama's justice department found "insufficient evidence to prove beyond a reasonable doubt a violation" of the relevant Civil Rights statutes, testimony gathered by FBI investigators from Zimmerman's friends and neighbors in 2012 made clear that, contrary to the prevailing narrative, "George acted in very non-racist ways. He took a black girl to the prom. His best buddy was a black guy. He mentored two black kids. He sought justice for a black homeless man beaten up by a white cop's son."

It was the erasure of that last episode by Martin's partisans that most disturbed me—even as I understood that a young civil rights activist like Zimmerman, raised in a multiracial family, could nevertheless have been soured on young black men in a problematic way by the wave of break-ins and burglaries that he and his fellow residents at Twin Lakes had recently been experiencing, incidents in which young black men were almost always the suspects.

It may seem perverse to use the term "civil rights activist" to characterize Zimmerman. But in the case of Sherman Ware, that is precisely what Zimmerman, an ardent Obama supporter in the 2008 election, had been. In December 2010, less than a year and a half before Zimmerman's confrontation with Martin, a homeless black man named Sherman Ware had been sucker punched and knocked out by Justin Collison, the white son of a Sanford police lieutenant. Although the assault was videotaped and uploaded to YouTube, the SPD took no action. Incensed at the preferential treatment Collison had received and the racial injustice it represented, Zimmerman and his wife, Shellie, printed up fliers that called out the Sanford police chief, Brian Tooley, and handed them out at local African American churches:

> I challenge you reading this to stand together and not "simply go away" as Chief Tooley and his corrupt subordinates wish, but to have our voices heard and to hold accountable those whom let this atrocious attack pass unpunished until the media revealed it. This animal could have attacked anyone of us, our children or loved ones in his alcohol fueled rage.

Note that *us*. That is George Zimmerman asserting his solidarity with the black citizens of Sanford, Florida. Zimmerman helped organize an early January 2011 meeting at Sanford City Hall—by this point his agitations had convinced the local NAACP to enter the fray—and he blasted the SPD, on camera, for laziness and unequal treatment under the law. Tooley was soon forced to retire.

This George Zimmerman, decrying an act of violence against an African American victim and a police force unwilling to take it seriously, was so at odds with the narrative of Zimmerman-as-predatory-racist as to seem almost unthinkable. More than that: his passionate advocacy for Sherman Ware and hyperbolic condemnation of Justin Collison anticipated, uncannily, the way in which the Martin family's attorneys, Benjamin Crump and Natalie Jackson, were advocating for Trayvon and savaging Zimmerman himself. Such a parallel, undercutting the established narrative, could not be allowed to stand. The local NAACP disavowed all prior knowledge of Zimmerman, and Jackson, who had represented Sherman Ware in an out-of-court settlement with Collison, dismissed any mention of Zimmerman's role in the Ware affair as "race baiting."

As the mainstream and alternative media and various blogs began to unpack the Zimmerman/Martin story in the spring of 2012, some facts became clearer and others remained obscure. Although progressive media outlets including the *Daily Kos* and the *Nation* had claimed that Zimmerman outweighed Martin by "almost" and "more than" a hundred pounds, respectively, as a way of casting doubt on Zimmerman's claim that he had fired in self-defense, the truth was that on the night of the encounter, the 5' 7.5" Zimmerman weighed 204 pounds and the 5'11" Martin weighed 158 pounds. (Those heights and weights are taken from a physician's assistant report and an autopsy, respectively; Martin was mistakenly described as 6'3" and 140 pounds in several early accounts.) Zimmerman was three and a half inches shorter and forty-six pounds heavier than Martin. Did this matter? Only if the facts matter. What to make of them would remain a contested issue.

Although the initial police report misidentified the large canned beverage found in Martin's pocket as Arizona Iced Tea, and although virtually every mainstream media outlet, academic scholar, and popular advocate for Martin repeated and continues to repeat this error, a photo taken at the crime scene clearly shows a can of Arizona Watermelon Fruit Juice Cocktail. I initially assumed that this seemingly trivial error, a failure of both popular memory and scholarly due diligence, was a way of avoiding the racist associations that the word *watermelon* might have in relation to a black Southerner like Martin. But a second explanation seems even more compelling: the image of Trayvon-as-innocent leans heavily on the snacks he was carrying home when Zimmerman shot him down. Iced tea and Skittles: what could be more harmless? What could be *less* like the forty-ounce bottles of malt liquor and marijuana-laced blunts that featured in white racist fantasies of gang-banging, hip-hop-spouting boyz in the hood? Trayvon had left the house merely to seek refreshment—not to get high, or burglarize neighborhood houses, or fight, or do any of the things that racist whites were always accusing young black men of doing.

It was at this moment, as a concerned father of a seven-year-old boy striving to see the situation clearly, that I watched the story split apart like the broken shell of Humpty Dumpty. Even as I resented the way in which my early sympathies had been played on by the media, I too felt the pull of Trayvon-as-innocent. He'd been that kid once, certainly, although it was unclear whether he was still that kid by the time he encountered Zimmerman. When President Obama stood in the Rose Garden and said, "If I had a son, he'd look like Trayvon," I was glad to have a president who could put it that way, framing it in family terms. It was easy to like and admire that kid—an ambitious young black teen, as his mother Sybrina Fulton attested, who loved planes, dreamed of a career in aviation, and had been mentored by a celebrated black aviator.

"He loved flying and working with his hands. Barrington Irving took him on his plane at the Opa-Locka Airport. He got a chance to sit in the cockpit and that did it for him," said Fulton, referring to the first black person to pilot a plane around the world solo in 2007. "He wanted to be a pilot or work as a mechanic in aviation. He was mechanically inclined and could fix just about anything." This was the Trayvon who, as *USA Today* put it, "liked the TV show 'South Park' and his mother's burgers and fries." One would have to have a heart of stone not to feel the tragedy represented by the violent end of such a promising young life.

But this Trayvon, it turned out, coexisted with another, somewhat older, and very different Trayvon, one known full well to, and celebrated by, the youthful peers with whom he exchanged texts, tweets, and Facebook messages: a boastful and aggressive young man with the Twitter handle "NO_LIMIT_NIGGA" who smoked pot, flashed guns, and had a reputation not just for fighting MMA style but for refereeing, filming, and uploading others' fights to his YouTube channel. This was the Trayvon whom one of his friends called "weedhead" and another called "a lil hoodlum"—to which Trayvon replied, "Naw, I'm a gangsta." The Trayvon Martin who was sojourning with his father at Twin Lakes was there because he had been suspended from eleventh grade for ten days, his third suspension of the academic year. The first offense was truancy; the second offense, writing "WTF" on a locker, resulted in a school police officer searching his daypack and finding twelve pieces of women's jewelry, a watch, and a large screwdriver that the officer described as a "burglary tool." The most recent suspension, according to the *South Florida Sun Sentinel*, came about when Martin was "caught with an empty plastic bag with traces of marijuana in it," plus a marijuana pipe.

The state medical examiner's autopsy determined that Martin had had traces of THC in his blood on the night he died, but whether he'd been smoking pot that night and deserved the word "impaired" remained unclear. The autopsy also discovered a form of advanced liver damage unusual in an otherwise normal seventeen-year-old. Anybody who dared to ask why that might be the case soon fell down the rabbit hole, landing in a world where Trayvon-as-innocent, bearing harmless snacks back to the townhouse, was supplanted by a profoundly troubled young man swimming in the currents of a homegrown drug known as "lean" or "purple drank."

Purple drank is a Deep South thing, a black Southern phenomenon that originated, according to hip-hop historian Lance Scott Walker, in Houston's blues subculture of the 1960s, where musicians would drink Robitussin cough medicine and chase it with beer or a wine cooler. The concoction evolved over the next several decades as it became a part of Houston's hip-hop scene and then, with the release of Three 6 Mafia's "Sippin' on Some Syrup" (2000), spread to other parts of the South, including Florida. Prescription-strength cough syrup, which contained codeine and promethazine, was mixed with a sweet soft drink like Sprite or Mountain Dew; a few Jolly Rancher fruit candies or Skittles were often thrown in to sweeten the mix. Robitussin, which contained the active ingredient DXM (Dextromethorphan), remained a popular substitute for prometh/codeine syrup, which was harder to obtain; getting high on purple drank and its variants was sometimes called "robo-tripping" or "skittling."

Trayvon Martin, by his own admission, prepared and consumed the drug cocktail, which he called "lean," and he discussed it with at least one of his Facebook friends, Mackenzie DumbRyte Baksh. In late June 2011, eight months before his deadly encounter with Zimmerman, he asks if Baksh can help him find some liquid codeine ("unow a connect for codine?") so that he can "make some more," because, he says, "I had it b4." Baksh tells him that Robitussin can be used as a substitute for codeine: "u could just use robitussin [a]nd soda to make some fire ass lean." Martin's reply—"codine is a higher dose of dxm"—betrays both a misunderstanding of the difference between the two drugs and enough familiarity with them to suggest that he's become an active member of this particular drug-concocting, drug-abusing subculture.

The following month, July 2011, according to the date stamps on his YouTube account, he began following the channel of comedian Andy Milonakis: a doughy white "boy"—actually a man with a growth hormone deficiency—who, as a contemporary incarnation of white minstrelsy on an absurdist trip, had sought to turn himself into the comic avatar of a ghetto bad boy by releasing a rap track entitled "Red Lean, Purple Lean," featuring lines like "Lean with it, lean with it, when I take a sip / Codeine ho, clean off my dick" and talk about his "big Glock."

Milonakis released "Red Lean, Purple Lean" as a YouTube video on June 21, 2011, at almost exactly the same moment, it would seem, that Trayvon Martin was beginning to explore that particular quadrant of black Southern hip-hop culture.

The watermelon-flavored juice and Skittles that Trayvon had in hand on the evening of February 26, 2012, were two-thirds of the recipe for purple drank. Combine them with Robitussin or codeine-based cough syrup and you were set. Given Martin's familiarity with, and interest in, the ingredients of "fire ass lean" as expressed in the Facebook exchange with Baksh, and given the liver damage disclosed by his autopsy, a damage consistent with heavy use of both prometh/codeine and acetaminophen-containing varieties of Robitussin, I found it easy to believe that between June 2011 and February 2012, the life of this promising young man was spinning out of control as he moved more deeply into a drug culture that his parents may have had no idea he was a part of. His long history of skipping school testified *some* problem, surely: not just the pair of ten-day suspensions that preceded his third and last ten-day removal, this time to Twin Lakes, but another twenty-three days' worth of absences: four and a half weeks of classes. Most young men intent on careers as aviators don't choose to miss that much school during the first six months of junior year.

I could find no evidence, circumstantial or otherwise, suggesting that Martin was high on purple drank at the time of the encounter with Zimmerman. But there was plenty of evidence in Martin's own words and the words of his friends about his attraction to dangerous pursuits: not just handguns (illegal to own or carry in Florida at his age), which he sought to buy in various calibers (.22, .380), but mixed martial arts (MMA) style fighting. In one notable text exchange between Martin and a female friend on November 21, 2011, he said he was "tired and sore" from a fight he'd had earlier that day. He and "dat nigga," he reported, had "thumped afta skool in a duckd off spot"; he'd "lost da 1st round: (but won da 2nd nd 3rd)" in a three-round format adapted from MMA. "Im not done with [the] fool …," he tells her. "He gone hav 2 see me again." Her flirtatious response betrays concern: "Nooo … Stop, yuu aint gonn bee satisfied till yuh suspended again, huh?" "Naw," Martin replied, "but he ain't bleed nuff 4 me, only his nosez."

Martin's tough-guy response suggests just how far he had drifted, at least in this part of his schoolboy's life, from the fresh-faced burgers-and-fries kid his mother, father, and legal team were intent on preserving as the sanctified image of innocence. I couldn't blame them, or his many passionate defenders, for recoiling in denial and anger from these text messages and the conservative bloggers who had brought them to the attention of Zimmerman's defense team. Martin's parents' attorneys fully understood that allowing *this* Trayvon into the conversation bolstered both Zimmerman's self-defense claim about having been mauled in the *mano a mano* struggle and witness John Good's initial statement to SPD investigator Serino, long before anybody knew what was at stake. Good, it's worth repeating, lived directly adjacent to the concrete walkway where the struggle took place and had the best view of any witness—although he'd missed the all-important encounter that precipitated the fight:

> So I open my door. It was a black man with a black
> hoodie on top of the other, either a white guy or now

I found out I think it was a Hispanic guy with a red sweatshirt on the ground yelling out help! And I tried to tell the, get out of here, you know, stop or whatever, and then one guy on top in the black hoodie was pretty much just throwing down blows on the guy kind of MMA-style.

When I thought about Trayvon's parents and their refusal to allow for the possibility that their bright and promising son, generous and loving within the family circle, had this other, much darker and less embraceable side, I was struck by an uncanny parallel between the Trayvon Martin story and another story about black life in central Florida: Zora Neale Hurston's novel *Their Eyes Were Watching God* (1937).

Although *Their Eyes* is primarily the story of its black female protagonist, Janie Crawford, and the search for love that leads her in and out of two bad marriages, it's also the story of Tea Cake, a guitar-and-piano-playing bluesman a decade her junior, who romances and wins her heart. What troubles this glorious third romance is the fact that Tea Cake, playful and passionate as he is—good as he is for Janie in almost every way—is also a violent man. Hurston makes clear that the violence he carries is of a piece with the juke-joint world he's a part of. It's intrinsic, not extrinsic; it's a core element of his personhood and masculinity. And it's something that Janie finds impossible, at least at first, to fit into her adoring vision of the man as a playful, tender lover. "Tea Cake had a knife it was true," she insists one night early in their relationship when he heads out alone to a juke joint, "but that was only to protect himself. God knows, Tea Cake wouldn't harm a fly." But Janie couldn't be more wrong. When he falls back through the door late that night, all cut up, he's bragging about having mauled the other guy:

> Baby, Ah run mah other arm in mah coat-sleeve and grabbed dat nigger by his necktie befo' he could bat his eye and then Ah wuz all over 'im jus lak gravy over rice. He lost his razor tryin' tuh git loose from me. He wuz

hollerin' for me tuh turn him loose, but baby, Ah turnt
him every way *but* loose.

Tea Cake's peers in the Florida jukes know what a brawler he is, as
Trayvon's friends knew and admired this side of their teen peer. Two
days after Martin's death, someone with the handle Skee Dollas Nickuhs
who called Martin "cuzz" posted on Twitter, "Ima miss yu till I die dog
I know yu whooped his ass doe." But Janie, for whom the violent contours of the juke joint are a world apart, bursts into tears as she cleans
her lover's wounds. Hurston leads us to understand that Janie's ability
to enlarge her love to encompass *this* Tea Cake—somebody for whom
hands-on mayhem and braggartry are important elements of masculine
self-possession—is a wrenching proposition but also a necessary next
step in her development.

Very few of Trayvon's partisans, as far as I could tell, were willing to
extend him the same enlarged understanding that Hurston demands of
Janie Crawford: allowing him to escape from the martyred innocence
of the boy who "wouldn't hurt a fly" into the complexities of troubled
young manhood. It was much easier and politically more effective to
suture Trayvon's memory to that of an innocent lynching victim like
Emmett Till or a tireless Civil Rights activist like Medgar Evers, both of
whom were assassinated within the evil and baroquely white-suprema-
cist precincts of Jim Crow Mississippi. But George Zimmerman wasn't
Byron de la Beckwith—although his post-acquittal behavior was, to be
sure, bizarre. By then, he'd become an angry and emotionally imbal-
anced man, threatening violent reprisal against anybody who tried
to fulfill the fatwah that had been put on his head by the New Black
Panthers. The young civil rights activist who had once called out white
injustice on behalf of a homeless black man had been transformed into a
caricature of the man his enemies insisted he'd been all along: a crackpot,
trigger-happy vigilante. Depending on how you looked at it, this development was either the tragic fall of somebody who had merely sought to
serve his beleaguered residential community or the barest beginnings of
deserved payback for a lying racist murderer who deserved much worse.
I didn't believe that he was a liar, at least about what had happened once

the fight began. But I didn't know what had happened before that, and he was no hero of mine.

Relitigating the case in my own mind, seeking usable advice to offer my son, I found myself circling around a key element of the story that hadn't received as much attention as it deserved. On March 18 and 19, 2012, ABC News reported in a pair of articles that Attorney General Eric Holder, responding to a letter written by Martin family attorney Crump and the pressure Crump had exerted through several members of Congress, was assigning both the FBI and the Justice Department's Civil Rights Division to the case. The FBI, according to Tampa-based special agent Dave Couvertier, was "the lead investigating agency for the DOJ"; when the FBI finished its investigation, the Civil Rights Division would "conduct a legal review of the facts and make a determination whether or not there is a civil rights federal violation."

Although I wasn't a fan of Crump, viewing him as an opportunistic hustler who sought to generate criminal charges even in borderline cases for the sake of the profits that could be generated by the civil cases that followed, here was one place where he and I saw eye to eye. Elections made a difference. With Obama in the White House, with Holder heading the DOJ, the administration had the power to compel procedural justice in this way, rather than allowing the case either to fall by the wayside, uninvestigated, or—more likely at this point—to fester in a never-never land of charge and countercharge, rumor and innuendo. The director of the FBI was Robert Mueller: a man of such unimpeachable integrity and demonstrated competence, by all accounts, that Obama had asked him to remain at the helm of the bureau he'd led for eight years under George Bush.

Here, as Mueller's agency worked under the direction of Obama and Holder, was black power in action, shining needed light. The standard for civil rights charges was high, to be sure, and the DOJ wasn't specifically looking into so-called "patterns and practices" at the Sanford Police Department, as they would later in Ferguson, Missouri. But when this was over we would have a much better sense of who George

Zimmerman was—and whether he was acting with racist intent when he shot and killed Trayvon Martin. And that was a good thing. In an older South, the death of a black teenager like Martin would never have received this sort of attention from the federal government. This was a small but important step toward equal justice under the law.

The FBI descended on Florida. On July 12, 2012, State Attorney and prosecutor Angela Corey released the agency's findings. The *Miami Herald* headlined their coverage, "FBI records: agency found no evidence that Zimmerman was racist." The FBI had interviewed thirty-five of Zimmerman's friends, neighbors, and co-workers. "None said Zimmerman had expressed racial animus at any time prior to the Feb. 26 shooting of Martin," the *Herald* reported. Especially in light of the continuing local agitation represented by "Justice for Trayvon" protests and the ongoing national publicity the case, and Zimmerman, were receiving, this unanimous response, a denial that Zimmerman was motivated by racial animus, was striking. Even his former fiancée, a Hispanic woman who had taken out a restraining order against him in 2005 after they'd pushed each other during a domestic dispute, told the FBI that he'd "never exhibited any biases or prejudices against anyone and did not use racial epithets of any kind." The investigation, concluded the *New York Times*, "found a man not prone to violence or prejudice and who moved easily between racial and ethnic groups—a 'decent guy,' 'a good human being.'"

The FBI had weighed in, but the DOJ civil rights investigation was put on hold while the state case was in progress. In the aftermath of Zimmerman's acquittal on July 13, 2013, as the DOJ prepared to reengage, the NAACP and its president, Ben Jealous, applied pressure in the form of an online petition at moveon.org demanding that Zimmerman's "egregious [civil rights] violation" be documented and prosecuted. Six weeks later, after a large march in Washington to commemorate the fiftieth anniversary of the March on Washington in August 1963, Jealous planned to present Attorney General Holder with the 1.7 million signatures that had been collected.

One lesson to be drawn here was that popular agitation, both early on and at this post-acquittal moment, was—or could be—a prod to procedural justice. Marches, demonstrations, and petitions put heat under situations and demanded that light be brought to bear. They helped frame priorities and, paradoxically, gave the cooler heads in Obama's FBI and DOJ a chance to do careful, fact-based work. The results of that work, of course, didn't always satisfy those who were marching in the streets. But with a black president and a black attorney general in charge, it became harder to dismiss disappointing results as the predictable outcome of what some progressives were fond of calling America's criminal injustice system.

On February 24, 2015, after meeting with Trayvon Martin's parents and their attorneys, the Department of Justice finally announced its findings. "After a thorough and independent investigation into the facts surrounding the shooting," read the press release, "federal investigators determined that there is insufficient evidence to prove beyond a reasonable doubt a violation" of the relevant civil rights statutes. "Accordingly, the investigation into this incident has been closed." In order to leave no doubt about what the word "thorough" meant, the press release spelled it out:

> Federal investigators reviewed all of the material and evidence generated by the state of Florida in connection with its investigation and prosecution of Zimmerman, including witness statements, crime scene evidence, cell phone data, ballistics reports, reconstruction analysis, medical and autopsy reports, depositions, and the trial record. Federal investigators also independently conducted 75 witness interviews and obtained and reviewed the contents of relevant electronic devices. The investigation included an examination of police reports and additional evidence that was generated related to encounters Zimmerman has had with law enforcement in Florida since the state trial acquittal. In addition, federal authorities retained an independent

biomechanical expert who assessed Zimmerman's descriptions of the struggle and the shooting.

Here, it seemed, procedural justice of a certain sort had finally been obtained. Although conservative bloggers and pundits were fond of attacking Holder as an agent of injustice—Obama's "deep state liberal wingman," in the words of Jeffrey Lord; "Obama's Enforcer" who had "racialized and radicalized the [Civil Rights] division to the point of corruption," according to authors John Fund and Hans Von Spakovsky—those accusations were significantly undercut by this outcome. By the same token, and unsurprisingly, the NAACP was "deeply disappointed" by the news. Anticipating that disappointment, the attorney general had offered his own statement, incorporated within the press release, which sought to clarify the high legal standard at stake in this case and frame the Zimmerman/Martin encounter, in human terms, as the "devastating tragedy" it clearly was:

> It shook an entire community, drew the attention of millions across the nation, and sparked a painful but necessary dialogue throughout the country. Though a comprehensive investigation found that the high standard for a federal hate crime prosecution cannot be met under the circumstances here, this young man's premature death necessitates that we continue the dialogue and be unafraid of confronting the issues and tensions his passing brought to the surface. We, as a nation, must take concrete steps to ensure that such incidents do not occur in the future.

Who could disagree with that call to action? I was grateful to the attorney general for crafting a "we" statement that all Americans, of whatever color or political persuasion, could embrace.

What concrete steps you specified, however, depended on how you viewed the case: the primal encounter between Zimmerman and Martin, the social context in which it was embedded. And the moment you did that, American reality split down the middle again, hamstrung between the sanctification of a martyred innocent and the odious reduction of Trayvon to some grill-flashing, Stormfront-style caricature, a poster child for what might, a hundred years earlier, have been condemned as "negro retrogression."

When I looked again at Holder's statement, I realized that he had, in fact, manifested the first-rate intelligence that Fitzgerald had called for, holding two opposed ideas in tension as he fulfilled his duty as America's chief law enforcement officer.

First, the conviction that something bad, something *wrong*, had happened here. Trayvon Martin shouldn't be dead. Regardless of how you arbitrated the issues, the promising young man evoked by his mother, his head full of aviation dreams, deserved a better fate.

Second, the knowledge that even the most thorough investigation, conducted under the watchful eye of a black president and black attorney general who had every reason to honor the concerns of Martin's many advocates and sympathizers—including a new organization called Black Lives Matter—could find no legitimate reason to prosecute George Zimmerman for a hate crime under Title 18, Section 249 of the US Code. If "death results from the offence," that statute specifies a penalty of ten years to life for "whoever, whether or not acting under color of law, willfully causes bodily injury to any person or, through the use of fire, a firearm, a dangerous weapon, or an explosive or incendiary device, attempts to cause bodily injury to any person, because of the actual or perceived race, color, religion, or national origin of any person." The evidence for a hate crime, given John Good's eyewitness account of Zimmerman being beaten up—which bolstered his claim of self-defense—and the FBI's inability to obtain any racial-animus-confirming testimony from Zimmerman's friends, neighbors, and coworkers, just wasn't there.

Where did this paradox leave us? I wasn't sure. But now that the state court and the Department of Justice had weighed in, now that I'd moved past my pique at the way the mainstream media had lied to me, now that I'd probed Trayvon's background and developed a more realistic sense of who he'd become during the last eight months of his life, and now that Zimmerman, post-acquittal, had morphed into a troubled, belligerent, entirely unsympathetic figure, I was suddenly with filled with grief—and fear for my son, who would have to navigate the world in which these two Americans, twenty-eight and seventeen, had had their fateful encounter.

So I decided to revisit the scene of the crime one last time, armed with whatever knowledge I'd managed to accrue. Or maybe it was the first time I'd dared to go there. Maybe I was afraid of what I'd find.

II.

It all started, according to his accusers, when he got out of his car. That's when he went from being a citizen volunteer, a Neighborhood Watch captain, to a vigilante creating trouble where no trouble existed. He was a wannabe cop, his accusers said—overeager, trigger-happy. The problems always started when the cops, usually white men, got out of their cars. Remember what happened to Rodney King? George Zimmerman never should have gotten out of that car.

In the slave South and later in the Jim Crow South, every white man had the de facto right to police black bodies. Demand papers, ask who was your owner or boss, what plantation you belonged to. That's just how it worked. God forbid you should talk back in a way that could be construed as sassy. You'd be dead then—or flogged to near-death.

But it was a new era now, and nobody put up with that slavery shit anymore. Not in the South, not anywhere. Not unless the cops had guns drawn—and even then there were always options, although they weren't necessarily good ones.

Our son, the psychologist told us when he was eight, had a tinge of ODD. We'd figured that out, although we didn't know the technical term. Shaun was stubborn; he'd reflexively contradict you in ways most parents would find annoying. He was a great kid, apart from that. But what would happen when he was a teenager, driving a car? What would happen the first time he was stopped by a cop for speeding, or failing to come to a full stop at a stop sign? Or for bicycling through the Wellsgate development at night, God forbid, with his Afro dancing in and out of view under the streetlights—weaving into the center of the road, perhaps, and catching an officer's eye?

On the three or four occasions when I'd been stopped by the police while driving, I was hyper-courteous and obliging. All my papers were in order, easily available in the glove compartment. I made a point, when stopped, of having them waiting on the dash so that I could place both hands on the steering wheel as the cop walked up. But that was just me: a law-abiding man who almost never interacted with the police and who, on those rare occasions when they had me in their sights, did everything I could to put them at ease. Would I be able to guide Shaun toward the same attitude? Sherrie and I kept trying to school him in how to be polite.

Worrying the line is a term used by blues scholars to denote the ways that the repeated A-line of a three-line AAB blues stanza, performed by a skilled blues singer, varies from the first iteration, adding emotional nuance. "Worrying the line," notes blues poet Sherley Anne Williams, "includes changes in stress and pitch, the addition of exclamatory phrases, changes in word order, repetition of phrases within the line itself, and the wordless blues cries which often punctuate the performance of the songs." Sometimes that second A-line is called the A-prime line as a way of marking that repetition-with-a-difference.

The Retreat at Twin Lakes wasn't an all-white gated community, as some had claimed, and it was no longer comfortably middle class. It may once have been like that, but in the aftermath of the stock market crash of 2008, the value of townhouses there had dropped precipitously—from $240,000 to $100,000, by one estimate. Of 263 units, 40 were empty. Half were rented, not owned. Brandy Green, Trayvon's dad's fiancée, was renting. Approximately 20 percent of Twin Lakes residents were black.

Another 20 percent, including Zimmerman, were Hispanic. Most of the rest were white: 50 to 60 percent.

A significant number of the residents, a Rainbow coalition—white, black, Hispanic—felt besieged by crime. Twin Lakes had "got bad," one resident told the FBI. There were break-ins, thefts, drug dealing out of townhouses, a few assaults, quite a bit of loitering and casing. More often than not, although by no means always, the perpetrators of these crimes were black and male. This was fact, not fantasy, a matter of police reports and eyewitness testimony—although facts can give rise to fantasies and precipitate misjudgments. Most of us are savvy enough to bracket such "facts" with scare quotes, sensitized as we've lately become to the phenomenon of racial bias within the ranks of American police departments.

"Let's talk about the elephant in the room. I'm black, ok?" the woman told a white male reporter from Reuters two months after Zimmerman shot and killed Martin, declining to give her name because she anticipated backlash for being honest. She looked him straight in the eyes. "There were black boys robbing houses in this neighborhood," she said. "That's why George was suspicious of Trayvon Martin."

In July 2011, neighbors told the Reuters reporter, "a black teenager walked up to Zimmerman's front porch and stole a bicycle.... A police report was taken, though the bicycle was not recovered."

In August 2011, twenty-one-year-old Olivia Bertalan was alone with her infant son in her Twin Lakes townhouse. She had moved there two months earlier. "[A] man came to her door," she told *The Daily Beast*, as she had earlier told FBI investigators and as she would testify during the trial,

> knocked, and rang the doorbell. She peered out a window, didn't recognize the man and called police when another man came to her back door. Bertalan...ran upstairs and locked herself and her son in a bedroom as the second man entered her home.... Terrified, she and her son cried as the man tried to turn the knob of the

door where they hid. Both men ran when police arrived, but not before stealing a laptop and digital camera.

Officers eventually identified the person who burglarized Bertalan's home as a neighbor. He was arrested but released because, as Bertalan understood it, he was a minor. Both he and the other man were black, according to the police report.

"There was definitely a sense of fear in the neighborhood after all of this started happening, and it just kept on happening. It wasn't just a one-time thing. It was every week," she said. "Our next-door neighbor actually said if someone came into his yard he would shoot him. If someone came into his house he would shoot him. Everyone felt afraid and scared."

The story is never just about what is happening now. It is always also about what happened in the long run-up to now. What they did to you, or us. What she did to you. What they lived through. What we did to them. A hundred, or two hundred, or three hundred years earlier.

All those things are, or can be, part of the story. They can help us see more clearly, and understand more deeply, what is happening right now. But they can also blind us to what is happening right now.

Twin Lakes was two miles from downtown Sanford, Florida. Sanford had a long and troubled racial history, as articles in the *Nation* and *Mother Jones* published a month after Martin's killing made clear. The town's founder, New England tycoon Henry Shelton Sanford, envisioned Sanford as a citrus capital; he imported Swedish laborers to build it in the 1870s. One of his friends was King Leopold, the death-dealing ruler of the Belgian Congo. Sanford viewed the Congo as a place where freed black Southerners—former slaves—could be shipped; a space in which their "enterprise and ambition" could flourish, rather than upsetting the established order by seeking outlet in stateside politics. The Congo, he believed, could be "the ground to draw the gathering electricity from that black cloud spreading over the Southern states."

In September 2011, after the rash of break-ins at Twin Lakes during the summer, the Sanford Police Department helped the residents start a Neighborhood Watch program. The homeowners' association asked George Zimmerman if he would be willing to head it. He said yes. According to Wendy Dorival, the Sanford PD official who worked with Zimmerman, he was "very professional" and "seemed a little meek." "He seemed like he really wanted to make changes in his community to make it better," she testified at the trial.

In the first two months of 2012, the Sanford PD received fifty-one calls from the residents of Twin Lakes, including Zimmerman. Most of the calls were for things other than actual crimes—sometimes merely to request information, sometimes to report suspicious activities and persons. But residents also reported eight burglaries, two bike thefts, and three simple assaults. One of Zimmerman's neighbors, Frank Taaffe, insisted to CNN's Soledad O'Brien that all eight burglaries had been committed by black males. The SPD had suspects in only four of those burglaries; all four suspects were black males.

Repetition is a fundamental constituent of the blues. So is *signifying*: saying one thing but meaning another, with the deeper meaning evident to those in the know but sufficiently masked so that the clueless remain oblivious. Signifying can be a way of speaking race—the inescapable trials of black life—without speaking race. *They call it stormy Monday, but Tuesday's just as bad / They call it stormy Monday, but Tuesday's just as bad / Wednesday's worse, Thursday's also sad.* But those trials ease up when payday arrives and party-time behind that. *Eagle flies on Friday, Saturday I go out to play.*

"Eagle flies on Friday means that he gets paid," B. B. King tells the reporter for National Public Radio, explaining T-Bone Walker's lyrics to noninitiates. It is November 7, 2008, three days after Barack Obama has been elected president.

In 1946, the year before he integrated major league baseball with the Brooklyn Dodgers, Jackie Robinson did the same thing, or tried to, with the Montreal Royals, the Dodgers' AAA team. The Royals held spring training in Sanford, Florida, a Jim Crowed town. Branch Rickey, the Dodgers' general manager, thought that the white people of Sanford would allow Robinson to play with the team as long as he avoided whites-only restaurants and stayed with a local black family instead of at the team hotel.

Rickey was wrong. After a couple of days of relative peace, the mayor of Sanford, according to sports historian Dave Zirin, was confronted by a "large group of white residents" who "demanded that Robinson… be run out of town." Capitulating, the mayor informed the Royals that Robinson would not be allowed to join them on the field. "Rumors spread," according to Robinson's biographer, Arnold Rampersad, "that a mob of angry whites was about to march on the home where he and [his wife] Rachel were staying." Rickey, concerned for Robinson's life, sent the Robinsons to Daytona Beach, then relocated the entire team there.

Robinson's daughter Sharon, born four years after the episode, carried the family memory. "The Robinsons," she wrote in *Promises to Keep* (2004), her own biography of her father, "were run out of Sanford, Florida with threats of violence."

"There's a lot of things that give you the blues, that give me the blues, that give any man the blues," John Lee Hooker told blues scholar Paul Oliver in *Conversations with the Blues* (1965). "It's somewhere down the line that you have been hurt some place.… My mother, my daddy and my stepfather, they told me these things and I know that they must have went through those things themselves. And so when you gets the feelin' it's not only what happened to you—it's what happened to your foreparents and other people. And that's what makes the blues."

Zimmerman was just doing his job as Neighborhood Watch coordinator. He had once been a civil rights activist. The Twin Lakes community was under siege. Most of the suspects were black males. Zimmerman was courteous and helpful to his neighbors—when he recognized them as his neighbors. All those things were true.

But he made a fatal mistake. A misjudgment. He was driving slowly behind a young Twin Lakes visitor, son of his neighbor's fiancée, when it occurred. He called the dispatcher at the Sanford PD:

> "Hey, we've had some break-ins in my neighborhood and there's a real suspicious guy, uh, Retreat View Circle... This guy looks like he's up to no good or he's on drugs or something. It's raining and he's just walking around, looking about."

> "...Now he's staring at me."

> "...Yeah, now he's coming toward me."

> "...He's got his hands in his waistband. And he's a black male."

> "...Something's wrong with him. Yep, he's coming to check me out. He's got something in his hands. I don't know what his deal is."

> "...These assholes, they always get away."

The Twin Lakes visitor told Rachel Jeantel, his friend on the phone, that he was being followed by a "creepy-ass cracker."

Trayvon wasn't innocent. He was rough. That was a key element of his self-conception. He was No Limit Nigga: a chronic truant, a weed smoker and fan of purple drank, a guy who liked to fight with his fists and elbows and brag about making people bleed. Zimmerman might have been right about the drugs, although the evidence was sketchy. Trayvon could have smoked a blunt between the time he left the convenience store and the time he walked back into Twin Lakes, roughly half an hour later—although the toxicology report found trace levels of THC far lower than one would have expected if that were the case.

But Zimmerman was mistaken about Trayvon's motives. Trayvon wasn't looking to commit a burglary that evening, regardless of what he may have done on some other occasion. He wasn't about to commit a criminal act. He was just walking back home to Miss Brandy's townhouse through the dark, under the streetlights, chatting with a girl, enjoying the cool damp night, wandering a little, taking his time.

And now some guy in a car, a white guy, was following him and eyeballing him like he was a fucking criminal.

That's why he got pissed off. And he did get pissed off. Because he wasn't doing anything wrong. And he was tired of this shit. That's what I'd suddenly figured out: his sense of justice was offended. He was just trying to be free, to feel free. And now this.

Or *thought* I'd figured out. But was I right? Or was I inventing the Trayvon I needed him to be? Were we all doing that?

You have seen how a man was made a slave; you shall see how a slave was made a man. Frederick Douglass was tired of being a slave. So he fought back against the slave-breaker, Covey. Shaun saw a YouTube video about this. He told me about it later. I knew the story well and always found it inspiring.

"I seized Covey hard by the throat," Douglass wrote, "and, as I did so, I rose. He held on to me, and I to him. My resistance was so entirely unexpected, that Covey seemed taken all aback. He trembled like a leaf. This gave me assurance, and I held him uneasy, causing the blood to run where I touched him with the ends of my fingers."

They fought for two hours in the middle of the barn. Douglass whooped his ass. Nobody had a concealed handgun back then.

"Mister Zimmerman was wrong to pursue," said Charles Barkley, "he was racial profiling, but I think Trayvon Martin—God rest his soul—I think he did flip the switch and started beating the hell out of Mister Zimmerman."

Zimmerman's failure was summed up in one sentence: "These assholes, they always get away."

The test of a first-rate intelligence is the ability to hold two opposed ideas in tension. For example: My community has experienced a crime wave in which young black males have played a major role, *and*, precisely because I'm inclined by this collective experience to be suspicious of people who fall into that category, I need to remain cool, dispassionate, and objective. I need to collect information and swing slightly behind the beat rather than jumping to conclusions.

It may have been true that the burglary suspects at Twin Lakes tended to be black and often got away. But the leap from that fact to the incorporation of Trayvon into "these" and "they" and "assholes" was unjustified. This failure of intelligence, a failure to hold two opposed ideas in tension—a failure even to entertain the second idea—wasn't prosecutable as a hate crime. But it was still a failure. Zimmerman flunked the test. Trayvon died as a result. That is a terrible thing, a tragic waste of a young man's life. People were right to get upset. But Trayvon, too, played a role in provoking his own death, after Zimmerman's critical failure of judgment, and *that* is a tragedy. Two opposed ideas. If we're willing to do the work, holding those ideas in tension, we can learn from what happened.

This is what I will tell our son.

I will also tell him: if somebody stares at you like you're a criminal just because he doesn't like the way you look, I won't blame you for eyeballing him right back, circling his car, or running away. Get as pissed off as you want in the privacy of your own mind. But please don't double back a minute or two later and try to beat him up. Do your best to avoid people like that. Live to fight another day, another way. Lag a little behind the beat and keep on swinging.

Hands Up, Don't Shoot

When an unarmed black teenager named Michael Brown was shot dead on the streets of Ferguson, Missouri, by a white cop, Darren Wilson, on August 9, 2014, when angry protests sponsored by Black Lives Matter poured onto the streets and rocked Ferguson for a full week, drawing live feeds from the cable networks, anyone would be forgiven for feeling that America was coming apart. The revolution was being televised; the fires were burning. Straw metaphors abounded: the straw that broke the camel's back; the last straw. Rodney King's plea in the midst of the 1992 Los Angeles uprising—"Can we all get along?"—sounded as quaint these days as an aging Princeton man in a straw boater saying, "Twenty-three skidoo." Nobody was interested in getting along.

Sherrie and I were keeping hope alive within our family circle; the beloved community we'd created there was never seriously tested. The Velvet Ditch, as Oxford was nicknamed, had helped insulate us from the turmoil, as had *How to Train Your Dragon, Cloudy with a Chance of Meatballs, Despicable Me,* all those big-screen distractions from the cable-news dynamo. But it had recently become clear that Shaun, now eight, would be coming of age in a far more troubled America than we'd hoped on that astonishing evening back in November 2008 when, as a two-year-old, he'd slumbered in his crib while we watched America's first black president take the stage in Chicago's Grant Park. "Yes we can!" had been Obama's battle cry, and ours. His dream of a more perfect union had faded badly in the aftermath of Newtown and Trayvon Martin. Now it had been blown out of the sky.

As the Michael Brown story emerged through the range of media outlets I attended to, the broad outlines felt familiar—so familiar that I refused to take sides, chastened by the way the Trayvon Martin story had been distorted early on. A longtime *New Yorker* subscriber, I was a fan of Amy Davidson Sorkin; her first take, published two days after Brown's death, was typical of the moment, if more restrained than many:

> Michael Brown didn't die in the dark. He was eighteen years old, walking down a street in Ferguson, Missouri, from his apartment to his grandmother's, at 2:15 on a bright Saturday afternoon. He was, for a young man, exactly where he should be—among other things, days away from his first college classes. A policeman stopped him; it's not clear why. People in the neighborhood have told reporters that they remember what happened next as a series of movements: the officer, it seemed to them, trying to put Brown into a car; Brown running with his hands in the air; the policeman shooting; Brown falling. The next morning, Jon Belmar, the police chief of St. Louis County, which covers Ferguson, was asked, at a press conference, how many times Brown had been shot. Belmar said that he wasn't sure: "more than just a couple of times, but not much more." When counting bullets, "just" and "not much more" are odd words to choose.
>
> 2:15 in the afternoon is not a time when you hide in your house. Among the people who ran out onto the street, quickly forming a crowd as the sound of gunshots

died down, were Brown's mother, Lesley McSpadden, and his stepfather, Louis Head, who were distraught. Head held up a sign that said that his child had been "executed"; someone took a picture. More came when they heard on social media what had happened. "The police just shot someone dead in front of my crib yo," someone using the handle @theepharaoh tweeted. "Dude was running and the cops just shot him. I saw him die bruh." (The feed, with other social-media witness accounts was collected and published by the St. Louis Post-Dispatch.) Brown's body was not removed from the street for hours; people saw that, too, as well as pictures of a tall SWAT vehicle on the street and dozens of officers.

Belmar, in his press conference on Sunday morning, told a story that involved Brown walking with another young man when the door of a police car they were passing opened and, for some reason, one of them forced his way into the police car and tried to get the officer's gun. Brown, though, was apparently shot more than ten yards from the car, and the police have said that he was unarmed. The officer was not identified. Belmar acknowledged that the police were still trying to work out what, exactly, had happened. For all the daylight on the scene—in part because this happened to a teen-ager walking in the open—there is a lot we don't know, and a lot we might yet learn. But the police story, that morning, was insufficient.

One thing people did learn Sunday was more about Brown, who was described as gentle, committed to sports and to his friends, working hard to make up classes when he fell behind, and excited about starting college. All of this added to the anger; people marched, with their hands in the air, chanting "Don't shoot me." Brown's mother, throughout the day, came out on the street near where he was killed. "I know they killed my son," she said, according to the Post-Dispatch. "This was wrong and it was cold-hearted." There was a vigil for him that evening.

"One way or the other," Sorkin added, "this happens too often to young men who look like Brown, or like Trayvon Martin, or, as President Obama once put it, like a son he might have had."

A gentle, unarmed black teen filled with promise had been shot dead by a white cop in full view of the black community. A tragic and infuriating story, one worthy of the rage it produced. But was it true, as told? Or would other salient facts emerge, forcing a reconsideration, a deeper reckoning? Once again I found myself combining the roles of concerned father and skeptical scholar, determined to see the facts clearly, arbitrate them dispassionately, and extract usable truth. Even as I held back from investing in the emergent narrative, I was aware of the downside risk this posture entailed, which was political quietism, a failure to rise to the moment's moral demands. King had harshly critiqued white moderates in "Letter from Birmingham Jail" for precisely this reason. Was there no middle ground? No space for a liberal centrist who followed the evidence where it led? I wrestled with this paradox, unable to resolve it. All you could finally do was love your family and do the work you were put here to do.

The riots in Ferguson continued as live coverage on CNN and MSNBC inflamed outrage. Black Lives Matter entered the fray, giving the group mainstream recognition overnight. Activists DeRay Mckesson and Shaun King worked Twitter as protests flooded the streets. The phrase "Hands up, don't shoot" exploded into public consciousness, anchored in the claim by witnesses that Brown had made that gesture in the face of Officer Wilson's gun and been shot dead anyway. "If you're angry, throw your arms up," the Reverend Al Sharpton told protestors. "If you want justice, throw your arms up. Because that's the sign Michael was using. He had a surrender sign. That's the sign you have to deal with. Use the sign he last showed. We want answers why that last sign was not respected."

Two days after the shooting, Obama's justice department, led once again by Eric Holder, sent in the FBI, headed by James Comey, to interview witnesses and collect evidence. The DOJ initiated two simultaneous investigations: one focused on the Brown/Wilson encounter and the question of whether Wilson had violated Brown's civil rights by using force in an objectively unreasonable way (for example, by shooting him when his hands were up, or in the back when he was running away), a second and much broader "patterns and practices" investigation looking for racial bias in the words and actions of the Ferguson police department itself.

Although riots and protests subsided after the first week, race relations in Ferguson remained poisonous as the DOJ's twin investigations simmered along. On November 24, when the grand jury decided not to indict Officer Wilson, riots and protests erupted once again. "Burn this bitch down!" Michael Brown's stepfather, Louis Head, told a crowd in front of City Hall. Twelve buildings and two St. Louis County police cars went up in flames that night.

By the time Londoners assembled en masse two days later to chant "Hands up, don't shoot" in solidarity with the Ferguson protestors, that phrase had already become an international slogan of resistance. As a contributor to the *Feminist Wire* had noted a month earlier, "Since Michael Brown's murder, we've seen photos of young black men and women in Ferguson, Tibetan monks from India, black Harvard law students, school children in Missouri, young people in Moscow, and a church congregation in New York City with their hands up. Some stand, some kneel, some bend their heads, some stare straight ahead. Each one symbolizes a bodily act of solidarity with Michael Brown and victims of oppression of state-over-citizen around the world."

On March 4, 2015, the Department of Justice released two reports, one on Wilson's shooting of Brown and one on the Ferguson police department. I neglected those primary documents at the time, although I went back later, downloaded them, and read them closely. But I paid attention to what one pundit, Jonathan Capehart, had to say about them. Capehart, a gay black columnist at the *Washington Post*, was a familiar progressive voice on MSNBC; one might have assumed, given the company he kept, that he would spin the bad news contained in the first report in the way that talking heads do when the facts are against them.

He did the opposite. He told a complex truth with the help of an incendiary headline: "'Hands Up Don't Shoot' was built on a lie." It was a brave column, not just because it was sure to incur the wrath of those who had heavily invested in the prevailing narrative, but because the truth it told—the truth told by Obama's and Holder's DOJ—was sure to be misleadingly framed and then applauded, as it was, by Fox News pundits, as a simple, one-dimensional retraction, a mea culpa that let sneering conservative doubters off the hook. It did nothing of the sort. But I knew that Capehart would take that double hit, and his willingness to do so for the sake of journalistic integrity was inspiring. He passed the test. He held two opposed ideas in tension. His bravery was enabled by Obama's and Holder's DOJ and the careful, detailed investigative work they produced, an object lesson in procedural justice that Capehart summarized with justified confidence.

There were two top-line conclusions drawn by the DOJ reports. First, Officer Darren Wilson, whose account of the incident proved to be unimpeachable, was justified in using deadly force to defend himself against Michael Brown. Second, the Ferguson police department in which he worked was racist, predatory, and morally bankrupt.

It was only by appreciating the gravity and scope of that department-wide malfeasance that you could appreciate why many in Ferguson's black community had no trouble seeing Officer Wilson as a violent, lying predator who had executed one of their own in cold blood—shooting him in the back as he was running away, then shooting him in the head as he stood with hands raised. The problem, as the DOJ had discovered and as Capehart reported, is that that narrative, the community's aggrieved view of the encounter blown up into an international meme, wasn't true. It was based on a lie told multiple times by Witness 101, Brown's friend Dorian Johnson, which was repeated and embraced by many others. It was rebutted by the physical evidence, including ballistics, DNA, and three autopsies, and by a careful assessment of conflicting witness accounts.

But without understanding just how ruthlessly the black people of Ferguson had been abused by "their" police force prior to the shooting, you couldn't understand the depth of rage that had instantly transformed Brown's death into myth—a myth that wasn't, in fact, based on a lie, but on a deep reservoir of shared experience.

The Ferguson PD was the textbook definition of systemic racism. But this damning fact wasn't the whole story.

Begin with the primal scene. A white police officer is cruising the streets of Ferguson, Missouri in an SUV and spies a pair of young black men walking down the middle of the street, single file along the double yellow line. The officer, Darren Wilson, pulls up alongside the younger men, Michael Brown and Dorian Johnson, and asks them to move to the sidewalk because cars were "trying to pass them." Is this true? Is it a reasonable request, or is it harassment and over-policing of the sort that black people in Ferguson and many parts of America were familiar with? Was this the last straw for Big Mike? Did Wilson say, "Get the fuck on the sidewalk," as Johnson claimed, or did Big Mike suddenly erupt with, "Fuck what you have to say," as Wilson claimed? None of this could be corroborated by other witnesses, except for the two-man walk along the double yellow line. But it all starts with that primal scene: a white cop, a police car, and young black men.

Trymaine Lee, a Pulitzer Prize–winning young black journalist and correspondent for MSNBC, was a familiar face and voice in cable news's saturation coverage of Ferguson, filing more than sixty stories between August and December 2014. Two years earlier, his reports for *Huffington Post's Black Voices* and appearances on Keith Olbermann's

MSNBC show had helped establish the Trayvon-as-innocent narrative. Lee was a good example of an advocacy journalist who, drawing on his own experience as a black man surveilled by the police, found it impossible to suspend judgment until all the evidence was in. The stories he filed pointedly sided with those in the community who saw Wilson's shooting of Brown as an inexcusable last straw, interpreting each known detail in a way that was most prejudicial to Wilson and most favorable to Brown. His strength as an advocacy journalist was his weakness as an arbiter of procedural justice. His commitment to social justice led him to unearth, in dozens of stories, the same racist policing practices that the second DOJ report ended up substantiating, but that commitment also blinded him to the possibility, as the DOJ's first report established, that Brown was the aggressor and Wilson was justified in shooting him.

Although unable to hold those two opposed ideas in tension, Lee evoked his lived experience of black precarity—an experience at the heart of the fatal Brown-Wilson encounter—with stark eloquence. "Being an African-American in this country," he told NPR's *Morning Edition*,

> experiencing what it is like to be black in this nation I think certainly gives you a perspective, and different vantage point than other people. We know what it's like to be stopped and harassed. We know that feeling of the police pulling up behind you with those flashing lights, and being concerned about how this encounter might end. You're always feeling that the eyes are watching you. It's almost like there's some sort of guilt of something that you can't necessarily put your finger on. But it's almost like there's this assumption of guilt; you're guilty of something simply for being who you are.

Only justice can stop a curse, I will tell my son, sounding like a broken record to myself as I think ahead to that moment. Truth be told, I'm tired of Alice Walker's fatuous mantra. But I believe in the truth it contains. The curse will continue until we live in a country where the presumption of innocence extends to all. None of us deserves to bear the stigma of the group we belong to—even when, as in the case of Darren Wilson and the Ferguson Police Department, the group we belong to is guilty and deserving of punishment.

Shortly before Officer Wilson encountered Brown and Johnson, the two young men had left a nearby convenience store, where Brown had stolen a package of cigarillos and shoved the clerk who tried to stop him. A later toxicology report showed that Brown had THC, marijuana's active ingredient, in his bloodstream and was "impaired" at the time of his death.

Brown's family and others invested in the "Hands up, don't shoot" narrative viewed anybody who invoked these facts as engaging in character assassination. Neither Brown's partisans nor those determined to view him as a thug were interested in making a space for his complexity—allowing him, for the sake of argument, to be somebody who was gentle with friends and kin, excited about starting college, happy to get high and engage in petty shoplifting with a pal to show he was still down with the hood, and pissed off at a baby-faced white cop who dared to mess with him over something as chickenshit as jaywalking.

What helped Obama's and Holder's DOJ determine that Officer Wilson had told the truth about his encounter with Brown wasn't just a careful evaluation of the physical evidence, but the testimony of half a dozen black eyewitnesses, male and female. Some of these witnesses were reluctant to go on the record; virtually all expressed a fear that others in the black community would censure them for corroborating Wilson's account and disputing the narrative of murder-by-cop that so many in the community were embracing. Nevertheless, they told the truth—a truth that aligned with the physical evidence, with Wilson's account, and with each other's accounts.

They are the unsung heroes of Ferguson. They, more than anybody, knew how badly the Ferguson PD had abused the community. But they also knew what they'd seen with their own eyes, and they refused to allow Wilson to be punished for his department's sins. I came to this realization in the summer of 2020, after downloading and annotating the eighty-six-page "Department of Justice Report Regarding the Criminal Investigation into the Shooting Death of Michael Brown by Ferguson, Missouri Police Officer Darren Wilson." Many people who clearly had no idea what was in the report had strong opinions about Brown's death and Wilson's purported malfeasance. "Listen to black voices!" was their cry. If you actually did that, the narrative retailed by Al Sharpton, Trymaine Lee, and BLM fell apart:

> At the time of his [Wilson's] interview, federal prosecutors and agents were aware of the autopsy, DNA, and ballistics results, as detailed below. Wilson's account was consistent with those results, and consistent with the accounts of other independent eyewitnesses, whose accounts were also consistent with the physical evidence. Wilson's statements were consistent with each other in all material ways, and would not be subject to effective impeachment for inconsistencies or deviation from the physical evidence. **Therefore, in analyzing all of the evidence, federal prosecutors found Wilson's account to be credible....**
>
> Autopsy results and bullet trajectory skin from Brown's palm on the outside of the SUV door as well as Brown's DNA on the inside of the driver's door corroborate Wilson's account that during the struggle, Brown used his right hand to grab and attempt to control Wilson's gun...There is no credible evidence to disprove Wilson's account of what went on inside the SUV....**The autopsy results confirm that Wilson did not shoot Brown in the back as he was running away because there were no entrance wounds to Brown's back....**
>
> **Several witnesses stated that Brown appeared to pose a physical threat to Wilson as he moved toward Wilson.** According to these witnesses, who are corroborated

by blood evidence in the roadway, as Brown continued to move toward Wilson, **Wilson fired at Brown in what appeared to be self-defense and stopped firing once Brown fell to the ground**. Wilson stated that he feared Brown would again assault him because of Brown's conduct at the SUV and because as Brown moved toward him, Wilson saw Brown reach his right hand under his t-shirt into what appeared to be his waistband. There is no evidence upon which prosecutors can rely to disprove Wilson's stated subjective belief that he feared for his safety....

While credible witnesses gave varying accounts of exactly what Brown was doing with his hands as he moved toward Wilson—i.e., balling them, holding them out, or pulling up his pants up—and varying accounts of how he was moving—i.e., "charging," moving in "slow motion," or "running"—**they all establish that Brown was moving toward Wilson when Wilson shot him. Although some witnesses state that Brown held his hands up at shoulder level with his palms facing outward for a brief moment, these same witnesses describe Brown then dropping his hands and "charging" at Wilson....**

§**Witness 102 is a 27-year-old bi-racial male.** Witness 102 told investigators that **he knew "for sure that [Brown's] hands were not above his head."** Rather, Brown made some type of movement similar to pulling his pants up or a shoulder shrug, and then "charged" at Wilson. It was only then that Wilson fired five or six shots at Brown.

Witness 102 did not stay on Canfield Drive long after the shooting, but rather started to leave the area after about five minutes because he felt uncomfortable. According to Witness 102, crowds of people had begun to gather, wrongly claiming the police shot Brown for no reason and that he had his hands up in surrender. Two black women approached Witness 102, mobile phones set to record, asking him to recount what he had witnessed. Witness 102 responded that they would not like what he had to say. **The women responded with racial slurs, calling him names like "white motherfucker."**

§**Witness 103 is a 58-year-old black male.** Witness 103 is a convicted felon. Witness 103 expressed concerns because **there were signs in the neighborhood of Canfield Drive stating "snitches get stitches."** Therefore, he agreed to be interviewed only on the condition of confidentiality…. When Witness 103 stopped his truck on Canfield Drive, although he did not see what led up to it, **he saw Brown punching Wilson at least three times in the facial area, through the open driver's window of the SUV.**

§Witness 104 is a 26-year-old biracial female….

According to Witness 104, she was leaning over, talking to her sister, Witness 107, when she heard two gunshots. She looked out the front window and saw Brown at the driver's window of Wilson's SUV. Witness 104 knew that Brown's arms were inside the SUV, but she could not see what Brown and Wilson were doing because Brown's body was blocking her view. Witness 104 saw Brown run from the SUV, followed by Wilson, who "hopped" out of the SUV and ran after him while yelling "stop, stop, stop." **Wilson did not fire his gun as Brown ran from him. Brown then turned around and "for a second" began to raise his hands** as though he may have considered surrendering, but then quickly "balled up in fists" in a running position and "charged" at Wilson. Witness 104 described it as a "tackle run," explaining that Brown "wasn't going to stop." Wilson fired his gun only as Brown charged at him, backing up as Brown came toward him. Witness 104 explained that there were three separate volleys of shots. Each time, Brown ran toward Wilson, Wilson fired, Brown paused, Wilson stopped firing, and then Brown charged again. The pattern continued until Brown fell to the ground, "smashing" his face upon impact. Wilson did not fire while Brown momentarily had his hands up. Witness 104 explained that it took some time for Wilson to fire, adding that she "would have fired sooner."

§Witness 105 is a 50-year-old black female....

Witness 105 explained that Brown put his hands up "for a brief moment," and then turned around and made a shuffling movement. Wilson told Brown to "get down," but Brown did not comply. Instead, Brown put his hands down "in a running position." Witness 105 could not tell whether Brown was "charging" at Wilson or whether his plan was to run past Wilson, but either way, Brown was running toward Wilson. According to Witness 105, Wilson only shot at Brown when Brown was moving toward him....

When Witness 105 contacted SLCPD detectives, she was reluctant to identify herself and ultimately met with them in a library parking lot. She explained that she was coming forward because in speaking with her neighbors, she realized that what they believed had happened was inconsistent with what actually

happened. She further explained that she had not been paying attention to media accounts, and had been unaware of the inaccuracies being reported.

§**Witness 108 is a 74-year-old black male** who claimed to have witnessed the shooting, stated that it was justified, but repeatedly refused to give formal statements to law enforcement for fear of reprisal should the Canfield Drive neighborhood find out that his account corroborated Wilson....

During the initial canvass of the crime scene on August 9, 2014, in the hours after the shooting, SLCPD detectives approached Witness 108, who was sitting in his car on Canfield Drive. They asked if he witnessed what happened. **Witness 108 refused to identify himself or give details, but told detectives that the police officer was "in the right" and "did what he had to do,"** and the statements made by people in the apartment complex were inaccurate. Both state and federal investigators later attempted to locate and interview Witness 108, who repeatedly expressed fear in coming forward. **During the investigators' attempts to find Witness 108, another individual reported that two days after the shooting, Witness 108 confided in her that he "would have fucking shot that boy, too."** In saying so, Witness 108 mimicked an aggressive stance with his hands out in front of him, as though he was about to charge. **SLCPD detectives finally tracked down Witness 108 at a local repair shop, where he reluctantly explained that Wilson told Brown to "stop" or "get down" at least ten times, but instead Brown "charged" at Wilson....**

Witness 108 refused to provide additional details to either county or federal authorities, citing community sentiment to support a "hands up" surrender narrative as his reason to remain silent. He explained that he would rather go to jail than testify before the county grand jury.

Integrity means telling the truth even in the face of community censure, I'll tell my son, which is why these witnesses deserve our admiration. But discretion in the service of self-preservation is a good idea, too. Live to fight another day.

As for the "hands up" surrender narrative, I'll tell him that angry people, people long abused by those in power, sometimes make mistakes, repeat untruths, and evolve stories that don't correspond with the facts. Black people in Ferguson were sick and tired of how they'd been treated by the overwhelmingly white police force. Their rage was as legitimate as the abuse was illegitimate, and they were justified in raising hell.

Only by taking to the streets and burning Ferguson did they ensure that the entire nation—and Obama's Justice Department—would take their abuse seriously and lay it bare in an official report so that the rest of the world could appreciate what they'd been dealing with for many years. The phrase "Hands up, don't shoot," although misleadingly applied to the encounter between Brown and Wilson, perfectly expressed the community's aggrieved desire not to be preyed upon by the men who were supposed to be protecting them. Had Obama not been in charge, had Holder not been his attorney general, had civil rights not been a top priority of the Obama administration, the truth would never have been known.

"In a scathing report issued in March [2015]," reported the *New York Times*, "the Justice Department called on Ferguson to overhaul its criminal justice system, declaring that the city had engaged in so many constitutional violations that they could be corrected only by abandoning its entire approach to policing, retraining its employees and establishing new oversight. The report described a city that used its police and courts as moneymaking ventures, a place where officers stopped and handcuffed people without probable cause, hurled racial slurs, used stun guns without provocation, and treated anyone as suspicious merely for questioning police tactics."

Although I had learned by then to greet the mainstream media's representations with reflexive skepticism, anyone who takes the time to work their way through the report will find it not just persuasive but infuriating, a damning indictment of police malfeasance:

> Ferguson's law enforcement practices are shaped by the City's focus on revenue rather than by public safety needs. This emphasis on revenue has compromised the institutional character of Ferguson's police department, contributing to a pattern of unconstitutional policing, and has also shaped its municipal court, leading to procedures that raise due process concerns and inflict unnecessary harm on members of the Ferguson community. Further, Ferguson's police and municipal court practices both reflect and exacerbate existing racial bias, including racial stereotypes. **Ferguson's own data establish clear racial disparities that adversely impact African Americans. The evidence shows that discriminatory intent is part of the reason for these disparities.** Over time, Ferguson's police and municipal court practices have sown deep mistrust between parts of the community and the police department, undermining law enforcement legitimacy among African Americans in particular....
>
> **Many officers appear to see some residents, especially those who live in Ferguson's predominantly African American neighborhoods, less as constituents to be protected than as potential offenders and sources of revenue....**

Officers expect and demand compliance even when they lack legal authority. They are inclined to interpret the exercise of free-speech rights as unlawful disobedience, innocent movements as physical threats, indications of mental or physical illness as belligerence. Police supervisors and leadership do too little to ensure that officers act in accordance with law and policy, and rarely respond meaningfully to civilian complaints of officer misconduct. **The result is a pattern of stops without reasonable suspicion and arrests without probable cause in violation of the Fourth Amendment; infringement on free expression, as well as retaliation for protected expression, in violation of the First Amendment; and excessive force in violation of the Fourth Amendment.**

African Americans experience disparate impact in nearly every aspect of Ferguson's law enforcement system. Despite making up 67% of the population, African Americans accounted for 85% of FPD's traffic stops, 90% of FPD's citations, and 93% of FPD's arrests from 2012 to 2014. Other statistical disparities, set forth in detail below, show that in Ferguson:

§**African Americans are 2.07 times more likely to be searched during a vehicular stop but are 26% less likely to have contraband found on them during a search.** They are 2.00 times more likely to receive a citation and 2.37 times more likely to be arrested following a vehicular stop.

§African Americans have force used against them at disproportionately high rates, accounting for 88% of all cases from 2010 to August 2014 in which an FPD officer reported using force. **In all 14 uses of force** involving a canine bite for which we have information about the race of the person bitten, the person was African American.

§African Americans are more likely to receive multiple citations during a single incident, receiving four or more citations on 73 occasions between October 2012 and July 2014, whereas non-African Americans received four or more citations only twice during that period.

§African Americans account for 95% of Manner of Walking charges; 94% of all Fail to Comply charges; 92% of all Resisting Arrest charges; 92% of all Peace Disturbance charges; and 89% of all Failure to Obey charges....

Our investigation indicates that this disproportionate burden on African Americans cannot be explained by any difference in the rate at which people of different races violate the law. Rather, our investigation has revealed that these disparities occur, at least in part, because of unlawful bias against and stereotypes about African Americans. We have found substantial evidence of racial bias among police and court staff in Ferguson.

The content of these communications is unequivocally derogatory, dehumanizing, and demonstrative of impermissible bias....

[All of these Ferguson officials] are current employees, almost without exception [these emails are sent] through their official City of Ferguson email accounts, and apparently sent during work hours. These email exchanges involved several police and court

supervisors, including FPD supervisors and commanders. The following emails are illustrative:

§A November 2008 email stated that President Barack Obama would not be President for very long because **"what black man holds a steady job for four years."**

§A March 2010 email mocked African Americans through speech and familial stereotypes, using a story involving child support. One line from the email read: **"I be so glad that dis be my last child support payment!** Month after month, year after year, all dose payments!"

§An April 2011 email depicted President Barack Obama as a chimpanzee.

§A May 2011 email stated: "An African-American woman in New Orleans was admitted into the hospital for a pregnancy termination. Two weeks later she received a check for $5,000. She phoned the hospital to ask who it was from. The hospital said, 'Crimestoppers.'"

§A June 2011 email described a man seeking to obtain "welfare" for his dogs because they are "mixed in color, unemployed, lazy, can't speak English and have no frigging clue who their Daddies are."

§An October 2011 email included **a photo of a bare-chested group of dancing women, apparently in Africa, with the caption, "Michelle Obama's High School Reunion."**

This documentary evidence of explicit racial bias is consistent with reports from community members indicating that some FPD officers use racial epithets in dealing with members of the public. We spoke with one African-American man who, in August 2014, had an argument in his apartment to which FPD officers responded, and was immediately pulled out of the apartment by force. **After telling the officer, "you don't have a reason to lock me up," he claims the officer responded: "Nigger, I can find something to lock you up on." When the man responded, "good luck with that," the officer slammed his face into the wall, and after the man fell to the floor, the officer said, "don't pass out motherfucker because I'm not carrying you to my car."**

…FPD officers routinely conduct stops that have little relation to public safety and a questionable basis in law. FPD officers routinely issue multiple citations during a single stop, often for the same violation. Issuing three or four charges in one stop is not uncommon in Ferguson. Officers sometimes write six, eight, or, in at least one instance, fourteen citations for a single encounter. Indeed, **officers told us that some compete to see who can issue the largest number of citations during a single stop**.

In October 2012, police officers pulled over an African-American man who had lived in Ferguson for 16 years, claiming that his passenger-side brake light was broken. The driver happened to have replaced the light recently and knew it to be functioning properly. Nonetheless, **according to the man's written complaint, one officer stated, "let's see how many tickets you're going to get,"** while a second officer tapped his Electronic Control Weapon ("ECW") on the roof of the man's car. The officers wrote the man a citation for "tail light/reflector/license plate light out." They refused to let the man show them that his car's equipment was in order, warning him, "don't you get out of that car until you get to your house." **The man, who believed he had been racially profiled, was so upset that he went to the police station that night to show a sergeant that his brakes and license plate light worked.**

While the record demonstrates a pattern of stops that are improper from the beginning, it also exposes encounters that start as constitutionally defensible but quickly cross the line. For example, in the summer of 2012, an officer detained a 32-year-old African-American man who was sitting in his car cooling off after playing basketball. The officer arguably had grounds to stop and question the man, since his windows appeared more deeply tinted than permitted under Ferguson's code. **Without cause, the officer went on to accuse the man of being a pedophile, prohibit the man from using his cell phone, order the man out of his car for a pat-down despite having no reason to believe he was armed, and ask to search his car. When the man refused, citing his constitutional rights, the officer reportedly pointed a gun at his head, and arrested him.** The officer charged the man with eight different counts, including making a false declaration for initially providing the short form of his first name (e.g., "Mike" instead of "Michael") and an address that, although legitimate, differed from the one on his license. The officer also charged the man both with having an expired operator's license, and with having no operator's license in possession. **The man told us he lost his job as a contractor with the federal government as a result of the charges.**

FPD engages in a pattern of excessive force in violation of the Fourth Amendment. Many officers are quick to escalate encounters with subjects they perceive to be disobeying their orders or resisting arrest. They have come to rely on ECWs, specifically Tasers®, where less force—or no force at all—would do. **They also release canines on unarmed subjects unreasonably and before attempting to use force less likely to cause injury.** Some incidents of excessive force result from stops or arrests that have no basis in law. Others are punitive and retaliatory...**Ferguson's pattern of using excessive force disproportionately harms African-American members of the community. The overwhelming majority of force—almost 90%—is used against African Americans.**

Our investigation showed that the disconnect and distrust between much of Ferguson's African-American community and FPD is caused largely by years of the unlawful and unfair law enforcement practices by Ferguson's police department and municipal court described above. In the documents we reviewed, the meetings we observed and participated in, and in the hundreds of conversations Civil Rights Division staff had with residents of Ferguson and the surrounding area, **many residents, primarily African-American residents, described being belittled, disbelieved, and treated with little regard for their legal rights by the Ferguson Police Department.** One white individual who has lived in Ferguson for 48 years told us that it feels like Ferguson's police and court system is "designed to bring a black man down...[there are] no second chances." We heard from African-American residents who told us of Ferguson's "long history of targeting blacks for harassment and degrading treatment," and who described the steps they take to avoid this—from taking routes to work that skirt Ferguson to moving out of state. **An African-American minister of a church in**

a nearby community told us that he doesn't allow his two sons to drive through Ferguson out of "fear that they will be targeted for arrest."

We also reviewed many instances in which FPD officers arrested [African American] individuals who sought to care for loved ones who had been hurt. In one instance from May 2014, for example, a man rushed to the scene of a car accident involving his girlfriend, who was badly injured and bleeding profusely when he arrived. He approached and tried to calm her. When officers arrived they treated him rudely, according to the man, telling him to move away from his girlfriend, which he did not want to do. They then immediately proceeded to handcuff and arrest him, which, officers assert, he resisted. EMS and other officers were not on the scene during this arrest, so **the accident victim remained unattended, bleeding from her injuries, while officers were arresting the boyfriend.** Officers charged the man with five municipal code violations (Resisting Arrest, Disorderly Conduct, Assault on an Officer, Obstructing Government Operations, and Failure to Comply) and had his vehicle towed and impounded.

My nephew Jamarrick was visiting Oxford from Dallas for the weekend; we were relaxing in the living room, chatting. Jamarrick—Jay, as his friends call him—is a dark, stocky man in his mid-thirties, shorter than me. His mother is Sherrie's twin sister. He speaks with a drawl, goes to church on Sundays, and, when he's truly tickled by something, giggles. For as long as I've known him, he's held down a full-time job with the Boy Scouts and a second job at Walmart or some other big-box retailer. He's one of the hardest-working guys I know.

We were talking about cars. I was starting to think differently, I told him, about my daily ritual of jumping in the car without a driver's license and driving to the beginning of the South Campus Rail Trail, five minutes away, to take my morning run. I'd always assumed that if I were stopped, I'd probably get a summons and then be given the chance to show up at the Oxford police station later in the day, show my license, and get the summons mitigated or dropped. I'd heard from one of my white colleagues that this was how things worked. It never occurred to me that driving license-less like that could result in any sort of real trouble. Not in a small town where I was a college professor.

But lately it had occurred to me that if I were black—one of my black colleagues at the university, for example—I might not be quite so cavalier about leaving my license at home during that daily jaunt. And the moment I thought about things in that way, I came up against the phrase "white privilege." It was a term I disliked, in part because a younger generation of social justice warriors had recently begun tossing it around sneeringly and indiscriminately, as though whiteness, especially in combination with maleness, were some sort of toxic stigma that got you thrown out of the party, and in part because what they considered white privilege struck me as something more like full citizenship.

Every citizen *should* be able to jump in the car in the morning without their license, it seemed to me, and drive to a nearby trailhead without worrying that disaster could strike if they were stopped. If my black colleagues at Ole Miss didn't have the same blithe confidence in the reasonableness of our local police force as I did, I wanted a world where they could have that confidence. Surely all of us wanted a world where the margin for error was wider rather than narrower; where precarity was a rare thing, not a black thing. I didn't want privilege; I merely wanted whatever legal and customary rights accrued to full citizenship in all relevant contexts, and I wanted every American citizen to enjoy those same rights. My wife, my son, my nephew. Everybody. Surely we could agree on that. Nobody could agree on anything anymore, but at least we could agree on that basic goal. Then we could figure out how to get there.

I shared this train of thought with Jamarrick. I'd rarely talked with him, or with anybody on his side of the family, in a way that explicitly foregrounded race like this, but we were living in a new era, the Black Lives Matter era, so I took that risk.

He listened. He's a mellow guy. Then he told me a story.

A couple of years earlier, he said, he'd been out at a club in Dallas, on the other side of town from where he lived. He was a careful drinker; he'd rationed himself to one drink per hour. At some point, after the third drink, he headed out the door, got in his Crown Vic, and got back on the highway. And he realized all of a sudden that he'd had a little too much to drink.

Rather than driving home, he pulled off the highway and turned into a small parking lot in back of a Target. He wasn't planning on spending the whole night there, just snoozing for a couple of hours, then driving home.

He turned off the engine, made sure the doors were locked, tilted the seat way back.

"I did one more thing before falling out," he said, smiling. "I took my keys out of my pocket and put them on the dashboard, along with my driver's license."

"For the cops," I murmured.

"To reassure the cops," he chuckled. "If they stopped, which they were probably gonna do. A little insurance never hurts. You don't want to be rummaging in your pockets when they're shining a light through the window."

I'd slept in my car a couple of times over the years, once after driving home half-drunk from a downtown blues club. It had never occurred to me to do that.

RECLAMATION

Master Ra's Gifts

Skinny and shirtless on our back porch in the Labor Day heat, hair cropped short, Shaun was brandishing his new blue plastic machine gun with the huge circular drum. It was modeled on the Tommy gun that Al Capone and his gang used to slaughter rival gangs during Prohibition. Shaun was seven at this point, in 2013—the long hot summer of George Zimmerman's acquittal and the birth of Black Lives Matter—and had just entered first grade: our beautiful brown boy, slick as an otter, about to give Mom and Dad a demo. I'd never heard of a Buzz Bee Air Warriors Side Winder Blaster, but then again: when I was his age, we used to pretend forked sticks were guns and make all the shoot-em-up sounds ourselves. Sherrie was handling the home video play-by-play with her iPhone.

"So, Shaun has a new gun that he bought with his money—nineteen dollars, money saved in his bank—and he's gonna demonstrate his new toy. Okay? Ready, set, go!"

Grasping the rear stock with one hand and the sliding front stock with the other, he rapidly fired off shots as the big drum rotated, thirty shots in all, spraying our back porch with orange foam bullets. Every shot made the same loud mechanical *Clack!* He emptied the thing. He spewed. He was already a pro. He shivered and jumped a little after it was all over.

You can hear Sherrie giggling, just before the clip ends. "To Dad's dismay! Alright, dude. Very cool!"

That was the last straw. I knew we needed help. Violence was all around us. Every time you turned on the TV—and I'd become something of a news junkie by that point—there was gun violence. Gabby Giffords, Adam Lanza, Zimmerman and Martin. Sure: it's a *toy* gun. Calm down, Dad. But when I saw what toy guns had become in the hands of corporate America, I knew we needed help. The snake had entered the house. Shaun needed more male role models. He needed *something*.

So we did what many other parents in Oxford, Mississippi, were doing with their kids at that point, which is show up at Master Ra's gym down on University Avenue, the one with the big windows, and sign up for classes in taekwondo. And we got lucky. Because Master Ra is a special man, although it took me a while to figure that out.

Most small towns have a handful of people who hold the whole thing together. Master Ra is one of those people. For the eight years Shaun worked with him, I had no idea that his real name was Sung Ra, or that he had arrived in Oxford as a middle-schooler, an immigrant accompanied by his Korean-born parents, or that he'd graduated from Ole Miss in 2004 with a degree in accounting, or that he'd started his martial arts school that same year. He was just a large, solidly-built, good-looking younger man who had figured out early on something that I'd slowly become aware of, which is that Oxford is crazy about youth sports. Shaun did youth soccer, basketball, and baseball, although he'd never played on away teams. But several of my colleagues had kids who did, and it was a huge commitment of time and money, traveling all over the state. TKD, by contrast, was relatively low cost—$125 a month, two classes a week—and the democratic melting pot was in effect. White, black, Asian, Hispanic, every sort of mixed kid. Boys and girls in the same classes, always. As with band camps, the hierarchy was color-coded, based on belts rather than bands. Newbies had no belt, which made that first belt, the white belt, a big deal.

Master Ra made a lot out of those belt presentation ceremonies. Students and their parents were sucked into the ceremonial element before they realized it, and they enjoyed it more than they expected to. Once Master Ra had called your kid's name and your kid had padded up to the front of the room to join him and a couple of his junior black belts while you were taking photos from the waiting room behind the windows or off to the side of the main room, near the front door, once Master Ra had dropped to his knees, looping and tying that new white belt around your kid's white cotton dobok, they were a champ. They were *in*. They, and you, were part of the great chain of TKD being. All this orchestrated ceremony, with soft music, ritual invocations, and lots of bows, took place in front of the bigger kids and their ascending belt-grades: yellow, orange, green, blue, purple, brown, red, and poom— which was red and black striped, the final stepping stone. Then first-degree black belt, which was a rare thing indeed, but which could and did happen, because one or two black-belted teens, quiet and respectful, worthy of emulation and devoid of false pride, helped run almost every class.

Like all martial arts, taekwondo was a way of channeling and stylizing aggression, disciplining and focusing it rather than spewing it indiscriminately. At the heart of the practice was a fusion of body and spirit, form and philosophy. The big, dramatic, hip-swiveling high kicks caught the kids' attention on Day One; the numbered and increasingly difficult forms, each of which incorporated and deepened the previous form's kicks and punches, were the route to the next colorful belt. But it was the catechism, the five tenets of TKD, that I yearned to see Shaun embrace: courtesy, integrity, perseverance, self-control, and indomitable spirit. The first three were long-term aspirations; the fourth, self-control, was particularly needed in a young man with my son's darting attentions. But indomitable spirit! That was the blues ethos: a survival skill, something that could carry you through life when the setbacks came, which they always did.

In 1967, when I was nine years old and a fifth-grader, the youngest in my class, I began taking judo lessons once a week at the New City Judo Center, across the reservoir and five miles away from where we lived. My father or mother drove me over. Sometimes they waited in the seating area while I changed into my gi, took my class, and changed back into street clothes; sometimes they ran errands and picked me up when I was through. I don't remember who came up with the idea of judo lessons, but I was more than game. I was beginning to get picked on by the bigger kids in school, for no good reason except I was one year younger, had red hair, and knew a fair number of big, unusual words like antidisestablishmentarianism, ptarmigan, and aardwolf and could spell them out loud, which I occasionally did. In Congers, the white working-class town where I'd grown up, any two of these three things were more than enough to put a target on your back; three was just too good to pass up. You've seen *Back to the Future*, with Biff beating on McFly. There were no black people for Biff to pick on in my town. So I was it. Sensing my angst, my parents thought it would be a good idea to give me some survival skills. What they couldn't sense was just how fearful I'd become inside—as though something out there, just out of the field of view, was waiting to jump me.

The New City Judo Center was run by a fifth-degree black belt named Walter Shumway. Decades later, curious, I Googled him and discovered that he'd been born in 1935 and served in the Navy during the Korean War. So he would have been thirty-two when I showed up. He was a big bull of a man, bellying out his gi, and he bounced slightly on the balls of his bare feet when he walked onto and across the tatami mat. He was a man of awesome power. He had a big square jaw. He looked brutal, but he wasn't, at least to his students. God save the fool who tried to mess with him in an alley. Everybody called him Mr. Shumway. Judo meant "gentle way"; it was second cousin to the much more violent jiu-jitsu. We had no kicks or blows, at least at the lower levels, just throws and holds—grappling holds, down on the ground, designed to immobilize your opponent without choking him out. Within that purview, Mr. Shumway was the man. He held the big stick. On the half-dozen occasions when he picked me out of the long line of students rowed cross-legged against the back wall, summoning me to the center of the mat so he could demonstrate—for example—how to unweight somebody by grabbing their gi-lapels and then foot-sweeping them, the compass of his power was so astonishing, immediate, and unopposable that it was like a wisdom-teaching. It thrilled and educated. And he never hurt a kid. Boys thrive when given a chance to dwell in the presence of this sort of masculine energy.

Mr. Shumway wasn't about esoteric Eastern wisdom. He didn't quote sages; there were no tenets to be memorized. He was about the sport. He was a big tiger teaching his cubs how to tiger. It was exactly what I needed—including the new and mellifluous Japanese vocabulary. O goshi, Uki goshi, Harai goshi, Tai otoshi, Ippon seoinage, Kesa-gatame, Kata-gatame. I'd quietly mouth the throws and holds while walking the halls at school. Week after week, for three years, I took classes, absorbed, and became infinitely more comfortable with the realities of hand-to-hand struggle. One never knew when Mr. Shumway would finger you for promotion, but periodically he'd do that, and I slowly moved up the ladder, from white to yellow to orange to green. Eventually, after the end of eighth grade and junior high school, I decided to move on. But by that point I had achieved what my parents hoped I'd achieve. Somewhere along the way, my moment of truth had arrived.

Joey Hudson was one of my neighborhood antagonists, a skinny adenoidal kid who lived at the end of our half-mile long block. When he hit you, he hit hard. Some of the neighborhood toughs were the sons of New York City cops; I had no idea what Joey's dad did. But one day Joey came after me, as he'd done before, and got more than he'd bargained for. We were midway between our houses, on Stephen Anderson's lawn. And I was ready. No longer cowed, I kept my cool, dodged a blow or two, and went in. I took a glancing hit to the head, as knew I would, but the simple fact that I went in on *him* unbalanced him enough that I was able to throw him onto the grass and enwrap him in the very first hold I'd learned from Mr. Shumway, Kesa-gatame. And I held on. I lowered my head—our heads were side by side, ear to ear—and squeezed. He couldn't get out. He couldn't do anything. He tried to beat me with his fists, but I squeezed harder. Time has erased all memory of what I said to him. I may have sobbed with righteous rage and relief as I realized what I was in the process of accomplishing. Or I may have told him never to mess with me again. But I could feel his fear. I owned him, the way my pet boa constrictor owned a mouse before it ate it.

And then I let him go. He ran away. He never messed with me again. I ran home and told my mom, who made me repeat the story to my dad when he got home. My fear abated, although it never fully went away.

Master Ra's dojang became the sort of clean, well-lighted place that Ernest Hemingway knew we all yearn for. Order prevailed; chaos was denied entry. Ra's ability to create and uphold this vibe, almost single-handedly, was one of his gifts. It was a remarkable achievement, considering that he was working with a cross-section of our town's kids, ages three to sixteen, and that he was teaching them how to kick each other in the head, chest, solar plexus, crotch, and shins while jumping and spinning in 360-degree circles like whirling dervishes. What could possibly go wrong? But safety was a priority. When sparring was on the program, the kids strapped on protective gear: head guards, chest guards, shin guards. Then they went at each other in a flurry, like fighting cocks without blades. Occasionally somebody got hurt, but never badly. One day a bigger kid with a whiff of sullen bully—an attitude I'd learned to recognize as a kid and steer clear of—blindsided Shaun with a kick to the solar plexus during a group sparring session and he dropped like a popped balloon, gasping and crying. Master Ra stopped the class and went down on one knee to attend. He was a careful, gentle man. Indomitable spirit may have been his dojang's guiding tenet, but he was no military-grade stoic and did not demand that of the kids.

Shaun, his attentions scattered by his proliferating musical interests, made slow but steady progress up through the belts: yellow, orange, green. The month or two before belt testing saw everybody focusing on forms: the eighteen-odd sequenced turns, blocks, punches, and kicks that each form required, executed with precision and, ideally, an audible *snap!*, like a crisp white napkin snapped across a waiter's outstretched arm. We bought an instructional DVD, *Tae Kwon Do: A Visual Guide to Forms*, and Shaun practiced in front of the big screen in the living room, matching the master, working for more *snap!* Then, over the months and years, came blue belt, purple belt, brown belt, red belt, each belt with its own season of sharpening into the forms; each with its own afternoon of belt testing, which included verbal recitation of the tenets, demonstrations of the forms, and board breaking; each, several weeks later, with the formal, front-of-the-room presentation of the new belt, which Master Ra wrapped and tied around the adept's waist. Shaun had left me far behind, belt-wise. Dad was delighted.

Sometimes, when board breaking was being tested, Master Ra would summon the testee's parent from the waiting room, where we sat kibbitzing behind the big window, out onto the padded mat. He'd give us a magazine-sized pine board, stiff but not thick, and ask us to hold it out away from us at hip height, one hand each gripping top and bottom. And our kid, waiting ten feet away, would bounce a little, then run towards us, jump, and whirl, bending sharply at the waist and shouting "Kiyah!" as the leg snapped out at a ninety-degree angle and the foot struck the board hard—snapping it in two with a loud *crack!* I held boards for Shaun more than once. Early in his career he'd strike the board glancingly or not at all, two or three times, before achieving the break. Then, as he got older, rising through the belts, he came into his full power, and I could feel it. What made me proudest, though, especially as he got bigger, is that he wasn't a bully. Working with Master Ra had disciplined him. He was particularly good with younger kids. They'd knock on our door sometimes—the pair of boys next door—and ask, "Can Shaun come out and play?" And he would.

I was out on the road in July of 2018 with my then-current duo, the Blues Doctors, when Sherrie called me one morning on my cell. She sounded uneasy, a little scared. I'd never heard that note in her voice.

"A package was left at our front door," she said. "It's a brown cardboard box. It doesn't have any address on it. Were you expecting some sort of drop-off?"

"No. That's weird."

We agreed that she should call the police and have them open it. Oxford was very safe, the sort of place where you almost didn't have to lock your doors at night—although we always did, storm door as well as front door, because Sherrie had grown up in the hood and that's what you did. But it wasn't the sort of place where people mailed each other bombs.

She called me back a couple of hours later. Same weird sound in her voice. "It wasn't a bomb."

"Well, *that's* good!"

"It was basically nothing. Just a bunch of trash, like you'd find by the side of the road." She mentioned leaves, sticks, paper, a dirty sock.

"Trash?" I said.

"That's all it was."

When something like this happens to you and your family, especially if it's never happened before, your mind starts working. One week earlier, the local paper had run a profile about me and my decades-long blues journey titled "Everybody in Harlem Knows Satan: The Story of Adam Gussow and Sterling Magee," headlined with a smiling double head-shot we'd sometimes used as a press photo. Black and white together! I was sure that the box of trash was signifying on this—expressing some local reader's anger at such a visible interracial partnership, or the fury of some ardent Christian who was incensed at the idea that an Ole Miss professor would dare to praise a man, much less a black man, who called himself by that name.

Sherrie disagreed—strongly. She thought that somebody was trying to intimidate our family.

"But why?" I asked. "Why now? We've never had a problem with anybody around here."

That was indisputably true. But there was something else. The previous year, not long after Trump had been elected president, she'd been walking through the Walmart parking lot towards the big front doors when an SUV drove slowly past her and, through the open back window, a kid of eleven or twelve had shouted, "Nigger, nigger, nigger!" It was the first time something like that had happened since she'd moved here in 2004, the month after we got married. Oxford just wasn't like that. Maybe things were changing.

Sherrie put a query out on our neighborhood Facebook page. It turned out that one of our neighbors had seen something curious on the night the box showed up. A passenger van, they posted, had stopped at the top of the hill near our house; three or four teenagers had gotten out, laughing. The neighbor thought they'd headed down the hill but wasn't sure.

That's all we knew. After a couple of days, Sherrie threw away the trash-filled box. I told her not to wait until I got home from the tour. I didn't need to see it. The whole episode put us on edge for a while. But nothing else like that ever happened to us. Oxford, Mississippi, just wasn't that sort of place.

Around the time Shaun got his poom belt, a significant pre-black-belt threshold, he began to lose interest in taekwondo. His musical dreams, first on trumpet, then on trombone and euphonium, were stealing bandwidth. Sherrie, to my surprise, transformed into Tiger Mom overnight. "We're getting that black belt," she said. "If you wanna stop once you do that, okay. But not until then."

Master Ra took visible pleasure in having guided Shaun and his fellow poom belts to the point where black-belt testing hovered on the horizon. He would seat them in the front row in mixed-level classes so the other kids could admire them; he'd have them guide the lower belts through their forms during pre-belt-testing. But he knew that not every kid he'd nurtured was there for the long haul. Shaun would talk about the kids who had drifted away, moved on. Even black belts: Rowan, the redhead, who became an Oxford police officer; Gus, the skinny home-schooler with long stringy hair who moved out to Colorado and got married. Then there was Aniah Echols, the black girl at Oxford Middle

School who left the gym, repurposing her TKD skills to play offensive line on the football team, the first girl in school history to do that. Everybody at Team Ra Martial Arts was talking about her appearance on *Good Morning America*.

It was fascinating to watch how Master Ra, having cornered the local market on taekwondo, slowly but surely wove his way into other parts of our lives. Birthdays, for example: he'd host birthday parties at the dojang—for a fee—and kids who didn't have a lot of friends would suddenly have cake, ice cream, party hats, a singalong, and lots of chasing each other around the mat with a bunch of their TKD pals. He'd host movie nights and advertise them in a way that gave parents a wink and nod, as if to say, "Movies for them, date night for you." He'd do Halloween, Easter. He knew how to make a buck and worked hard for it. I was almost tempted to get cynical. He clearly had a desire to create and recreate his large and rangy TKD brood, several hundred kids and their parents, as one big family. In that sense, his whole ministry was devoted to the creation of beloved community: bringing us together, fostering productive mutuality and spiritual health, helping us dwell in the joy of connection. He didn't overcharge, so he wasn't profiteering. I never once saw his ego engaged. Quite the reverse: he was modest to a fault. Apart from a love of taekwondo and the pleasure he took in sharing that love with young people, I couldn't quite figure out what made him tick—until one day when he quieted the kids down near the end of class and told them a story, which I was lucky enough to overhear from the waiting room.

It wasn't the sort of story that my own martial arts master, Mr. Shumway, would have told. It was about his mother. He wound into it slowly, so that later, when I thought back, I couldn't remember how it began or what the motivating pretext was. He would occasionally talk about his family, especially his father, the retired professor, who traveled back and forth to South Korea and was a fan of the blues. Master Ra and I had spoken about the blues more than once. His father was a fan of my books, he said. Ra brought several of my books to the gym one day and asked if I'd sign them for his father, dipping his head in a little bow, as was his way. I was delighted but embarrassed. That was the day he told me that he played blues guitar. Stevie Ray Vaughan, B. B. King. Master Ra! Who knew? But on this day he was telling the kids, all of us, about his mother.

"My mother and I," he said, "had a pretty good relationship. It wasn't perfect, but it was pretty good. How many of you have a pretty good relationship with your mom?" He raised his hand. Almost every kid raised a hand.

"Good," he said. "I like that. Sometimes we have harsh words with our parents. Sometimes our parents have harsh words with us. But family is important. Your family is your team. They're there for you. They take care of you when you're down. They inspire you with their strength. We're all a big family here. Can I get an amen?"

"Amen!" the kids said.

He kept talking about families, parents, and ideals. I wasn't sure where he was going.

"So what happened with me," he said, "is that I was talking with my mom on the phone a few years ago, and we were having a fight. We were not using kind words. It's terrible when this happens, but sometimes it happens. We get angry, we get upset. Does that ever happen to you?"

"Yes," a few kids murmured.

"Well, it happened to me." He gazed down at his hands. "My mother and I had harsh words on the phone. And then we hung up. And later that day, I got a phone call from my father. My mother had been in a car wreck. It wasn't her fault, as far as they could tell. But she was... not alive."

He paused and let that sink in.

"So when I tell you to be nice to your parents, to be nice to your mom and dad, I mean it. You only have one of each. They love you. They raised you to be the best you can be. Sometimes harsh words can happen. But we can also try to be a little nicer to the people we love. You know I love all of you, right?"

"Yes, Master Ra."

"Good." He dipped his head. "Good."

219

South of Haunted Dreams

I had touched the past, which is one thing. The difficult
part is carrying the past into the future, carrying
it without pain and without shame, remembering
how we came to be here, remembering that without
the past there is no present, no future. It is here in
the present, in us, that past and future meet.

—Eddy L. Harris, *South of Haunted
Dreams: A Memoir* (1993)

I t was 2022, a couple of years after the racial reckoning. My mother, who was in her early nineties at that point and who loves her only grandson, kept nudging me. Shaun was about to get his driver's license. My mother knows, because she reads the *Nation* and the *New York Times* religiously and watches *Democracy Now!*, that American roads are a killing field for young black men when they're stopped by cops.

"You need to have the Talk," she said. "You need to warn him what's out there."

I'd taken the trouble to educate myself about the data by then, with the help of Coleman Hughes, Roland Fryer, and the *Washington Post*'s searchable database. So I knew that things weren't nearly as bad as she thought. But I understood why she thought what she thought:

because bad news travels much further than good news, especially on social media, and because death-driven narratives and videos with a social justice valence—cops vs. blacks—had become the American national pastime, the highly monetized contemporary instantiation of racial melodrama. Still, I knew that basic due diligence was called for. Sherrie agreed.

One afternoon when Shaun was in his room playing *Black Ops III* with his gaming buddies, I asked him to take a break and join me in the living room. He came out, sat on the sofa, pushed his glasses up on his nose. He's gotten big: six feet tall, two hundred and thirty pounds. Except for the first year of his life, when we were living in rental housing across town, this was the only living room he'd ever known.

I wasn't sure how to start, so I eased into the subject almost philo-sophically, the way a professor would.

"Are you familiar with something called 'the Talk'?"

"No."

I was surprised. "The Talk is when a father—a black father—sits down with his son at some point before the son gets his driver's license and gives him some tips about how to interact with the police if he gets stopped. Like if he's speeding or goes through a Stop sign. Because the cop might respond differently to the kid *because* he's black. So the father—"

Shaun waved his hand. "I won't have that problem."

"Why not?"

"Because people who don't know me think I'm Mexican. Or Egyptian. That's what everybody in school thought at first, until I told them about my mom and dad. So the cops won't be a problem."

I had rehearsed many scenarios over the years, thinking about how this moment would play out—the cloud that might pass across my son's face as I helped him take on the full burden of his blackness, etc. But the Mexican-Egyptian angle hadn't occurred to me.

We kept talking, of course. We had our version of the Talk. It was a good talk, an open exchange. We talked about politeness and other prac-tical things; about having your driver's license and insurance card ready to go, right on the dashboard, and about putting your hands on the steering wheel when the cop came up, if a traffic stop ever happened. It's possible that I even referred to Fryer's research—his statistical analysis showing that unarmed black men aren't, in fact, killed more frequently by the cops than unarmed white men, although they suffer proportionately more sub-lethal violence.

I was weirdly cheered by my son's revelation, and by the fact that he was moving ahead confidently, not fearfully, into a deeper engagement with the public space of his native Mississippi. I knew what I knew of the state's, and our country's, dark history—more than most white fathers, surely, thanks to my graduate training and several decades of teaching. But what did I know, really? *Should* I have alarmed him? Was it paternal malpractice on my part not to have thrown a haunting across his dreams of the future? Or would doing so have merely proved that I hadn't quite come up to speed about the world he actually inhabited?

One reason I was so determined to arbitrate the deaths of Trayvon Martin and Michael Brown in a thorough and non-ideological manner back in the summer of 2020 is because a younger generation of black writers and scholars had been insisting and continues to insist that black boys like my son—and by extension their fathers and mothers—need to be very, very afraid. This cohort sees black death and anti-black racism everywhere: an ongoing holocaust in post-millennial America. Black women, as a group, have taken things particularly hard, beginning with the trio who founded Black Lives Matter in 2013. Trayvon's death, the trial and acquittal of George Zimmerman, had pushed several of my former black female colleagues over the edge, although it wasn't until later, when I saw the writings of Imani Perry and Jesmyn Ward, that I began to connect the dots.

In the fall of 2012, nine months after Zimmerman killed Martin, I was team-teaching Southern Studies 101 with sociologist Barbara Harris Combs. A decade later she would publish a long, deeply researched study, *Bodies Out of Place: Theorizing Anti-Blackness in U.S. Society*, which offered a pitiless, Manichean vision of an America frozen in

place, in racial terms—black people tracked, corralled, with all escape
routes cut off:

> Despite Black gains, the new social structure looks and
> operates a lot like the old one. Blacks today can attain
> heights not permitted under the old system with this
> one exception: Blacks belong in subservient positions
> to Whites in America. White supremacy is about
> maintaining a social order with Whites on top, and the
> regulation or control of bodies is key to that. In this
> stratification system, Black bodies are on the bottom.
> This hierarchy is totalitarian in nature; it undergirds
> and preserves White supremacy, and it is so deeply
> ingrained in society that even subordinated groups
> can be complicit in maintaining and defending this
> order…. Any Black person outside his or her societally
> designated "place" is presumed to be a malevolent actor
> and must be pushed back into position.

Combs writes candidly about the emotional substrate, parental concern, that underlies her research. "I do not take mobility for granted," she
writes. "Safely navigating social spaces and physically moving from one
location to another is something few Blacks in America have the luxury
of taking for granted. Over the last few years, my husband and I have
been compelled to have that conversation with our son and daughter
on several occasions—too many occasions." And she invokes Trayvon's
death as a touchstone that haunted her kids. "My children wanted to
know why Zimmerman thought Martin looked suspicious."

I have already made clear how I would have answered that question, had my own son asked it. The Retreat at Twin Lakes in Sanford,
Florida, had "got bad," according to many of its residents—white,
black, Hispanic—in the aftermath of the housing market collapse in
2008. There had been eight break-ins in the weeks leading up to the
Zimmerman-Martin encounter; black men, more younger than older,
were almost always the suspects, generally because they'd been seen try-

ing to break in or running away, and the police had arrested black men in four of those eight cases. The community was on edge. Still, even with that solid pretextual background and with no ascertainable evidence of anti-black animus in Zimmerman's personal history, I found it easy to believe, as Charles Barkley believed, that Zimmerman had erred in Martin's case, presuming criminal intent where none necessarily existed, thoroughly pissing off Trayvon and leading him to circle back ninety seconds later and jump the neighborhood watch captain. Reasonable people could disagree about such things, or so I believed. Reasonable parents with skin in the game had a common concern here, or so I hoped.

I paused halfway through *Bodies Out of Place*—awed by Combs's theoretical sophistication and command of the literature, depressed by her unappeasable pessimism—and walked into our bedroom. Sherrie was watching her favorite show on HGTV, *My Lottery Dream Home*, in which a couple who has just hit it big tours three available homes with the help of David Bromstad, a muscular, gay, heavily tattooed, and extremely fun real estate agent, and, in the last five minutes, reveals their pick. This episode featured an interracial couple: a stocky black man and his white wife, both of them beaming. As I entered the room, the couple and their agent were standing on the back deck on a brilliantly sunny day and the black husband was leaping with delight into the backyard swimming pool of the house they'd chosen, making a huge splash.

Bodies out of place? Or a contemporary America where interracial marriage and multiracial families have become no big deal, and where theories of who belongs in what sort of space, public and private, need to be updated?

As I brooded on such questions, I thought back to the Thursday morning after the 2012 presidential election, when Barb and I were due to team-teach our Southern Studies 101 class. It had been a troubling Tuesday night on the Ole Miss campus, as the *New York Times* made clear:

> A student protest at the University of Mississippi against
> the re-election of President Obama turned disorderly

on Wednesday morning, with some students chanting racial epithets and two arrested for disorderly conduct.

The university said in a statement that a crowd of 400 people formed at the student union shortly before midnight after reports of a riot spread on social media. Some students yelled racial slurs and profanity in anger over Mr. Obama's re-election, the statement said. Photographs posted online showed students lighting Obama campaign signs on fire.

The university's chancellor, Dan Jones, said, "All of us are ashamed of the few students who have negatively affected the reputations of each of us and of our university." No one was injured, and no property was damaged, but Dr. Jones said the campus police were investigating....

On Sept. 30, the university marked the 50th anniversary of the riots that followed its racial desegregation. In recent years, it has taken steps to address complaints of insensitivity, changing its mascot to a black bear from a Confederate soldier and dropping "Dixie" as its unofficial fight song. Students elected the first black homecoming queen this year.

Barb and I had agreed to spend the first portion of class contextualizing and unpacking what had happened—the riot, the protest, whatever the hell it was. When she showed up at the big lecture hall for our 9:30 AM start, her smile was taut. "I'll start things off," she said. I sat in the back of the room as she went to work. She said nothing. She cued up Nina Simone's "Mississippi Goddamn" and played it through the sound system, the full-length recording, all of it, at top volume. A deliberate assault, it communicated her rage with exquisite power and precision. The students sat there cringing, bathing in her fury, unable to escape.

All of us were unbalanced, overwrought, by the national obsession swirl-ing around Trayvon Martin and George Zimmerman, Michael Brown and Darren Wilson, between 2012 and 2014. The Mother Emmanuel AME church shooting in Charleston, South Carolina, in the summer of 2015, which left nine black parishioners dead by the hand of a cold-blooded young white supremacist, Dylann Roof, shredded any remain-ing faith we might have had in the redemptive promise of the Obama presidency. Nobody who lived through those years could deny the pro-phetic acuity of Houston A. Baker, Jr., who had lamented a decade ear-lier that "Now, in the present, black male death is everywhere, every-where around us." Black female death, too: six of the Charleston nine were women. Whose dreams were *not* haunted in those days?

And yet: as the best young writers of the hip-hop generation began to respond to the apocalypse with anger, rebellion, and existential despair, I began to notice a strong whiff of sentimentality where Trayvon was concerned. This sentimentality was connected with each writer's desire to configure Trayvon as a member of the family—a son, a brother, a surrogate for the author's own child—and it had the unfortunate result of infantilizing the seventeen-year-old, babying him, denying him his troubled young manhood. Two of the books, Ta-Nehisi Coates's *Between the World and Me* (2015) and Imani Perry's *Breathe: A Letter to My Sons* (2019), were explicitly addressed to the authors' sons; the third, *The Fire This Time: A New Generation Speaks about Race* (2016), edited by Jesmyn Ward, was dedicated "To Trayvon Martin and the many other black men, women and children who have died and been denied jus-tice for these last four hundred years." Sentimentality in *Between the World and Me* manifests in a curious way: not as Coates's affect, which is stringent and fatalistic—the opposite of sentimental—where black death is concerned, but as his willingness to allow his teenaged son, bro-ken-hearted in the aftermath of the events in Ferguson, wholly to iden-tify with Michael Brown:

> That was the week you learned that the killers [sic] of Michael Brown would go free. The men who had left his body in the street like some awesome declaration of

their inviolable power would never be punished. It was not my expectation that anyone would ever be punished. But you were young and still believed. You stayed up till 11 P.M. that night, waiting for the announcement of an indictment, and when instead it was announced that there was none you said "I've got to go," and you went into your room, and I heard you crying. I came in five minutes after, and I didn't hug you, and I didn't comfort you, because I thought it would be wrong to comfort you. I did not tell you that it would be okay, because I have never believed it would be okay.

As the Department of Justice report issued in March 2015 made clear, Brown's killer, Officer Darren Wilson, was not indicted because all the available evidence, including the autopsy results, ballistics, and the statements of six believable black witnesses, substantiated Wilson's claim of measured self-defense against the hard-charging Brown, who had already attacked and bloodied him once in his car and tried to wrestle his gun away. The "men who had left [Brown's] body in the street" had done so, the DOJ report explained, because Dorian Johnson's "hands up, don't shoot" lie had so inflamed the community that several successive teams of police reinforcements needed to be called in to maintain the integrity of what was then a crime scene, making it impossible to remove Brown's body for several hours.

Coates's book was in press when the DOJ report was issued; he wouldn't have known all these details. But he wasn't interested in these details. Nor was he interested in helping his son arbitrate the complexities of what had taken place on the ground between Brown and Wilson—complexities that might, if probed, have increased his son's long-term chances of survival. He was interested in contrasting his son's heartfelt naïveté with his own hardboiled fatalism, generating out of that contrast an existential challenge: "that this is your country, that this is your world, that this is your body, and you must find some way to live within the all of it."

227

Yes! Coates and I agree on that much. Our job as fathers is to help our sons take full possession of their birthright, including the bodies they inhabit as they make their way through the world. What Coates fails to see is that his son's tears, the tears he takes grim pleasure in remaining stoically insensate to, are the product of his refusal to help his son think critically, allowing him instead to dwell within the charmed circle of a disempowering mythology. This reflex carries forward into the way he frames his son's relationship with Trayvon, despite his son's own relative privilege. "You have seen the wonderful life above the tree-line, yet you understand that there is no real distance between you and Trayvon Martin, and thus Trayvon Martin must terrify you in a way that he could never terrify me." No real distance? One can appreciate the totalizing majesty of Coates's faith here—his son and Trayvon are both black bodies; black bodies are all that the murderous white American law has ever seen—and, in the next breath, make a space for advice about behavioral protocols. But one can only do the latter if one is willing to grant what the fullest possible accounting of the evidence suggests, which is, as Charles Barkley opined, that Trayvon Martin is dead because, after having been racially profiled, he returned to seek vengeance and messed with a fool who happened to have a concealed handgun. What is the best available fatherly wisdom in such cases, and is that what Coates offers? *Between the World and Me* forces conscientious readers to ask such questions.

Jesmyn Ward, a native of the Mississippi Gulf Coast, is a stunningly gifted novelist and memoirist: winner of awards, kin to Wright, Welty, and Faulkner. I've had the privilege of teaching *Men We Reaped* (2013) three times in introductory Southern Studies courses and *Sing, Unburied, Sing* (2017) once in a graduate seminar. Ward has taught many of us to see things we didn't know were there to see. Like literary scholar Christina Sharpe, who begins her study of the afterlives of slavery, *In the Wake: On Blackness and Being* (2016), with an autobiographical account of the two times in her life when a trio of close family members died in relatively short succession, Ward's vision of the world has been profoundly shaped by the death of her younger brother Joshua in 2000, and—the subject of *Men We Reaped*—the deaths of four other young black men over a four-year period in her hometown of DeLisle. Like Sharpe, Ward circles outward from evocations of the personal, familial, and community-level shattering inflicted by these deaths into a broader indictment of systemic racism and anti-blackness over the decades and centuries. That is her mode: worrying those interconnections, those multiple and overlapping threads.

This mode works superbly well for Ward in her longer works. It works much less well in her introduction to *The Fire This Time* when the subject is Trayvon Martin. There, her reflexive desire to leverage personal loss into social insight results in a problematic intermingling of the personal with the political, a sentimental reduction of the 5'11", seventeen-year-old fan of mixed martial arts fighting into a harmless boy-child. To her credit, Ward is candid about this intermingling. Speaking about the weeks after Trayvon's shooting, when she began following the developing story, she writes, "I was pregnant, and I was revising a memoir about five young black men I'd grown up with, who all died young, violent deaths. Every time I logged in or read another article about Trayvon, my unborn child and my dead brother and friends sat with me." Yet, curiously, as though the gravitational pull of her unborn child and deceased kid brother are just too strong, she is incapable of seeing Trayvon as the young black man he is:

> I returned often to the photo of Trayvon wearing a pale hoodie. As I gazed on his face—his jaw a thin blade, his eyes dark and serious, too big in the way that children's eyes are—I saw a child. And it seemed that no one outside of Black Twitter was saying this: I read article after article that others shared on Twitter, and no major news outlet was stating the obvious. Trayvon Martin was a seventeen-year-old child, legally and biologically; George Zimmerman was an adult.... How could anyone look at Trayvon's baby face and not see a child?

Children, child, child, baby face, child. It may be true that a seven-teen-year-old teenager is not legally a man, but he is certainly no child. Ward is consoled a couple of pages later by the idea that those who were "agitating for justice…could not get Trayvon's baby face out of their heads." This is infantilization, not insight. It is a mother's sentimental refusal to honor Trayvon's full and tragic complexity. Anybody who has a son that age, on the cusp of adulthood, knows that complexity. Our job as parents *is* to know it, to work skillfully with it, and to help our sons avoid whatever tragedy is waiting for them out there—or in them. Sentimentality critically interferes with this process.

Imani Perry, a Princeton professor and native of Birmingham, Alabama, is as justly celebrated these days as Ward, thanks to her mon-umental travelogue-cum-memoir, *South to America: A Journey Below the Mason-Dixon to Understand the Soul of a Nation* (2022), which won the National Book Award for nonfiction. Although she can be a subtle and uncompromising truthteller, one who sees clearly and speaks with poetic insight, her overweening disdain for George Zimmerman leads her in the new book, like Ward, to infantilize Martin. "Then he [Zimmerman] tried a criminal justice program and was one credit shy of completing an associate's degree when he killed a Black child named Trayvon Martin." Child, not teenager. In *Breathe*, directly addressing her sons Freeman and Issa, she reminds them of a sentimental bond that she and they share: "We cried for Trayvon. You heard every bit of how a child was made a demon. And hunted. A child like you." Again, twice, the word "child." Again, as with Coates, the parental urging that the sons see themselves *as* Trayvon, hunted by whiteness like Trayvon, foreclosing their own indi-viduality to fuse with the sacred victim. The specious idea of Trayvon as "hunted" by Zimmerman was vividly dramatized in the six-part docu-mentary, *Rest in Power: The Trayvon Martin Story*, which aired the year before *Breathe* was published and which may have contributed to the gothic atmospherics of this fleeting invocation.

We agree, Imani, that those who sought to transform Trayvon into a demon, a subhuman and racist Stormfront caricature of black mas-culinity, are nothing we want any part of. But we disagree profoundly about what happened on the night Trayvon died, and about what sort of young man he had become in the months leading up to that terrible moment. And we disagree, as a result of that disagreement, about what lessons we should draw from his death and shape into useable wisdom for our sons.

What saddens me is that we agree on other deeply important things, as *Breathe* makes clear. The thrill you and your young sons felt on the night Obama was elected president was my family's thrill as well:

> You were both little bits when President Obama was elected. That night was jubilant. We celebrated with friends, then, on the ride home, Black people cheered and danced in the streets. It reminded me of the night when Harold Washington won as mayor of Chicago, and strangers hugged me and my father. Such joy. It was a palate cleanse for a fragment of a moment. A season in which pundits speculated we might be postracial, in which scholars speculated that Black children would be less wounded; they called it a turning point, a point of no return. When Obama won, for a time Black tongues were scraped of bitterness and bile. Then the aftertaste came back like an earthquake.

Neither of us can turn back the clock, much as we might like to. But we can agree that we, as the parents of our sons, took immoderate joy in that brief, shining moment. The reclamation we now seek might be founded in an assertion of that shared joy—and in our shared grief at how badly that dream faded in the years that followed, haunting us with the promise of what might have been.

In the fall of 2001, when I was a visiting assistant professor of English and Africana Studies at Vassar College in Poughkeepsie, NY, and the tenure-track job down in Mississippi was no more than a distant possibility, I worked up a new freshman course on American road narratives. The subject had always interested me; I'd published an essay on Jack

Kerouac's *On the Road* fifteen years earlier and, after putting in thousands of miles as a touring blues player between 1991 and 1998, had grown even more fascinated with the shifting geographic panoramas and sociocultural thermoclines one encountered when one took to America's highways—especially the narrower, slower "blue highways" William Least Heat-Moon had written about in his book by that name. Road narratives were a way of reclaiming America, especially the off-the-beaten-path parts: the people, places, ideas, forms of soulfulness, and ways of life that the mainstream media had ignored or missed.

The form took a while to evolve out of disparate materials, including William Bartram's travels through the Revolutionary-era South—he was surrounded one night in the swamps of north Florida by a hundred hungry alligators—and, decades before that, Sarah Kemble Knight's 1704 journey on horseback from Boston down to New York. Mere survival is a key trope early on, along with the idea of encountering the unknown. We read George Catlin's *North American Indians*, Twain's *Roughing It*, John Muir's *A Thousand-Mile Walk to the Gulf.* There was Frederick Law Olmsted's massive volume, *The Cotton Kingdom*, which offered a Yankee traveler's view of the slave South in the decade before the Civil War, from large and deceptively beautiful "show plantations" near Natchez, Mississippi, to hardscrabble backwoods farms in Tennessee. By the time the form enters the twentieth century, however, and especially once automobility arrives on the scene, road narratives begin to yearn for more: an escape from the soulless, commercialized, over-administered world modern America has become.

I was aware of the need for racial representation, and aware, too, that the whole idea of an African American road narrative was problematic. There had been Nat Love, of course, the famous black cowboy, a.k.a. Deadwood Dick, who had found interracial brotherhood as a part of a "free and wild life on the range" that he celebrated with great gusto. But he was the exception. Once Jim Crow clamped down, black automobility was a challenged concept. John A. Williams's 1965 travelogue, *This is My Country Too,* which indexed one black man's fraught solo journey through the civil rights South, was the exemplary text. But it was out of print, and I wanted to give my students hope. So I ended with a pair of books that did that: Eddy L. Harris's *South of Haunted Dreams: A Memoir* (1993), and Erika Lopez's *Flaming Iguanas: An Illustrated All-Girl Road Novel Thing* (1997).

Lopez's novel, which features fearless, voluptuous, trash-talking, bisexual Mestiza protagonist Jolene Gertrude "Tomato" Rodriguez on a motorcycle trip across America, was just for fun, a lagniappe for the final week. It presses every button, crosses every line. It fucks everything in sight, without regret. I wanted to free up my students to take big risks, think new thoughts. I wanted them to claim America's promise as their own. (You could safely assign a book like *Flaming Iguanas* on an American college campus back then; these days I'd probably be strung up.) Harris's memoir, also organized around a motorcycle journey, is something different. A black Stanford grad, a screenwriter and journalist with a massive chip on his shoulder, Harris hops on his BMW, the uneasiest of riders, and swoops down across the Ohio River into Kentucky, determined to confront the South.

Burdened with rage, grief, and paranoia, keeping every part of the South's dark history—slavery, segregation, racial violence—quivering in consciousness as he cruises along back roads and pauses in small towns, he hopes to find freedom but fears, he confesses bluntly, that "before this trip ends someone will have died." He is addicted to racialism, he discovers: addicted to the negative feelings produced by worrying the rosary beads of black history, the crimes against his family and tribe, in familiar ways now supercharged by his proximity to the scene of the crime. Yet he is energized, too, by a yearning to reclaim his ancestral land, a hunger awakened by the South's evocative natural vistas and smells:

> This is my land. Here in this southern soil, my people were known. Long before I was a glimmer in my father's eye or a worry in my mother's womb, my roots were planted, fertilized by the living, perhaps the suffering, and the dying of my ancestors. Here in these hills my ancestors walked and toiled. They breathed this air, and tilled these fields. They lived and died to become these

233

hills, these trees, this land. They became these things so that I might be. And their voices whisper in my ears....

This land is mine. I have come to reclaim it. My roots are here. This land is me. Fear or no fear, I cannot distance myself from these hills, from this soil, these smells, this past. Nor should I want to. I am these hills.

It is a wrenching journey, one in which, like Milton's Satan, Harris repeatedly watches his own mind make a heaven of hell, a hell of heaven. The black people he meets on the road counsel him, challenge him, encourage him to keep questing; the white people surprise him with their unforced kindness but occasionally challenge him as well, pushing him to acknowledge what he's beginning to understand, which is that the contemporary South can't be reduced to its darkest history and that his haunted dreams are blinding him to what is right in front of his eyes.

The moment of truth arrives late in his trip when, after a couple of friendly young white surfer dudes in coastal North Carolina named Greg and Jack chat him up about his bike and offer him a hammock for the afternoon, he drifts off into an uneasy swoon and comes face to face with who he has become:

It was a hallucinating sleep, at once fitful and deep, troubling and confused. The rage that had been stored inside me came pouring out like poison vomited after a long night's debauchery.

It was like some hideous malarial nightmare. I was hot and cold at the same time, wet and clammy. I tossed in the hammock and could not get comfortable. Finally I fell into a noisy sleep. Eventually my snoring wakened me. When I awoke, drool coated the corners of my mouth and dripped into my beard.

The South had done this to me, turned me into some kind of paranoid schizophrenic, outraged one minute and at peace the next, forever questioning motives, ever on the lookout for evil directed at me and then finding it, real or imagined, behind every tree, suspicious of every good turn, reminded by every person I talked to and by everything I saw and did and felt that I am black, and that I am hated for it....

In focusing on this race thing, I have missed the life and world around me. I have seen it, but I have not seen it, have not held the crystal orb up to the light and watched the sparkles dance.... The journey has been all inside my head and in my soul, hardly on the road at all. I have traveled my black self, but I have missed the South.

Harris ends up staying three days with Greg and Jack. They talk deep into the night on a verandah overlooking the sea. They talk about affirmative action and the rebel flag and many other things. "Greg and Jack were young enough, their minds not yet made up, and they were willing to listen and think." This is the turning point. The fever has broken. "I had calmed down. I was making peace. I slept on their sofa, snored resoundingly. When I awoke, peace was all over me, in my beard and in my eyes, it covered the front of my shirt and bathed all of me."

Later he will realize that he has started to like the South. "Then," he says, "I fell in love."

For as long as I can remember, Sherrie, Shaun, and I have taken an Alabama beach holiday over the Memorial Day weekend. It's become a thing we do—a ritual that sustains us.

It began with a trip to Pensacola back in 2010, the year after I had remanufactured myself into a one-man blues band, playing foot-drums as well as amplified harp, when I was crazy to make music and willing to drive anywhere for a gig. I found a street fair in Pensacola; we packed four-year-old Shaun into the back seat of the Honda along with my amps, drum bag, suitcases, and beach toys, and we drove down there in one long day, about seven hours with breaks, and stayed at some crappy motel nowhere near the beach. The gig was forgettable, but the beach, once we drove over to the public lot and walked out past the outdoor showers onto the sugary sand, was fantastic: hot, sunny, with beers and fried fish for Sherrie and me and chicken fingers and a Coke for Shaun, all at some shack down in front of the condos. I took Shaun into the water and we splashed around while Mom snapped photos. Two days later we had that tired, happy, been-to-the-beach feeling as we headed north toward home, up through the middle of Mississippi. The beach was the key part—that free feeling on the beach with surf gently crashing and summer about to begin. Nobody gives a damn about a mixed family on the beach. There's a sort of pirate vibe in that part of the South, as though anything goes. Wrap a bandanna around your head and pretend you're Jimmy Buffet. So we decided to do it again.

It took a couple of years for the location and the driving route to consolidate. But eventually we figured out that Gulf Shores, Alabama, was the place, a hi-rise condo on the beach. Then when you wake up in the morning and pull the curtains aside, the beach is right there, spread out below as the sun rises on your left, tickling the water—which is huge, because it's the Gulf of Mexico as far as the eye can see. People call that part of the gulf coast the Redneck Riviera, but that gives a false impression. There are quite a few black people, families and some teens, although the overall mix is more white than not. Families like ours notice that sort of thing. But nobody is nasty. They're just unpretentious. It's not a bunch of drunk rednecks messing with people. There's a nice scene late in the day as the sun slowly sinks and the air cools, where the people who are still scattered across the sand fold up their umbrellas, kick back in their beach chairs, and have cocktail hour, drinking wine or beer and nibbling whatever appetizers they've brought with them in whatever cooler they've dragged along. Eventually everybody packs up and heads inside, sliding around barefoot on the cool sand, but it takes a while for things to clear out because the vibe is so mellow. At night, when you stand on our terrace and look down, the dark beach is spotted with small down-facing flashlights: people hunting for crabs.

At some point we figured out with the help of a talkative GPS nav unit that the eastern route made more sense than heading down through Jackson and Hattiesburg. Less stress; more country. After loading up the rooftop carrier with boogie boards and towels—by myself early on; with Shaun's help once he got big enough—I'd assemble all the bags on the driveway, spread out behind the Lexus with the hatchback up, and carefully load in. I'd think about Mr. Satan and how he and I used to do the same thing every morning, out on the road. "I am the packing master!" he'd declare. And then, fifteen minutes behind whatever departure time I'd specified the night before, because Sherrie is always taking care of last-minute things in the house as Shaun plays some game on his tablet in the back seat behind her seat, we're all suddenly in position, ready to go. The summer begins! And we're off. Hungry for that same old freedom-feeling down on the beach.

The drive itself is relaxing. I always take the first hundred miles or so, out Route 278 thirty-five miles to Pontotoc, veering sharply right and then straight, five miles down the shaded country road past battered auto repair shops and country estates and Lep's Barbecue, then southeast through rolling hills to Okolona, home of a young country singer named Chance Moore who recorded the only country song I've ever written, "Rattle On," which is about persisting through the ragged patches. We usually take a short pit-stop at Dodge's Southern Style, right around the corner after a quick left-right, which is one of those combination gas station/groceries you find all over Mississippi, with black women in charge of dispensing fried chicken, fried catfish, and fried potato wedges out of the steam table display case to a line of hungry men and working the cash register as well. Shaun, as a kid, would scamper through the front door, hunting for soda—which I hated, because it's crap and bad for you—while I found myself a cup of coffee. Then I'd pay for both of us with my brown kid standing in front of me, wondering whether that little smile and "Thank you, baby," was meant for me, a welcome-to-the-family nod, or just routine friendliness, Mississippi-style.

Everything opens up once 245 joins 45 Alt; the US Route is a divided highway, two lanes in each direction, and you can cruise safely at seventy without worrying about cops. Sunny skies, few cars, greening cotton and hip-high cornfields carpeting away on both sides. Things slow as you curve into West Point and roll through town—it's Howlin' Wolf's hometown, Shaun's probably yammering for a Happy Meal as we pass McDonald's—and then, after the car wash and thumpity-bumpity railroad crossing and another ten miles, you slide under the overpass past the exit for Starkville and drift out of farmland into rolling hills. It feels like Deep Mississippi, a different part of the state. Every time we pause at the crossroads in Brooksville and I see the sign for Aliceville, Alabama, pointing left, Sherrie and I remember the only night she ever got scared in my company, early in our dating relationship, when we drove out here on a wild-goose chase after hearing from Scott Barretta at *Living Blues* that bluesman Willie King was hosting Saturday night blues parties for all comers deep in the woods down in Aliceville. Off the grid is putting it mildly! We were *deep* down in the woods, that's what it felt like, parking on some shadowy back road—you could hear music down there, you could see flickering lights, and for the only time since I've known her, as we walked down the road into the woods, Sherrie actually got apprehensive. I kept reassuring her, almost laughing. But it was the back woods of Alabama and I was a white guy leading her into the darkness toward some distant bonfire, and I suddenly realized what was going on. I took her hand, rubbed it, and we walked slowly towards the light and the grooving music, and when we finally found our way to the structure, it was a wide-open juke-joint—literally wide open, no doors or windows—with lights strung up, benches and chairs scattered across the floor, and about twenty white college kids and another fifteen black folks kicked back, sipping from paper bags and beer cans, and Willie King in his trucker's cap with his scraggly beard was playing electric guitar on a little stage, with a black drummer and bass player and a longhaired white woman on a second electric guitar. Incredible music! It took Sherrie a little while to relax. Then she was okay. We had a great time after all. We laugh about it now. But she was not happy at the beginning. Chasing the blues, especially down South, will take you to some places.

All that is behind us. Sherrie's at the wheel and she drives with a heavier foot than I do, sailing us along at eighty. She hasn't been stopped by the cops yet, although I warn her she will, but she's unconcerned, even amused, like the Texas woman she is. This is the wide-open part of the trip, straight down 45 past signs for Shuqualak and Wahalak; trying to figure out how to pronounce those Choctaw names keeps us chattering as we blow past little crossroads communities. Scooba is next: home of East Mississippi Community College, "Last Chance U," where talented but troubled football recruits go for a second chance at Division 1. Sometimes we stop for early lunch at the Scooba Junction gas station, where they have pizza; after Shaun gets bigger and less fussy, we usually put off lunch and shoot straight through, another hundred miles past the Meridian loop and Shubuta, all the way down to the Chevron in Buckatunna, which we're never sure how to pronounce—"TOON-ah" or "TUN-ah"—but which has a couple of lunch ladies behind a steam table serving up the sort of soul food that makes you gaze longingly: fried chicken, fried catfish, rib tips and rice, turnip greens, big trays of pinto beans in gravy with succulent little slabs of floating ham hock, baked beans, crusty homemade corn bread. Tell the lady what you want and she ladles it into a white Styrofoam tray and hands it to you with a scrawled receipt for when you pay up at the register.

Early on, I'll confess, I felt self-conscious walking into that gas station with my wife and kid. I didn't know how a family like ours would be taken by the locals as we stood on the lunch line, discussing our options. An uncertain mind, in a space like that, can produce a low frequency, waiting-for-the-other-shoe-to-drop vibe, even with zero evidence that a shoe is waiting to drop. Race mixing! But nothing ever happened. Nobody said anything; nobody disrespected us. No glares. At a certain point you realize that there aren't, in fact, any shoes. It's all phantasmic, self-generated. We're just a Mississippi family on vacation, sitting quietly at one of the tables in back, having lunch. Dreaming about boogie boarding the big waves, and relaxing in a shaded chair reading *Becoming Beyoncé: The Untold Story*, and dribbling remoulade on one of those fried oyster po'boys at The Flying Harpoon down the road in Orange Beach.

Mississippi Band Kid, Part Two

2021, as America limped along under the shadow of COVID lock-downs and reopenings, was the year of the trombone. Shaun, who had changed his school band instrument over the years from tuba to bass clarinet to trumpet, threw one more curve at his band director. The other trumpet players were delighted, since this finally gave them a shot at first chair; the trombone players were resigned. Shaun was Shaun. He'd made a place for himself as the kid who could play anything—your own instrument, most likely, better than you.

That summer, to my surprise, he took his trombone up to the Square and busked. No pressure from me; he just had it in him. He set up in front of the mildewed marble statue of the Confederate soldier who keeps guard over Oxford's big white-columned courthouse. There'd been a lot of fuss around Confederate monuments in town over the previous two years. Back in 2019, some angry sons of the Confederacy, including a famous black reenactor named H. K. Edgerton, had marched up University Avenue into Ole Miss—it was an organized, pre-approved protest that sent the whole campus into an uproar—and rallied around the big statue at the foot of the Lyceum circle, not far from where the 1962 riot over James Meredith had taken place. The next summer, after

George Floyd was killed and statues were being toppled all over the country, the Ole Miss administration quietly relocated our monument to the Confederate graveyard, an out-of-the-way spot across campus. There'd been marches around the Square protesting the town's Confederate monument and its high-visibility location at the top of South Lamar. But that good old boy had stayed put. And that's where Shaun stationed himself. Because buskers want to be seen and heard.

Shaun had learned the Ole Miss fight song by that point, along with "Stars and Stripes Forever" and a handful of other marches, including "The Imperial March," Darth Vader's theme from *Star Wars*. His curly brown hair was ramping towards a full-blown Afro. He's fearless, Shaun is. I don't know where that comes from, but I approve. He called me on my cell phone, after he'd been at it for fifteen minutes.

"Some guy literally stopped his car in front of the statue, jumped out, and threw a one-hundred-dollar bill into my bucket!" he said.

Later that summer we took a family vacation up to Monhegan Island, Maine, and Shaun busked on the dock—entertaining the line of departing vacationers, greeting the arriving boats. He cleaned up. He harvested cash. He came home crowing. He bought junk food with his hard-earned cash—except it didn't feel hard-earned. It felt magical. In hourly terms, he did better than I'd ever done—and I'd been busking on and off for more than thirty years. I almost felt jealous, but that was silly. The kid had a gift. Something had been given to him by a power that was beyond me.

A few days after we got back to Oxford, he came to me with a new proposition, a stunner. "I want a euphonium," he said.

"A euphonium?"

I had a vague idea of what it was, which put me ahead of most people. Years earlier, around the time of the pawn-shop trumpet, we'd taken Shaun to a Sunday afternoon concert on campus. It featured a euphonium trio: three grinning men hugging small tubas. Shaun seemed interested in a general way—most kids appreciate shiny toys—but I'd

242

never have imagined we'd arrive here. Yet here we were. Riding the roller coaster once again.

"It's the same range as the trombone," he explained. "But the parts are better." Meaning in band.

Any reasonable person in my place, having invested in a good trombone, would have said no. But I was learning to dance with the universe—or the devil, or whoever was pulling the strings. Kali the Destroyer was waiting in the wings, but she no longer scared me.

"I'll tell you what I'm willing to do," I said.

It turned out, as I'd hoped, that IQ Instrument Rentals, the mail-order purveyor who'd rented me the bass clarinet three years earlier, had a decent euphonium for a reasonable monthly fee. So I did that. Because this is what band dads do.

The day it came in its big cardboard box, the moment Shaun unzipped the black case, lifted it out, and began blowing, the universe fell into place. Whatever instrumental sweet spot he'd been triangulating towards since that first pawn-shop trumpet suddenly manifested. And it made sense: pitched halfway between tuba and trumpet, with essentially the same mouthpiece as the trombone but with fingered valves that put his trumpet skills back to work, the euphonium instantly took center stage in his instrumental armamentarium. Within a week he was busking it at the Watermelon Festival in Water Valley, twenty miles south of Oxford: sitting in a fold-up chair, blowing his way through a dozen Sousa marches, raking in cash, and pausing to have several conversations with older men—a former band director, a former Marine—who knew what a euphonium was and were surprised to see a fifteen-year-old playing one.

The band dad had been convinced for a long time that the world outside Mississippi needed a chance to appraise his son and make its mark on him. Distant galaxies beckoned; fresh challenges awaited. In the summer of 2019 we'd spent a week in Memphis, billeted at an Extended Stay America, while Shaun took part in the Prizm Ensemble, an educational nonprofit centered on chamber music with a hearteningly diverse faculty and student cohort. He was playing trumpet at that point; it was a successful test flight. Now, after his recent swerve into euphonium, I hungered for more.

I knew very little about the organized world of classical music and its band camps, but I'd heard of Interlochen, as I'd heard of Tanglewood, and as the summer of 2022 beckoned, I set my eyes on Interlochen's Tuba, Trombone, and Euphonium Intensive, a retreat that would, according to the promotional materials, bring together distinguished faculty and students from around the world "for an in-depth study of the techniques and repertoire unique to low brass instruments."

Here, an attentive reader will notice from the presence of the imperial "I" that my dreams for my son had outpaced and supplanted my son's dreams for himself. This is true. Despite my best intentions, I had morphed into Tiger Dad. When I first broached the idea of attending Interlochen, or of simply applying and seeing if we could get in, Shaun was uninterested. He was deep into his latest venture: the creation of multi-track iPhone videos using Adobe Audition, uploaded to Tik-Tok and YouTube, in which he played eight different band parts on trombone and euphonium. (The second euphonium part of Sousa's "The Gallant Seventh" differed from the first, he informed me, because it included the lower "divisio" notes. I was unfamiliar with the term.) Pushing hard, I found him a euphonium teacher, Dr. Micah Everett, the resident low brass guru at Ole Miss, and they went to work: correcting bad breathing habits, focusing on scale exercises, working their way through repertoire, including the Curnow étude requested by Interlochen as an audition piece.

As with Terrell, we had lucked into the perfect guide for the next stage of Shaun's journey. Focused, taciturn, and unflappable, Everett had, I found out later, been something of a boy wonder himself: a band kid who'd held first chair in the Mississippi Lions All-State Band, three years straight. Younger than me but with some crust, he'd seen it all, knew what it took, and was disinclined to flatter. But he got my son—better than I did, in some ways.

Knowing that contemporary DEI initiatives would make a biracial euphonium player from Mississippi a hugely attractive applicant for a progressive institution like Interlochen, I still wanted to leave nothing to chance. So I submitted a carefully crafted letter to the low brass admissions committee on behalf of my son. I told the story of his humble beginnings on the pawn-shop trumpet; his conspicuous abilities on multiple rental instruments, including the euphonium he'd played on his audition video; the resilience he'd demonstrated through busking and the handy cash it had earned him. No child of privilege, this one. He was a Mississippi band kid from the low-down, hoping for a shot at the big time.

I really milked it. I was embarrassed by the letter even as I wrote it. I knew Shaun was good enough to hold his own on the merits, not an affirmative action tip-in. But America was what it was in the aftermath of the racial reckoning, and, in my Tiger Dad fever, I was determined to work every angle.

He got in. We were excited. He was feeling it.

I'll never do that again, I swore to myself.

Now that he'd gotten in, of course, I couldn't send him off with that dented rental horn to rub shoulders with national-class band kids. So we took another drive up to Amro, early in 2022. I called Leslie with a heads-up. "This time we're just coming to look," I said. "Not buy."

"That's fine," he drawled softly. "I'll put a few things aside for you."

Shaun had already explained the difference between the standard euphonium we'd been renting and a so-called compensating euphonium. The standard three-valve euphonium tended to go sharp in the lower register. The compensating euphonium had a fourth, thumb-operated valve that, when depressed, eased those low notes down into tune. Shaun had done his best on the rental instrument to lip the notes down a little, but still: compensating euphoniums were just better. They were also twice as expensive.

Sometimes I felt like Wile E. Coyote chasing the Road Runner off a cliff, or Charlie Brown trotting towards the football as Lucy got ready to yank it away. I knew exactly what was in store for me, but I was foolishly convinced I could outsmart it. Except this time I'd made peace with what was about to happen—not because my kid was heading off to the major leagues, but because, for the first time in his long and winding journey, my gut told me that he'd settled on an instrument, one that would vault him forward into a career. That's why we'd brought along his step-up trumpet, with his blessings. Time to trade in and move on.

A rising junior at Oxford High School, Shaun attended two back-to-back band camps in the summer of 2022 with his silver-plated Eastman Professional Series compensating euphonium in hand. At Northeast he made first chair in Red Band: top of the heap. I drove out there on the final afternoon to pick him up, out past Toccopola and Pontotoc on US 278, then north on US 45 at Tupelo past Saltillo and Guntown. Mississippi's rolling green hills are uncluttered, peaceful, speckled with occasional herds of cattle, easy on the eyes. The series of brief band concerts in the packed gym was a familiar pleasure, a staged pageant of progressively higher talent levels that gave every band kid an aspirational image of the Great Chain of Being. As always, I was moved by the easy transracialism, the just-country-people-hanging-out vibe so at odds with Mississippi's long and tragic history of white people fighting tooth and claw *not* to let black kids and white kids just be band kids. And all for what? A few of them might end up marrying and producing a kid like my kid? The horror! But Bilbo was dead now, and nobody could remember where he was buried.

Early the next morning, thanks to Sherrie's ministrations, Shaun and I tossed his freshly packed duffel loaded with freshly laundered clothes back in the SUV and drove nine hundred miles north. Up through the middle of Illinois, east around the bottom of Lake Michigan, an overnight motel just off I-94 near Michigan City, then rising early on a cool, crisp June morning for the cruise up along the lake's huge endless flank and a quick zig-zag to Grand Rapids. We got lost several times but found our way and kept pushing. After eighty miles of wilderness-adjacent highway arcing north below cool bright skies, Shaun took the wheel for the final fifty and ran us in, up and over a long series of gravel farming roads, then straight to the front gate of Interlochen Arts Academy, just off a country highway in the middle of leafy green June woods. We'd made it by noon.

Shaun's audition later that day snagged him third chair out of five. He'd proved he was national class. But the camp experience, as we talked it through later during the long drive home, left him underwhelmed. The rustic woodland dorms had no air conditioning, which killed him on the two warm nights; the food was too healthy; most of the kids were on meds.

"It's a little different up in Michigan," I agreed. I'd noticed that right away, including a somewhat wider gender spectrum than he would have been exposed to at Mississippi band camps—a good thing, in my view. "But what about the music? We really enjoyed the concert," I added.

Sherrie had flown up to join me; we'd stayed at a hotel in Traverse City but driven down to join Shaun on the final afternoon. The covered outdoor performance space on the lake was spectacular. Interlochen gleamed with carefully curated tradition and privilege. That was why you came here: for proximity to that. Whatever they'd figured out over the decades about how to nurture the best young musicians in the world. To learn from that and be certified by association with it. An indelible line on your CV.

That's when Shaun told me that the tuba-trombone-euphonium intensive didn't have a dedicated euphonium teacher, like Dr. Everett. Nor did any of the guest artists they'd brought in for workshops play euphonium.

"*What?* Seriously?"

"Seriously. I mean they showed us a lot of stuff about breathing. And the music was pretty good. But the tuba players and trombone players had actual teachers, and we didn't."

"Man. That surprises me. I don't blame you for being bummed."

He was fiddling with his AirPods and iPhone, drifting away like the tired sixteen-year-old he was.

"How good was the first-chair euphonium guy? Did he deserve it?"

"Oh yeah."

You've already figured out how this story ends, but I'll tell it anyway, because that's what band dads do.

Things simmered along on all fronts after that summer, driven by Shaun's weekly lesson in Dr. Everett's campus office and his willingness to practice without cajoling. It became clear not just that Shaun was made for the euphonium, but that the University of Mississippi, where Sherrie and I both worked, would be the perfect next step when that moment arrived. After Dr. Everett handed him a poster for a two-week Euphonium Tuba Institute at the Eastern Music Festival in the summer of 2023, my Tiger Dad instincts flared. This was the perfect next step, I insisted. You can do this! You'll kill. I don't care what it costs. It's a step up.

I pushed. I enthused. I stared at the poster photo of the impassioned young Asian man with glasses holding up his shiny silver euphonium, a smile of quiet triumph playing across his lips.

Shaun resisted. He was stubborn. He had his own ideas. He wanted to stay local, attend all the camps he'd previously attended one last time as a rising senior. Prizm, Northeast, Itawamba. He wanted to have *fun* for once. No stress.

Let's ask your teacher, I finally said. I'll abide by what he says.

Dr. Everett, to my surprise, was fine with Shaun's plan.

So that's what happened. In the summer of 2023, Shaun used his music as he saw fit. He'd picked the trombone back up at some point and was doubling on that; since Dr. Everett was a master of both, he helped dial Shaun in. By late spring Shaun had decided to test himself yet again by playing trombone, not euphonium, at all three camps, although he auditioned on both instruments. We weren't surprised to hear that he'd notched first chair in Red Band at both Northeast and Itawamba. On both instruments. He went with trombone, which was a relief to the euphonium players. That's my son.

The awards, though, were a surprise. He'd never won one. An in-your-face kid who laughed loudly at his own jokes, he hadn't always been Mr. Popularity with the in-crowd. He face-timed from Northeast to let us know: they'd given him the Avant-Brown Memorial Leadership

Award. Itawamba, the following week, was an embarrassment of riches. Most outstanding Red Band member. Most outstanding in trombone ensemble. Most improved in jazz band. And the Robert P. Chase award for most outstanding band camper.

"Jesus," I said, squinting through my own iPhone at the certificates he held up to his iPhone. "You cleaned up!"

"I just had fun, Dad. I was myself."

For once I had nothing to say. Wise men sometimes don't.

Parchman Blues

"**W**hat I wanna know," he said in a low growl, eyeing me skeptically as he leaned in, "is what can a white man *possibly* teach me about the blues?"

Chris, short but solidly built, had drifted in my direction soon after entering the classroom with the other men, all of them wearing the same green-and-white-striped pants and bulky dark grey coats with "MDOC CONVICT" stenciled on the back. We were standing face to face in the Education and Pre-Release building, a one-story structure next door to Unit 25, three miles inside the front gates of the Mississippi State Penitentiary. It was a few minutes before the bell on the first day of class in the spring term of 2023: English 367, The Blues Tradition in American Literature, the first time I'd been given a chance to participate in the Prison-to-College Pipeline Program (PTCPP) that my English Department colleague and supervisor, Dr. Patrick Alexander, had helped usher into being a decade earlier. Patrick had schooled me in the weeks leading up to my debut: we don't say *convict*, we don't say *inmate*. Those words are designed to dehumanize. These men are our students.

As Chris and I eyed each other quietly, eyes locked, I was disinclined to back down. I'd been teaching this course for twenty-five years—at The

New School, Vassar College, the University of Mississippi—and I'd written five books about the blues: its cultural and historical underpinnings, its literary extensions. I'd spent four years on the streets of Harlem with Sterling, another seven years touring America and overseas. I'd paid my dues, or hoped I had. Still, this was Chris's world, not mine. I'd already lost half a dozen students since the previous week's get-acquainted session, an introduction to the class open to all potential enrollees. From eighteen down to twelve. I couldn't afford to lose many more.

"I, ah…," I started to say.

He winked, his face relaxing as he bumped my elbow gently with his. "Just testing," he said.

"You got me." I chuckled, relieved. Surprised but also, somehow, not surprised. "You got me."

"I got you, doc."

"Yes, you did."

That was how the term began, in late January 2023. By the time it was over, in mid-May, a month after we were profiled on NPR's *Weekend Edition* and *All Things Considered*, I would find myself telling anybody willing to listen that this class, the ten men I'd been given a chance to spend time with at Parchman, had been the most meaningful teaching experience of my career. When I finally worked up the nerve to look at the course evaluations Patrick asked me to have students fill out before the final exam, the only criticism that they—including Chris—offered was, "The course ended too soon."

Something profound happened in that classroom. I've been trying to figure out what it was. Maybe it's as simple as focus: the men showed up, and dug down, in a way that undergrads in the outside world rarely did. They did the reading and hung on the words—books splayed open, pointing at the stanzas, paragraphs, arguing with each other, dialoguing. The characters were people they knew. They knew Honeyboy, Tea Cake.

"I've *been* Tea Cake," Mitch laughed, eyes flashing over the top of his reading glasses. "Sometimes you need to step away from a card game with a hand in your pocket."

251

Everybody chuckled. Seven black men, three white men. Melvin, dark brown and slim with heavy black prison-issue glasses, my age but older-seeming, spoke in a soft, rough, feathery, broken-up voice. He came to class one day, excited.

"I know that street," he said, holding up *The World Don't Owe Me Nothing*. "Where they took Robert Johnson when he got poisoned. That's in Baptist Town, down in Greenwood. My wife lives right around the corner!" Tickled at the connection.

He'd been in and out, multiple times, Morgan told me later. All the men in Unit 25 were looking to get out within the next year or so. Release status of the two long-timers—thirty-five and forty-four years— was less certain, more pained, and depended on the whim of parole boards. They carried the wisdom and were looked up to as elders.

"We help settle down the hot-heads," one of them told me. "They throw some young guy in the unit who's only doing a year, he's got a bad attitude, doesn't wanna follow the rules. We smooth that out."

Patrick's guidance played a huge role in the success of the course. Patrick and I went way back, so there was trust. He'd come to us in 2012 as the leading candidate in a joint search with African American Studies, a prison-studies scholar at Duke finishing up his PhD. I was familiar with the Duke mystique, abetted by their flagship university press: cutting-edge approaches, left side of the dial, heavy on theory. Disarmingly warm and soft-spoken, passionate but peace-filled in a way I was later able to connect with his churchgoing background, he relaxed in our faculty lounge, dark-suited, chatting with me about his work in the Durham prisons. That was Patrick's thing: bringing knowledge to those men. He'd worked up a new course on Martin, Malcolm, and Barack.

"If you end up coming here," I told him, "I'll connect you with Bryan Ward, who's part of a Kairos prison ministry at Parchman."

A local musician and recording engineer, Bryan had pulled me into the studio, produced my solo album in 2010, and become a friend. One day he'd brought me inside Unit 29 to play a show with his duo. It was day three of the walk; the men were blown open with Jesus, almost vibrating as they moved, floating. Luke Woodham, the guy who'd killed six people at Pearl High School in 1997 was there, Bryan told me later. He'd found Jesus a couple of years back. We'd played right down on the floor, fifty men half-circled around us, only five or ten feet away. I'd never felt that sort of yearning energy in my life. Once or twice in Harlem, when things were swinging on the street.

Patrick's eyes glowed. "I know what you mean. Hey, thanks for the offer."

That faculty-lounge conversation sold him, he told me later. His Duke PhD could have landed him any job in the country. But he'd joined us at Ole Miss, hooked up with Bryan, eased his way through Parchman's front gates. Within a year or two he'd co-founded the Prison-to-College Pipeline Program. Now we were teammates for the first time, a decade down the line. He was my supervisor, my guide to the ministry he had created. The wisdom he carried was inspiring. I've never been supervised more closely, skillfully, or compassionately. Patrick knew that I wasn't a prison studies scholar, like him. I'm not an activist—a prison abolitionist with fist raised. One of my early mentors, Marcus Rediker, falls into that category, although he uses words, not fists. A brilliant historian of pirates, maroon communities, the Amistad Rebellion, and the slave ship as an institution, Marcus used to tell me about visiting Mumia Abu-Jamal on death row—his eyes glowing with admiration, his Kentucky-accented voice soft but determined, his faith undimmed. He viewed Abu-Jamal, a former Black Panther, as a Christ-like figure, a prophetic voice for social justice.

I'm not Marcus, although we're still good friends. I'm just a blues scholar and blues musician: a skeptical liberal questing for our common humanity. I'm the guy who reads *Assata*, by Assata Shakur, the former Joanne Chesimard, convicted cop-killer, as I did in Rampersad's black autobiography seminar back in grad school, and thinks, "Well, she never actually says that she *didn't* shoot the state trooper." I'm the guy who buys Abu-Jamal's *Death Blossoms: Reflections from a Prisoner of Conscience*, and reads it closely, looking for the same thing: the place where he full-frontally denies having done the thing that put him on death row, shooting

ADAM GUSSOW

and killing a Philadelphia cop. When I realize that it's not there, I feel
a little spasm of heterodox righteousness, which I sit on quietly, like a
hen on an egg, confirmed in my belief that the left sometimes fudges
the facts for the sake of the larger struggle. But I watch *Amistad* and I'm
inspired by the black freedom struggle! I'm that guy.

Patrick took me as I was. He was there to introduce and vouch for
me on Day One—the preliminary meeting with prospective students,
which included our TA, Morgan McComb, a PhD candidate in English.
Morgan had taken my graduate seminar in blues lit two years earlier, in
COVID/Zoom format, and was a specialist in the Black Arts Movement.
There weren't many Mississippi-born white women, to be honest, who
could pull that gig off—or walk into the Mississippi State Penitentiary
as centered, generous, and unafraid as she had. But she'd been schooled
well up at Kansas State, taking her MA with Maryemma Graham and
my friend Tony Bolden, the preeminent theorist of the blues-funk continuum. She'd aced my class from the jump. So she had the chops and
was, along with Patrick, the ideal companion for this particular journey.

When the men first drifted single file into the room, they shook Patrick's
hand, then mine, establishing a baseline intimacy that continued for the
rest of the term, deepening week by week. That first day, as I held each
man's hand and looked into his eyes, I was conscious of a shadow that
hung between us, a question produced by my own unfamiliarity with
this space: what had he done to end up here? As the term continued and
we got to know each other, this question faded, then disappeared. It was
irrelevant to the purpose that confronted us, which was digging deep
into the richness of the blues literary tradition—breaking open those
walnuts, extracting the meat. Yet it was also, without being uttered in
so many words, a burden each man carried within him: a core element
of his personal blues. It became clear as the term proceeded that this
burden was, if handled right, a kind of talisman: the defining existential
challenge of each man's life, something that needed to be wrestled with,
explored, accepted as a part of who one was and made peace with in

order to move on. It was his personal blues, but it wasn't his *only* blues. A man could sing more than one song.

I remember being offended, on that first day, by the needlessness of the stenciling on each man's coat. MDOC CONVICT? Wasn't that obvious from the green and white striped pants? Did they really need to be *labeled*? This slap in the face seemed like a calculated administrative insult. I bridled on my students' behalf, and not for the last time. (Mississippi, I found out later, is the only state that still stripes and labels its convicts.)

"One thing we do," Patrick had counseled me, "is give our incarcerated students a chance to help shape the course by weighing in on a specific course element or two. We do this because the prison doesn't give them much chance to exercise agency in the rest of their lives."

Professors are accustomed to exercising full control in the matter of what we teach, but I was game. The wisdom of Patrick's advisory only became clear later, when I got a better sense of how capricious the governing powers could be. Two things, in any case, needed deciding at the intro session. The first—should we read B. B. King's autobiography, or Honeyboy Edwards's?—resolved itself in favor of the latter. *The World Don't Owe Me Nothing*, I'd told them, offered a somewhat grittier view of Depression-era Mississippi than King's *Blues All Around Me*, and more direct confrontations with the criminal justice system: vagrancy laws, prison farms, lynching. I'd taught Honeyboy many times over the years, especially in Southern Studies 101, but never in this blues lit class. King was my go-to, a natural fit. Honeyboy was who they wanted, though; the raised hands made that clear. So he was in.

The second decision concerned harmonicas. I was an official endorser for Hohner; the company, at my request, had offered to supply every student with a free harmonica. I was happy to give the men a lesson during the twenty-minute break in our weekly three-and-a-half-hour class. But there was a catch: prison administrators would not allow anybody to bring their harmonica back to Unit 25. I would have to schlep a box of them with me each time class met, hand them out, teach a quick-hit lesson, then collect them before I left and cart them home.

255

That was the deal. Was it worth accepting? A free instrument, a few licks, but no practice time outside class.

Nobody had to spell out the rationale behind the policy: harmonicas can be disassembled and the cover plates sharpened into shivs. We all got that. The men voted yes regardless. Later in the term, after we'd had a lot of call-and-response fun with the instruments, we'd laugh off the no-harmonicas-in-the-unit policy.

"Can you imagine what would happen if ten bad harmonica players went back to the unit and put in a lot of practice time?" I joked. "You'd drive everybody crazy. You'd have a riot."

"Man, I'm telling you," laughed Mitch, one of our best students. He'd spoken more than once in class about having been a gang-banger, twenty years earlier. "I did stupid things back then. We all did." But that was then; this was now. "I'm getting the hang of this thing, Doctor Gussow," he'd say, holding up the harp. "I really think if I had a chance to practice, I could play for real."

Black women held all the power at Unit 25, or at least they did in the pre-release and education building where our classroom was located. Mirinda Frison—Ms. Frison to us, rhymes with bison—was the presiding administrator. A graduate of Mississippi Valley State University with an MS in Criminal Justice and Corrections, she was solidly built but not intimidating, with a flat affect and a straightforward, no-nonsense demeanor. She wielded her power discreetly; I never once heard her raise her voice. We worked well together. When Morgan and I arrived at the unit each Wednesday just after twelve noon and pushed through the pair of unlocked front gates and front door into the small anterior lobby, wheeling my hand truck filled with books, writing supplies, and harmonicas, she usually checked us in. We signed the guest log and surrendered my car keys, then wove our way around through another door and down a central hallway through one more pair of swinging doors into the portion of the building devoted to classrooms.

Our classroom was clean and spacious, with lots of south facing windows looking out through several layers of barbwire-topped chain-link fence across endless fallow fields that stretched away towards a large building on the horizon that was, the men told me, the spiritual life center. Five minutes after we arrived, Ms. Frison would wheel a portable A/V unit into the classroom, topped with her personal laptop. I'd plug my zip drive into it, along with a small powered speaker, and get some blues rolling: Albert Collins, Denise LaSalle, Lou Rawls singing "Stormy Monday" with Stanley Turrentine blowing sax. It felt righteous to throw that energy into this space.

There were three or four other women working in offices down the hall from our classroom whose faces became familiar, although I never learned their names because our interactions were glancing: surrendering or claiming my car keys, passing in the hallway. They were women of a certain age, mostly older rather than younger, and were uniformly cheerful stewards of their command. They wore business casual attire, slacks and blouses and nice shoes, which contrasted with the men in their green-striped prison garb and off-brand sneakers. They kept things humming along smoothly. The men respected them and vice versa.

The only time Ms. Frison ever gave me the equivalent of a "hell no"—and she was gentler than that—was the day I asked whether Morgan and I could bring the men healthy snacks. Like oranges, for example. Because we'd discovered that they loved candy bars and other junk food—potato chips, anything crunchy or salty. We were allowed to bring that stuff into the unit; we'd done that twice. But the men had complained about the prison food, and I hated to throw junk on top of that.

"No!" she said. "No oranges. No fruit allowed."

"Really? Dang, that's too bad."

She shook her head. "The men ferment it. They make wine."

I asked the guys later if this was true. They all started talking at the same time. Laughing.

"Noooo," said Arthur, one of the elders. A big man with a soft voice, he spoke with a slight stutter. "That's, that's forbidden."

"You give us some fruit, doc, we've got our ways."

Chris laughed. "Party *time*, baby!"

Ledale, one of our best students, was a quietly intense guy in his early forties with a residual smile, as though he were savoring a private joke, although the smile sometimes shifted into something edgier. He shook his head slowly and grinned. "It's a nice thought, those oranges, but we've got some evil ways up in here and we're proud of what we know how to do."

"It's all about survival," said Eskimo Joe, a small unshaven white guy whose real name was Christian. He was book-smart but canny, with a streetwise hipster vibe, and had quickly mastered my course concepts. "If they're gonna confront us with blues conditions, then we're gonna do our best to work some of that blues ethos into the mix."

"We watch out for him," Arthur told me quietly later, during the break. Meaning Eskimo Joe. "We are a caring place, but you got some mean people, too."

At the heart of our term's work was a series of classic blues texts, many of which I'd been working with since the beginning: *Father of the Blues* by W. C. Handy, *Ma Rainey's Black Bottom* by August Wilson, *Their Eyes Were Watching God* by Zora Neale Hurston, plus poems by Langston Hughes, Sterling Brown, and Sterling Plumpp, critical works by Kalamu ya Salaam and Angela Davis, blues stories collected by Barry Lee Pearson, and the 1986 film *Crossroads* starring Joe Seneca and Ralph Macchio. I'd bring along my flash drive every week, plug it into Ms. Frison's laptop, and aim the projector at the white cinder-block wall.

Recorded music and downloaded video clips were critically important to the loose, inquisitive, free-swinging vibe I wanted to create—but also to a lesson I hoped to teach about the blues ethos: the way in which blues, grounded in setbacks, pain, and despair, fostered resilience and enabled moments of triumph. Blues could spin defeat, or seeming defeat, into victory, as long as you kept your eyes open and jumped when the chance presented itself.

Music, according to Patrick, had never been part of a PTCPP course at Parchman; that element alone distinguished our class. Yet when you utter the words "Parchman" and "blues" in the same sentence, you're forced to confront a long and uncomfortable history. It's the story of white men, especially song collectors like Alan Lomax and his father John Lomax, who entered carceral spaces like Parchman Farm and Louisiana's Angola Prison, hungry for pre-modern song forms uncorrupted by contemporary pop trends, and, with the help of wardens, overseers, and other powerful white men, extracted those songs and stories from the inmates, then vanished into the big wide world.

I was intimately familiar with this history. Inspired by Patrick's thoughts about ethics inside the walls, I was determined to get things right, not reinscribe age-old power dynamics. Sometimes this meant that I played my harmonica when the men demanded it—like the day I tossed off the beginning of the *Sanford and Son* theme at the end of class in response to a request and the men hooted and swarmed my desk shouting, "Go, doc!"

Sometimes it meant that I threw out the lesson plan—my concept-heavy lectures at the board rarely worked—and let five men speak at the same time, or in sequence, or both, about a specific set of lines in a poem, like "Double Clutch Lover," Eugene Redmond's double-entendre-laced praise song to an oversexed femme fatale:

> Funk-junction lady with a jack-knife jump!
> I said funk-junction lady with a jack-knife jump!
> If you cain't sprout your tree before she counts to three
> She might leave you with a stump

It's a long and uproariously raunchy poem that Redmond, the late poet laureate of East St. Louis, was fond of reading live; I keep it in the coursepack of assigned readings but have never dared to explore it in depth in Ole Miss classrooms, skittish about running afoul of sexual harassment statutes. Not a problem at Parchman. The men took it apart with great gusto, leaving it quivering on the floor. All-male classrooms have their advantages.

"She's bad woman. You don't want to mess with her."

"Hell no!"

"*Fuck* no!"

Mitch raised his hand. "Doc, correct me if I'm wrong now, but I'm seeing some worrying going on there with that funk-junction thing— that repetition of funk-junction lady the second time with 'I said' added up front."

"You're, ah…wow. Yes, that's exactly right."

He saw my double-take and grinned, then veered off into poetry, which he sometimes wrote. "Worrying, signifying, testifying, and sanctifying that ol' funk-jumping, double-clutchin' goddess."

Knowing how much the men were enjoying the reading, I scoured YouTube every week for powerful clips to download and bring along. I'd assigned them several poems by Etheridge Knight but stumbled across "Feeling Fucked Up" at the last minute, a live reading by Mississippi's best-known black male poet, and knew I'd hit the jackpot. "Lord she's gone done left me done packed / up and split / and I with no way to make her come back…." Once Knight got rolling, the men hung on every word: talk of dope, death, and jiving driving away her laughter and softness and smiles, all of it followed by a litany of Fucks. "Fuck Coltrane and music and clouds drifting in the sky," fuck birds and alligators and trees, Marx and Mao, communism and democracy, Jesus and Mary, Fanon and Nixon, Malcolm and the revolution and red ripe tomatoes too—take it all, the poet says, the whole goddamn mess. Just give me back my woman so my soul can sing.

Our classroom exploded with shouts of "God *damn!*" and "Watch out!" and "Play that again, doc!" They wanted more of that same freedom-feeling. So did I.

I've had some terrific students over the years. But I've never had a group of students who worked together, as a community, to go deeper and more dynamically into the material we covered than those ten men. Yet even as I use that word, *material*, I'm stopped short. *Material* suggests an object, something out there that is not me. But once we got rolling, the conceptual distance that separates professor from students and students from texts broke down. The songs and stories we were investigating— the hardships they contained, the paradoxes they crystalized, the spiritual journeys they narrated—were the stuff of my students' lives. Objectivity was impossible. So we let it go. We ran with whatever came up. We freed ourselves and each other for the space of an afternoon, week after week. Teaching to liberate? That had never been my conscious goal. But that's where we'd taken each other.

The day that remains etched in memory is the day I played a recording of Bukka White's "Parchman Farm Blues" as we read along with the lyrics I'd handed out. White, a Mississippi native, spent two years at Parchman in the early 1940s. His song cuts close to the bone. He sings about how the judge gave him "life," and how he left his wife back home to mourn. "Oh, listen you men," he sings, "I don't mean no harm / If you wanna do good / You better stay off old Parchman farm." He talks about having to start work "just at dawn of day," and how "work is done" when you "see the setting sun."

When the recording finished playing, the feeling in our classroom was deep, heavy, impossible to deny. I didn't know what to say. We had passed far beyond the usual classroom mode. But where were we? I didn't know. I took a deep breath, struggling to find the right words.

"Where are you guys right now?" I finally asked.

Chris pointed at the boombox out of which White's song had just emerged. "I'm with him."

Then Chris and the other long-timers, those who had been inside for twenty or thirty or forty years, began to talk about how life was back in the day. What it was like to get up before dawn and ride out to the fields to chop and pick cotton until dusk.

"I *remember* the first day they took me out to those fields," Chris said, jerking his head toward the window of our classroom. "Oh, man. No way no way no *way* did I want to be out there. I threw a carrot across the field. And everybody started laughing." He rolled his eyes over his shoulder at Mitch, Joe, Arthur.

"Why did they laugh?" I asked.

"Because they knew what I was in for when the men on the horses came over."

"We were still doing this until 2006," Mitch said. "That's when they finally put a stop to it."

"That's right," Melvin responded.

"Wait, 2006?" I said, incredulous. "Look, tell me about it. Educate me. I've read the books, but that's not something I knew about—that you guys were still living like that."

And then my students started to share stories about life back then, which wasn't that long ago—angry, rueful stories filled with remembered details. Being woken up by a supervisor before dawn. Pulling on clothes, grabbing breakfast before the second bell rang. Climbing into the carts and being towed into the fields behind the tractors. The guards on horses, watching over them. Blues stories. They bore witness. They bounced it around the room. They were gracious enough to share their knowledge with the professor, who was more than willing to be a student. And by sharing the stories with each other, and with me, they took ownership of a way of life, back then, that had tried to own *them*. They threw it off and put it in its place. And that was inspiring.

So we schooled each other. We learned from each other. However you look at it, that's a gift.

Where We Are Now

Creole began to tell us what the blues are all about. They were not about anything very new. He and his boys up there keeping it new, at the risk of ruin, destruction, madness, and death, in order to find new ways to make us listen. For, while the tale of how we suffer, and how we are delighted, and how we may triumph is never new, it always must be heard. There isn't any other tale to tell, it's the only light we've got in all this darkness.

—James Baldwin, "Sonny's Blues"

As the class at Parchman drew to a close in the spring of 2023, the men and I deliberated briefly over a curious question: what would happen to their harmonicas, once the term was over? Each man had had his own assigned instrument in a blue plastic case, his name written on a label Morgan and I had handed out on Day One. We brought them with us in a Tupperware tub every Wednesday, handed them out at the beginning of class, collected them three and a half hours later after whatever practice and jamming time we'd managed to squeeze in between book-talk, and took them back to Oxford when we left. Since the men weren't allowed to have harmonicas in the unit, my hope was that the prison administration would hold them in storage until each man was released. But that couldn't happen, I was informed. So what to do? It seemed a shame to throw them out.

I thought about storing them in my campus office and having each man get in touch with me for pickup at such time as he was at liberty to do so. Then I had a better idea.

"Give me an address," I said. "Anybody who wants me to, I'll mail your harmonica to the person of your choice, for safekeeping. Wife, girl-friend, whatever."

Five of the guys jumped on this. They were avid about it. They wrote names and addresses on slips of paper and piled them on my desk. Mitch's mother in Texas. Melvin's wife down in Greenwood. Joe's sister back in Pontotoc. It became clear from the way they spoke about this sacred transfer-mission that we weren't just talking about harmonicas, or mementos from class. We were talking about hope. Freedom dreams. They wanted that harmonica waiting for them when they got out. Because it would be waiting for them, and because it would be safekept by their chosen designee, they *would* get out. This thought cheered us all up as the term raced to a close.

"I'm gonna practice *hard* when I get back home, doc," Mitch swore with a smile. "I'm gonna show up at your door some day and sur-prise you."

A few days after graduation, I sat at my dining-room table with a stack of blue-boxed harps and shipping supplies. I carefully wrapped each box in a sheet of white copier paper, taping the ends like a Christmas present. I took a sheet of stationery with my name at the top, something I hadn't had occasion to use in years, and wrote a note to the man's designated recipient. I introduced myself and explained the situation. I bragged on the student. And I ended every note with a variation on the same thought: he wants you to hold this for him until he gets back.

One thing the men of Parchman had been curious about was the life I'd lived as a touring blues performer, back in the day. I'd brought in a poster of my current blues trio, Sir Rod & the Blues Doctors, which was fronted by Sterling Magee's nephew, singer Rod Patterson. I told them that Sterling—Mr. Satan—had died of COVID-19 in the fall of 2020, and that we were keeping his sound alive, after a fashion, although nobody could ever do what he'd done on guitar. It was a family thing now; my son had even played bass with us at a recent gig. So the future was looking bright. But they wanted to know more. If I was teaching the blues, I must *have* the blues, right?

"I don't really have the blues anymore," I protested. "Not the same way I used to. My wife took care of that."

But they kept pressing. So I played them the trailer from the 2018 documentary, *Satan & Adam*, which featured Al Sharpton, journalist Peter Noel, the Edge from U2, and some footage from 125th Street. And I did my best to fill them in.

Between 1991 to 1998, Satan and Adam was a national touring act, playing clubs and festivals east of the Mississippi, with a handful of trips abroad: Canada, the UK, Finland, Ireland, Australia. Then, just as *Mister Satan's Apprentice* was published and things were about to take off, Sterling had a nervous breakdown and disappeared down south. My heart attack followed two years later. Sterling and I wandered in the wilderness for a while—broken, separated, out of the public eye. It was during this period that documentary filmmaker Scott Balcerek, who had begun filming us in 1995, cold-called every Magee in Mount Olive, Mississippi, and, through his cousin Joshua, finally located Sterling at the Boca Ciega nursing home in Gulfport, Florida, where he'd been placed by a couple of his sisters who lived in metro Tampa/ St. Pete. Scott had flown me down in the summer of 2002, just before I'd moved to Mississippi, and filmed our reunion, which took place on an outdoor patio at the home. The change in Sterling's appearance and demeanor was shocking. In the space of four years he'd been reduced from an explosively vital presence, a presiding elder in full flower, to a gap-toothed, over-medicated simpleton slouched in a chair. He had an acoustic guitar in his lap but was unable to strum it—unable even to pick up his own pick. I gently assisted him; Scott's camera registers my stunned dismay.

Against all odds, the forces of resistance and rebirth began to reassert themselves. Sterling, discovered and embraced by the local blues community, began showing up at local jam sessions, shepherded by Kevin Moore, an earthy, bespectacled Vietnam Vet and activities director at Boca Ciega who discovered Sterling's previous life as a blues star with the help of Google and sensed that this particular resident had more to offer the world. Sterling's incendiary guitarism had disappeared, never to return, but his voice was intact, resonant and distinctive. When I got calls from Florida saying, "We need you down here!" I was dubious. But I jumped in my car and drove down in May 2005, after spring term grades had been handed in. Gulfport, a town I would revisit many times over the coming decade, was a cozy mix of greying Parrot Head retirees, Jewish lesbian couples from Brooklyn, and hippie eccentrics who sold art and trinkets on the sidewalk. Sterling, famous bluesman on the comeback trail, had become a local celebrity. And there he was, standing with Kevin and several other men just outside the Neptune Grill, where I'd been told to show up at Friday cocktail hour.

"Hello, Mister Adam Gussow!" he roared happily as I thrummed into a diagonal space and jumped out. His back was slightly bent and his upper teeth were still missing, but he was standing tall, new Kangol cap cocked at a rakish angle.

"Look at you!" I said. "The one and only. You're looking good, Mister Magee."

"Just as sure as you are handsome. I *see* you got you some wheels."

Kevin chuckled. "Mister Satan is ready to go."

"Yes!" he shouted.

He was set up against the back wall inside. Although his percussion gear and Ampeg SuperStud guitar had disappeared after the breakdown, Kevin and the local blues community had come to the rescue—purchasing two new hi-hat cymbals, reverse-engineering the wooden sounding board from the *Living Blues* cover photo, raising money to purchase another SuperStud on eBay. I'd brought along the same pair of old tube amps I'd used during our road years. A third musician, introduced as Dave on Drums, was set up on Sterling's far side: a big, happy man with thinning blond hair slicked against his head, sitting behind an array of electronic drums, sweating profusely. Jealous of our longstanding duo format, I asked him to sit out the first few songs.

And he did. Sterling and I sounded more like our old selves than I could have imagined—even with his herky-jerk strumming and faltering groove. A roomful of newly minted fans was roaring as we kicked into "Sweet Home Chicago," his voice shadowing mine on "…back to the same old place…." But things weren't dialed in quite right; I knew that, even if our fans didn't. Dave on Drums, it turned out, was the key to what happened next.

Between December 2005, when Satan and Adam played the "Rebirth of the Blues" ball as a rhythmically unstable twosome at the Gulfport Casino, and November 2011, when his bad liver finally took him out at the age of sixty, Dave Laycock became, as he jokingly called himself, the third member of the duo. He enabled our renaissance. I'd badly underestimated him, perhaps because his crash-bang groove didn't swing the way we'd swung for so many years. What I'd missed was his heart, which was generous to a fault. He'd spent so much of his life on the road—he was touring nationally at fifteen—that he appreciated everything, never complained, and always had a laugh ready. He was a bodhisattva put on Earth to keep things loose and bring everybody into harmony.

The Satan and Adam comeback made a test flight up to New York City in June 2007. It was the first time Sterling had been north since his breakdown nine years earlier. Scott was there with his camera; he'd flown everybody up from Florida and himself in from San Francisco while I drove northeast from Mississippi, 1150 miles in two days. We descended on my mom's house in Piermont—Sterling and me in the second-floor bedrooms, Kevin and Dave sprawled on living-room sofas, Scott at a nearby motel. Kevin had become Sterling's roadie, heaving his gear around in a shoulder bag and duffel bag; his black T-shirt had the words "Satan's roadie" stenciled on back. The reunion was warm, an explosion of festive energy.

Later, before we drove into the city for our big gig down on Bleecker Street, Scott showed us a trailer he'd cut together. It was vivid and fast moving, a vortex of swooping closeups that began with us kicking and stomping on 125th Street as a black woman clapped and black kids danced. Then came a rapid-fire assemblage. "It's called co-acceleration," I said, describing our groove as I relaxed in the studio. "That's a great big ol' mess that ain't worth a *damn*," Sterling interrupted, puncturing my pretensions. "It's almost like he was challenging God," said a Harlem denizen in a winter coat, remembering Mr. Satan with awe. "I had a nervous breakdown," Sterling told the camera as he sipped a beer, the dynamism of Harlem fading into the quiet back streets of St. Petersburg. "Coming soon...*Satan and Adam*."

We made Scott replay it three more times. It was strange to see yourself as a coming attraction. Somebody was finally telling our story. I'd done that in *Mister Satan's Apprentice*, but Sterling's breakdown hadn't happened at that point, and this was a whole other level of whirling filmic energy.

In absolute terms, our touring was negligible: seven or eight gigs a year for the next four years, with another gig or two that I'd drive or fly to at the Peninsula Inn down in Gulfport, where Sterling held court at a weekly jam session. But we squeezed the juice out of it.

The run kicked off in July 2008, when Kevin and the band drove up to Mississippi for a couple of gigs—the first at my house, a delayed fiftieth birthday party, the second over at Red's, a juke joint in Clarksdale. Kevin had one of those semi-beat midsize Pontiacs that can hold lots of stuff and cruise for days. Shaun was a toddler at that point: babbling up a storm, bouncing around the house with his sippy-cup, but also intimidated by the strange men who were sleeping and relaxing in Daddy and Mommy's living room. Dave had brought along a house-gift: a Thomas the Tank Engine train set, which got Shaun hooked on those cheerful melodies. Sterling, who'd gotten new upper teeth by that point, was tickled by the fact that his harmonica player had a baby.

"You finally gone and got you one," he laughed. "He's *gonna* give you the blues now, all the money you be spending on diapers."

"He's cleaned up his act, Sterling," Kevin added. "He's got the wife, the kid, the house...."

"Yes!"

"Don't forget my bluesman's car."

"Hey, Sterling," Dave called out, "I bet you had a nice car or two, back in the day."

"You're damned right. And a nice woman to go along with it."

Clarksdale was a sixty-mile drive out through Batesville into the heart of the Delta. Red's Lounge, just across the tracks on the black side of town, had recently been discovered by white blues tourists from around the world who hungered for a rough-edged juke joint that merited the word "real" without requiring them to confront armed black patrons. The owner, Red Padden, was grizzled, taciturn, and notoriously hard to read. We pulled up in our two cars; I got out and strolled towards the club, happy to see that somebody had put a poster in the window with our old publicity photo from the 1990s. Red was standing by his cast-iron smoker, near the door. I'd never actually met him, but I knew who he was.

"We're your band for this evening," I said, nodding at the poster. "That's us. Satan and Adam."

He glanced at me, then the poster. "That doesn't look like you."

We had a great night regardless. The room was dim and dingy, with tattered posters of Ike Turner and his Rhythm Kings on the walls; we drank big cans of beer that Red sold us without comment. The audience was two-thirds European tourists and one-third local black folk. The old deathless groove, the soaring feeling of a song never wanting to end, came back in the middle of the second set on "Big Boss Man." We'd broken through; Dave was part of it now.

After that there was no stopping us. We'd get a gig or two, a little week-end tour, and we'd rendezvous at our designated motel, tacking in from our respective home ports. An outdoor festival in Greenwood, South Carolina, a club date up in Knoxville where the pretty girls danced to "Thunky Fing," Mr. Gip's juke hidden in the hills above Bessemer, Alabama. Gip's, like Red's, was that rarity in the modern American blues scene, the sort of black-owned establishment that was being hyped as a real-deal juke joint because it retained the visual feel and residual black customer base of a stop on the chitlin' circuit—a relic from the days before white kids discovered blues. By now, of course, white adults had discovered these places; sometimes they booked the talent and curated the Facebook page. We didn't care. We just wanted to play and get paid.

Sterling loved the road because it meant escape. Under Kevin's supervision, he'd been granted a rare exemption from the protocols that governed federally funded retirement homes. Kevin handled his meds and allowed him a couple of beers a night, which had the wondrous effect of transforming him back into Mr. Satan: prophet, scourge, and inspired performer. Needless to say, Boca Ciega did not want any of their aged residents declaiming "I am Satan!" in the dining room. But on the blues stage, it was just intriguing eccentricity. Kevin and I thought it was fantastic, a sign of soulful life. He'd grin at me the moment Sterling started preaching and whisper, "Mister Satan is back!"

There were all kinds of gigs. One fall weekend it was the King Biscuit festival over in Helena, Arkansas, with the crystalline blue skies that remain after the cotton has been picked and ginned. The next time it was the elegant dining room of the Kiawah Island Country Club in the lush, swampy low country below Charleston. In the spring of 2009 the Jazz Foundation of America flew us up to New York to play the afterparty at "A Great Night in Harlem," an all-star concert at the Apollo Theater. We stayed at a hotel out in Queens, near LaGuardia Airport; the promoters sent a stretch limo. Sterling was wearing a black trucker's cap and shirt that Kevin had found for him, both of them spattered with yellowish-red flames.

"You first, Sterling," Dave said, yanking open the long back door.

"Thank you, sir."

270

Kevin was squinting through the viewfinder of his videocam. "Satan and Adam finally make it to the big time."

The driver let us off on 125th Street—across the street from our old spot, just down the block from the Apollo. Kevin took a photo of us with the famous sign in the background. Dave's head is thrown back, his arms cradle our shoulders; it's the high point of his life.

By the summer of 2009, energized by the Satan and Adam mini-renaissance, I'd transitioned into a one-man band, sitting in a chair like Sterling and playing a foot drum and tambourine pedal with my feet as I blew harp. I had a reservoir of buried memory to draw on: sitting and standing at Mr. Satan's side on 125th Street back in the spring of 1987 after he'd added the second hi-hat cymbal. He hadn't yet settled into the new configuration back then—his feet were "confused," he'd laughed—but he was giving things a chance to figure themselves out. The process had its own internal logic. By August I was burning so hot that I got Sterling and Dave to let me debut my solo version of Stevie Wonder's "Superstition" at World Café Live, a club date in Philadelphia. They joined me on "Crossroads Blues" after I'd spun it up: Satan and Adam had exploded into *two* one-man bands plus a drummer!

The energies that possessed me during that period were like nothing I'd ever experienced, yet they echoed Sterling's earlier blossoming at exactly the same age, just past fifty. With Sterling's and Dave's help, I had finally come into my own sound. I recorded a solo album, *Kick and Stomp*, the following summer. My debut music video, which got five million plays on YouTube, featured "Crossroads Blues," with its shout-out to my aging blues master, guardian spirit of the crossing-point where transformations occur:

> You can run, you can run…tell my good friend Sterling Magee
> You can run, you can run…tell my good friend Sterling Magee
> I'm standing at the crossroads…I hope he'll wave to me

In 2011, after a final Satan and Adam gig at Hill Country Harmonica, a festival and teaching intensive I'd organized just north of Oxford, the magic carpet ride came to an end. Dave's liver had been bad for a while; in 2009 he'd been taken to the emergency room after spitting up blood in the control room on the day we began work on a new studio album down in Florida. On tour up in New England the following summer, he cratered at the motel, ashen-faced and weak, and left Sterling and me to hold down the gig; we barely made it through. By November 2011, he was dead.

Some things worth doing take time to manifest. The premiere of *Satan & Adam* at the Tribeca Film Festival in New York in the spring of 2018 was something I never imagined I'd see. During the twenty-three years that Scott had been tracking our long partnership, laboring to finish his documentary, America's racial gyroscope had come full circle. Our pepper-and-salt act had been forged on the streets of Harlem in the late 1980s, a moment when the murders of Michael Griffith and Yusef Hawkins by Italian American thugs in Howard Beach and Bensonhurst were answered by Spike Lee's *Do the Right Thing*. Even as Sterling and I left the streets behind to make our way through America's thriving blues scene in the mid-1990s, O. J. Simpson's trial and acquittal for the murders of Nicole Brown Simpson and Ron Goldman revealed a stunning divergence in black and white attitudes towards the American criminal justice system.

Then, in the late 1990s, as Sterling and I broke down and lost touch before pulling things back together, America's racial antagonisms slowly receded. Obama's election in 2008 seemed to change everything. There was a charmed feeling on election night, a promise of rebirth and renewal.

But it didn't last. White racial anger had flooded back into view— in the assassination of black parishioners at the Mother Emmanuel AME church in Charleston; at a "Unite the Right" tiki-torch rally in Charlottesville—and was matched by the fears and frustrations of a younger black generation galvanized by the emergence of Black Lives

Matter. The deaths of Trayvon Martin and Michael Brown, misunderstood as they may have been by a public force-fed racial melodrama by a media seeking market share, revealed fault lines in American society, unresolved wounds that needed to be addressed.

None of this could have been anticipated when Scott began following us in 1995. But here was his film at last: a blues partnership that had prevailed over the forces that sought to tear it apart.

Everybody showed up for the New York opening. Sherrie, Shaun, and I flew in from Memphis; Myla flew in from Little Rock, where she was teaching elementary school. Kevin flew down to Florida, picked up Sterling at the nursing home, and brought him back up to the city. Sterling's sister Janet Gammons and her husband, Bufus, flew up from Tampa. A tall hearty man, Bufus had always been the life of the party; Sterling and I had once stayed with him and Janet when we were touring down South. When I introduced Sherrie just before the red carpet photos, he did a double take.

"Adam!" he said with feigned astonishment. "You didn't tell me your wife was black!"

"I didn't tell you she *wasn't* black," I laughed. "I just didn't put my business out in the street."

Suddenly, thirty-two years after we'd first jammed on a Harlem sidewalk, there we were: the guitar man and his harmonica man, standing on the red carpet in the mezzanine of a huge downtown theater with several dozen cameras flashing. Sterling, fragile these days, had arrived in a wheelchair, a houndstooth hat on his head and, in his hand, an impressive wooden walking stick topped with a cobra's head, courtesy of Kevin. Sherrie had outfitted me with a trim black suit.

"You doing okay there, Mister Gussow?" he chuckled as we smiled towards the surging array of photographers angling for the right shot.

"I've been worse!" I laughed. "Do you believe this?"

"Hell, I don't have to *believe* a damn thing, I can see it!"

Much later, back at the hotel room, it occurred to me that he'd been right all along—that little saying he'd laid on me every time I'd complained about a girlfriend, a cold sore, some inconvenience on tour.

"You'll live through it." And I had. We both had. Breakdowns, heart attacks, a bike wreck, Dave's death. We'd made it through. The phrase "beloved community" was never mentioned, but that's how I saw our story—and the life I'd made with Sherrie and Shaun, which shows up near the film's end, a gauzy long shot of the three of us relaxing on our back porch in the lush green embrace of a Mississippi summer.

One of the nice things about having a musical phenom in the house is that instruments cycle in and out of use, leading to periodic surprises. The electric bass, for example: it never really went away, although Shaun hasn't taken lessons with anybody in four or five years—not since the six months with Clint Jordan at the Oxford House of Music and another couple of terms jamming out at Roxford Academy, our local school of rock. Several Christmases ago, I bought Sherrie a battery-powered cube so she could have music on the back terrace, but Shaun commandeered it almost immediately and has been working it hard ever since. He likes to drag it out of his bedroom into the center of the living room, pair it with his phone—"Bluetooth...connected!" a humanoid female voice barks—and jam along with Earth, Wind & Fire's greatest hits. You can find anything on YouTube these days. Shaun's bass teachers are those guys, a random assortment of pros uploading free lessons. And he's learned what they have to teach.

When he's in the mood, he'll emerge from his lair, plug everything together, and bump along to "September," "Sing a Song," and "Shining Star," singing as he plays, treating us to a pop-up concert. And because he has perfect pitch, he makes it work. Sherrie and I both sing along. Although we grew up in different worlds, Earth, Wind, & Fire crossed from her world into mine back in the seventies, along with Gladys Knight, Billy Preston, and other R&B that got played in heavy rotation on Top-40 AM radio out of New York. Four decades ago I played "Sing a Song" and "Shining Star" on electric guitar in my college band—the same Fender Telecaster now leaning against an old tweed amp in Shaun's room. So it's our music he's playing, something Sherrie and I both know and feel, something we associate with happy memories. Sometimes we dance along while Shaun plays and sings. We get happy, even silly, making up steps. Shaun and the family band! Sometimes, for a long moment, we are living happily ever after, although the song always eventually ends. But that's where we are for a minute or two—with the song, the groove. With each other.

Where we are these days is in flux. I am speaking about America, not my family. My family and I are solid. Sherrie and I will celebrate our twentieth anniversary in 2024. Shaun, a senior at Oxford High School, will be a freshman at the University of Mississippi next fall—a music performance major, euphonium and trombone. He'll continue his studies with Dr. Everett and is looking forward to scything his way up through the ranks of the Ole Miss marching band. I remain grateful to James Meredith for breaking things open back in 1962 and making our lives possible. Myla, thirty-three, just got her master's in education and has been married for most of a decade to her old Oxford pal, Solomon Bozeman, thirty-five, who is head basketball coach at the University of Arkansas Pine Bluff. When my son-in-law and I cross paths, we are aging athletes bellyaching about recalcitrant body fat. One Thanksgiving we went for a three-mile power walk around my neighborhood, chattering about favorite workouts. There are people in America—well-intentioned people, self-described antiracists—who would insist that we see ourselves first as a Black man and a White man. I feel sorry for them. It must be stressful to live like that, with that compulsion.

When the family and I head west for the holidays, we always take the southern route down I-55 towards Jackson, merging onto I-20 West, rolling down through Vicksburg, across the Mississippi, and out past Tallulah into the lake-flat Louisiana Delta. Every time we approach Monroe, we gaze left at the scattering of camp grounds and auto dealerships until—

"There it is!" one of us calls out. The Days Inn where we met on that Match.com blind date back in 2002. It looks exactly the same. Just a beat-ass chain motel that's done some hard living.

And we always go *Awwww*, and smooch or squeeze hands.

"Cringe!" Shaun calls out from the back seat.

This is what the fullness of time means. This is what reconciled lives look and sound like. Dr. King died, John Lewis fought to the end of his days, so that Sherrie and I might have a kid who calls out "Cringe!" from the back seat at a moment like that and it's no big deal. It's just ordinary family life.

Bilbo is dead. I think I'll make that my mantra.

Do I sound as though I'm losing patience for the lies my country feeds me? Afropessimists insist that anti-blackness is America's foundational attribute and that racial progress is a delusion. Jared Taylor and the Great Replacement theorists think I'm a race traitor—someone who should be feeling a whole lot more white extinction anxiety than I'm feeling, which is none.

This is where we are now.

For many years, Sherrie's mother wanted nothing to do with me. It wasn't anything I'd done. I hadn't beaten her daughter, or abandoned her, or dragged her down. I'd done the opposite of those things. It was the simple fact that I was a white man living in Mississippi who had married her daughter and spirited her away to that godforsaken state. Sherrie was disconcerted by this maternal rejection, but she has never been one to cultivate a grievance. We moved ahead with our lives, which are good and fulfilling lives.

Occasionally, on a weekend when I was away on a gig or otherwise occupied, Sherrie and Shaun would drive to Dallas without me, and she'd make a point of stopping in to see her mom. Her mother had no problem with Shaun. She was fine with our son. She had a photo of him on her desk, Sherrie reported. I remember being miffed about this. "What am I, chopped liver?" I thought. That was the way my Jewish grandmother would have put it. I didn't like the idea that my mother-in-law was able to have a relationship with my son that excluded me. But interracial marriages were supposed to encounter *some* rejection, I knew. That's what everybody said. I'd also heard that when hearts and minds changed, it was sometimes the grandchildren that brought the grandparents around. So I made peace with what was, and Sherrie and I kept on living.

When the three of us drove out to Dallas for a holiday, grandma's place wasn't on our list. Every other member of Sherrie's extended family, which consisted mostly of her sisters and aunts and nieces and nephews and the good men who were a part of their lives, was fine with me. There were big Thanksgiving meals at her eldest sister Kay Nelson's house, with kids, including Shaun, running around and yelling, and a free-for-all in the kitchen when the turkey, sometimes two turkeys, were served, along with ham and several kinds of greens, turnip and collard, and yams, pinto beans, mac and cheese, biscuits, and cornbread, all washed down with sweet tea concocted by Sherrie's twin sister, Sharon, that would knock your head off. I'd bring along a bottle of red wine, but nobody else drank, although Jamarrick might have a taste. Dinner was always eaten in front of the Cowboys game on TV. Everybody had a good time, even when the Cowboys lost. But grandma wasn't there. Somebody, one of Sherrie's sisters, would always make a plate and take it by her place. And nobody, not once, ever, made me feel unwelcome. Tribalism, at its best, works like this. I was part of the tribe. We were, and are, family.

But there was always that asterisk. Until suddenly there wasn't.

One year, in the run-up to Thanksgiving, word came down that dinner was at grandma's house and grandma wanted me there. Sherrie and I had been married for fifteen years, so this would have been the fall of 2019, just before COVID. Grandma had had a change of heart. That was the word that came down.

We loaded up the SUV and headed south towards Jackson. We cruised past the Days Inn in Monroe. I wasn't apprehensive, but I was curious. I'd only met Sherrie's mom once, outside her small church when we were courting, and she certainly hadn't looked happy back then.

On Thanksgiving day, early afternoon, we showed up at grandma's front door. She lives in a small, neat ranch house in a nice neighborhood in the black part of South Dallas. The last time we'd cruised down her block was Easter weekend 2003. We'd been turned away. Sharon had come out to tell us; Sherrie had gone inside, then returned a few minutes later, scowling. I'd never even gotten out of the car. This time the three of us got out and walked up the front walkway. Cars filled the driveway; the clattering buoyancy of family life and warm soulful smells greeted us the moment the front door swung open. Shaun pushed inside first with his trumpet case in hand, looking for Tavy and his other cousins. Sherrie was next, greeted by Jamarrick or Kay Nelson or Sharon. I was last through the door. The front room, I noticed, had quite a few potted plants: lots of green in the space.

A hand or two on my shoulder guided me gently to the right. And suddenly we were face to face, my mother-in-law and I. She's a small, compactly built woman with grey hair and glasses. She took my hand in the midst of the loose scrum.

I smiled. "Thanks for inviting us to—"

"No," she interrupted me, "I need to say something. I do."

And then she apologized. From the heart, for the past fifteen years. Simply, directly, unambiguously. "I was wrong," she said.

"I, ah…that's alright. I mean—"

"You are welcome in my house," she said, gripping my hand firmly.

"Thank you, Mrs. Gardner," I said.

And that was that. Grandma had spoken.

Later, as fifteen of us in the living room lazed back in chairs and crammed shoulders into sofas watching the Cowboys lose to the Bills, I glanced over at her desk and noticed a photo holder with three photos of Shaun at different ages. Our son. Happiness ricocheted off the walls, half a dozen different conversations over the hubbub on TV. Sherrie and her twin were sitting under the light at a table in the kitchen, nibbling on sweet potato pie.

Acknowledgments

My *Family and I* began life as a substantially different manuscript under a different title. The fact that it managed to find its way into print as the book it has become is the result of the generous and insightful editorial guidance of two longtime friends, Anne Matthews and Adam Bellow.

It was Anne who first saw promise in the scattered pieces of memoirist silver that I had tossed onto her desk, buried within a disjointed pile of essays, and who found the right words, always, to keep me on track as I tossed out, rearranged, and freshly conceived. Without Anne's patient ministry, this book would not exist. Nor would it exist had not Adam come along, understood intuitively what I was trying for, and inspired me in a way no previous editor has managed to do, so that thirty thousand words poured out in the space of a month, flowing into a mold I hadn't realized was there and helping this book achieve close-to-final form. Any writer who finds an editor capable of catalyzing his best work knows how rare that is. I am immensely grateful for Anne's and Adam's visionary faith in this project.

I also owe thanks to a handful of periodical editors, two of whom risked their reputations to publish me at a cultural moment when contrarianism could get you canceled. I'm thinking of Greg Brownderville, editor of *Southwest Review*, who published an earlier version of Chapter 12 as "The Test: Rethinking Trayvon" (Summer 2021) and Clifford Brooks, editor of *Blue Mountain Review*, who was delighted to run the essay that forms the core of this book's prologue, "White Antiracist Allies in Training: My Social Justice Workshop Troubles (and Yours)" (June 2021). Leslie Spencer and Stuart Taylor, Jr., stewards of the Princetonians for Free Speech website, solicited and published my essay about Joshua Katz's excommunication at Princeton, "Of Dissent and its Discontents: Beloved Community, the Black Justice League, and the Curious Case of Professor Joshua Katz" (10 June 2022), which, considerably expanded, appears here as Chapter 11. (It was Leslie who, when I sought her counsel about heterodox publishers, first pointed me toward our mutual friend Adam, for which I can't thank her enough.) Jimmy Thomas, editor of *Southern Register* and my colleague at the University of Mississippi's Center for the Study of Southern Culture, asked me to share my thoughts about a blues literature course I'd been teaching at the Mississippi State Penitentiary; that essay, enlarged here into Chapter 17, was first published as "Parchman Blues: A Teacher Becomes the Student in the Prison-to-College Pipeline Program." (Fall 2023). Finally, several short scenes from the "Mississippi Band Kid" chapters (4 and 17) first saw light in the online *Journal of Free Black Thought* as part of an April 2024 op-ed titled "Bilbo is Dead." Thanks to all for giving me the chance to share my thoughts in your pages.

Mister Satan's Apprentice, published by Pantheon in 1998, was brought back into print by the University of Minnesota Press in 2009 and remains in print; UMP has generously allowed me to reprint the preface to that new edition in full as Chapter 8.

I'd like to thank the Leila Wynn Summer Support Fund, housed in the Center for the Study of Southern Culture, for a grant in the summer of 2024 that gave me needed time for writing and reflection, and CSSC director Katie McKee for directing this support my way. Along the way, I've benefitted greatly from conversations with, and suggestions offered by, Charles Wilson, W. Ralph Eubanks, Gerry Howard, David

Shields, Tommy Franklin, and Peter Herman. I will always be indebted to my colleague Patrick Alexander for working me into the rotation at Parchman as part of the Prison-to-College Pipeline Program and opening my eyes to the wit and wisdom of the incarcerated students I came to know there in the spring of 2023.

A special shoutout to Rod Patterson, lead singer for Sir Rod & the Blues Doctors, who came into my life shortly before the summer of 2020 and whose friendship and musical fellowship have deepened my faith in the beloved community ideal. His uncle Sterling, were he still with us, would delight in this new chapter of the continuing saga. I'm grateful as well for three organizations, emerging during the time of troubles explored in this book, that have given me hope in our ability as Americans to have challenging but civil conversations, speaking truth without fear and finding our way toward common ground: the Common Ground Committee, Braver Angels, and the Foundation Against Intolerance and Racism (FAIR). Bruce Bond, a co-founder of Common Ground and one of my oldest friends, died much too young in December 2023, but his spirit lives on in people like John Wood, Jr., Monica Guzman, Darryl Davis, and Monica Harris.

No list of acknowledgments would be complete without thanks to my agent, Murray Weiss of Catalyst Literary Management, whose skillful stewardship of this project I greatly appreciate.

My son Shaun's musical gifts—including perfect pitch and preternatural sight-reading ability—continue to amaze. I wish I could take credit! But I'm just the instrument-provider and cheerleader. His teachers, though, deserve their props: Terrell McGowan, who first showed him the ropes on trumpet, enabling his meteoric early rise into band camp dominance, and low brass maestro Micah Everett, who patiently schooled him in euphonium and trombone and helped him navigate a bump or two along the way. Shaun enters the University of Mississippi this fall as a music performance major. His parents are thrilled.

It takes a village. Big thanks to my daughter and son-in-law Myla and Solomon Bozeman in Pine Bluff, Arkansas, and the rest of the Dallas-based crew: Jamarrick, Sharon, Sasha, Freda, Kay Nelson, Marion, Tavy, and of course Mrs. Gardner, who is an inspiration to us all. My mother, Joan Dye Gussow, never doubted for one moment that her son had chosen well.

As for Sherrie: better than I deserve, as Dave Ramsey is fond of saying. She was nice enough to let me share what I've shared of our life here, and I'm truly grateful for that, since she values her privacy, as do I. Twenty years and counting. True love is its own reward.

Oxford, Mississippi
June 2024